In Search of Nanny's Grave

ETHNOGRAPHIC ALTERNATIVES BOOK SERIES

Series Editors: Carolyn Ellis and Arthur P. Bochner
(both at the University of South Florida)

Books in the Series

In Search of Naunny's Grave

Age, Class, Gender, and Ethnicity
in an American Family

Nick Trujillo

ALTAMIRA
PRESS

A Division of
ROWMAN & LITTLEFIELD PUBLISHERS, INC.
Walnut Creek   Lanham   New York   Toronto   Oxford

ALTAMIRA PRESS
A division of Rowman & Littlefield Publishers, Inc.
1630 North Main Street, #367
Walnut Creek, CA 94596
www.altamirapress.com

Rowman & Littlefield Publishers, Inc.
A wholly owned subsidary of The Rowman & Littlefield Publishing Group, Inc.
4501 Forbes Boulevard, Suite 200
Lanham, MD 20706

PO Box 317
Oxford
OX2 9RU, UK

British Library Cataloguing in Publication Information Available

Library of Congress Cataloging-in-Publication Data

Trujillo, Nick, 1955–
  In search of Naunny's grave : age, class, gender, and ethnicity in an
American family / Nick Trujillo.
    p. cm. — (Ethnographic alternatives ; v. 14)
Includes bibliographical references and index.
  ISBN 0-7591-0499-9 (hardback : alk. paper) — ISBN 978-0-7591-0500-3
paper)
  1. Hispanic American women—Social conditions. 2. Hispanic American
families. 3. Hispanic Americans—Ethnic identity. 4. Hispanic Americans—Social
conditions. I. Title. II. Series: Ethnographic
alternatives book series ; v. 14.

  E184.S75T75 2004
  305.48'868073'092—dc22

                                                        2003019364

Printed in the United States of America

For Nanny, and grandmothers everywhere

Contents

Acknowledgments

A book is never the product of a single person, and I wish to thank many people who helped me along the way. I thank all of my relatives who shared their Naunny stories and their homes with me. I could not have written this book without their stories and their support. I also thank relatives who sent photographs of Naunny and other family members, especially my parents, Bill and Claudia Trujillo; my uncle and aunt, Charles and Penny Trujillo; and cousins Tom and Kim Trujillo, Bill and Marilyn Trujillo, and Dan and Terri Trujillo. I would thank the photographers of these photos, but unfortunately I was not able to determine who took the pictures, except for the ones that I took myself.

I thank publisher Mitch Allen and series editor Carolyn Ellis for their support, their careful reviews, and their insistence on pushing me to write more evocatively and probe areas that I was reluctant to explore. This book is so much better because of their influence. I also thank Erik Hanson, Katie Wadell, and Lynn Weber of AltaMira for their support and efforts in producing this book.

I thank colleagues who read earlier drafts of this work, including Robin Clair, Suzanne Daughton, Patricia Geist Martin, Bud Goodall, Judith Hamera, Anneliese Harper, Ronald Jackson, Stacy Holman Jones, Tamie Kanata, Sally Perkins, Pam Sanger, Bryan Taylor, Janet Yerby, and anonymous reviewers for *Qualitative Inquiry*, *Text and Performance Quarterly*, and *Women's Studies in Communication*. I also thank Jenny Stark and Sonia Rodriguez for scanning the photographs that are included in Naunny's family album.

I thank Diane Martin for her information about Trinidad, Colorado, as well as Sara Murphy at the Carnegie Library and Evelyn Rios at Trinidad State Junior College for helping me find information about Naunny's family history. I thank Pat McGinnis of the Media Relations Department at Boeing for giving me permission to search the Douglas Aircraft archives for materials about Naunny's work during the war years.

I thank the publishers and copyright holders for permission to reprint material for this book that appeared earlier in the following sources: "In Search of Naunny's Grave," in *Text and Performance Quarterly* (October 1998), reprinted with permission of Taylor and Francis (see www.tandf.co.uk); "Shopping for Family," in *Qualitative Inquiry* (June 1999), reprinted with permission of Sage Periodicals Press; "In Search of Naunny's History: Reproducing Gender Ideology in Family Stories," in *Women's Studies in Communication* (Spring 2002), reprinted with permission of the Organization for Research on Women and Communication; and "In Search of Naunny's History: An (Auto)Ethnographic Study of a Family's Ethnic Identity," reprinted by permission from *Expressions of Ethnography: Novel Approaches to Qualitative Methods,* edited by Robin Patric Clair, the State of New York University Press ©2003 State University of New York; all rights reserved.

Finally, and most important, I thank my friend, colleague, and spouse, Leah Vande Berg, who supports me in so many ways.

Introduction

For many children, a departed grandparent lives on, immortalized in their hearts and minds.
—ARTHUR KORNHABER, *Contemporary Grandparenting*

And so Eloysa's eternal life in heaven has just begun. But her life on Earth has not completely ended, because her life with us will continue in the memories we will always have of her and in the stories we can still tell each other about her. So I ask all of you friends and relatives here today to hold on to your memories of Naunny, of Grandma, of Aunt Elsie, of Mom, and to share your stories about her.
—from her eulogy

"Nick, Leah, I've got some bad news." My stomach tightened as I recognized my father's solemn tone on the answering machine. "Naunny passed away this morning."

Falling to my knees, I started crying and praying for my grandmother. I had not knelt down in my bedroom to pray since I was a little kid going to Catholic school in Las Vegas, Nevada. My dad's voice kept talking, but I could not hear the rest of his message above my litany of Hail Marys.

I was devastated that evening in January 1994 when I learned about my paternal grandmother's death. She lived in Los Angeles, and we saw her every summer and every Christmas, unlike my maternal grandmother, who lived in Chicago and whom we saw only on special occasions like our First Holy Communion and graduation. My sisters and I called each of them "Naunny," a name I coined when, as my mom told me, I tried to say "Grandma" as an infant and "Naunny" came out. So we had our "Naunny Los Angeles" and "Naunny Chicago," but since we saw Naunny L.A. so often, we ultimately dropped the city designation from her name.

I knew Naunny had been moved to a nursing home because of her dementia and that she had come down with the flu, but I had no idea that her flu had turned so quickly into pneumonia. To this day I wish my father had called me earlier so I could have traveled to Los Angeles to see Naunny one last time. Instead, I went there to attend her funeral and deliver her eulogy.

Two summers after Naunny's death, I visited relatives in Los Angeles for the first time since her funeral. Whenever I came to L.A. in previous years, I always spent time with Naunny and Pete, her second husband who had died in the late 1980s, and it felt strange not being able to see Naunny in her little apartment in East Los Angeles. Instead of going there, I decided to visit her at her grave.

I called my uncle Chuck, the older of Naunny's two sons, to see whether he wanted to go with me. He agreed to go because he had not been to his mother's grave since her funeral. He called Tim, his eldest son—and her very first grandchild—who joined us and brought his ten-year-old grandson, Lance. So the four of us—a son, two grandsons, and a great-great-grandson—crammed into the front seat of Tim's truck and went in search of Naunny's grave.

I don't know whether my first memory of Naunny is an actual one or whether I have heard the story so many times that I have transformed it into one. In either case, I cherish the idea that at least part of it is true.

When I was about four years old, my cousin Tim, who then was about thirteen, took me to Lincoln Park, a neighborhood park near my parents' apartment in the Lincoln Heights area of Los Angeles. Tim probably should have been holding my hand as I leaned over the edge of a small pond to get a closer look at some fish, floating leaves, my reflection, or whatever held the fleeting attention of a little boy. I'm sure that Tim was stunned when I fell face first into that pond.

Tim dove in, not realizing that the pond was only a couple feet deep. I think he hurt himself on the bottom before he pulled me out and carried me back to the apartment.

Naunny, who lived with Pete in an apartment in the same building, saw us and ran outside to help. She grabbed me from Tim and took me into my parents' place, where I immediately received a warm bath, clean clothes, and my favorite blanky. I have a hazy memory of sitting in Naunny's lap, feeling warm and comforted.

My mom scolded Tim as he sat there drenched and bruised. I'm sure that Naunny ultimately comforted him, too, since he was her grandson as well.

My family moved to Las Vegas, Nevada, in 1960 when I was five years old, and I lived there until I went to college in 1973. But every summer, we took a family vacation back to Los Angeles to see Naunny and Pete in the one-bedroom house they rented in East Los Angeles after they moved from Lincoln Heights. We left Vegas around two o'clock in the morning, because that is when my father, Bill, a musician in one of the hotels on "The Strip," finished the late show and because our 1960 Rambler station wagon could not survive the heat of the desert during daylight hours. My two younger sisters, Michelle and Lisa, and I would sleep in the car while my mom, Claudia, kept my dad company in the front seat. When I was old enough, I sat up front and helped to keep him awake during the five-hour drive.

A visit to Naunny's house was always a joy. When I was very young, she used to give me beer shampoos in the bathtub. I remember how cold the beer felt running down my head and how awful the liquid smelled when it first came out of the can. But my hair always felt so soft after one of those shampoos.

Naunny also taught me how to make bubbles in the bathtub with the Palmolive liquid soap that she used to clean dishes. She would put a squirt in the tub, make an "A-OK" sign with her finger and thumb, and dunk her hand in the water. When she pulled her hand out of the water, she would blow a massive bubble that floated toward the ceiling until gravity pulled it back toward the tub. I loved to pop it just before it hit the water.

When I was old enough to get an allowance, Naunny and I would play 500 Rummy during our visits. At first, we played for $1 and then upped the ante to $5 when my allowance was increased. These games were epic marathons that always seemed to go down to the bottom of the deck. I took great pride in my card-playing skills, which seemed to be validated by the fact that I only lost one time to Naunny, even though she played Rummy and other card games on a regular basis. That one loss occurred when I was about nine years old, and I pouted for the rest of the night. But then my apparent mastery of the game took over, and I never lost again for the remainder of my Rummy career.

When I was about twelve years old, I finally recognized that Naunny had been letting me win. One night I noticed that she kept throwing away the same cards that she had picked up earlier in the round. When I confronted her, she denied that she had been letting me win, even though it was pretty obvious. At first I was a little upset, having had my pride burst like the soap bubbles that I used to pop in her bathtub. Then I realized that she was letting me win because she loved me and wanted me to have a little extra money. I wondered how much money Naunny had let me win over the years.

THE MEANING(S) OF "GRANDMOTHER"

Since older people become grandparents at different stages of life, the meaning of grandparenthood is varied.
—TERRY HARGRAVE and SUZANNE MIDORI HANNA,
The Aging Family

Your grandma showed different faces to different people.
—HUSBAND OF FORMER DAUGHTER-IN-LAW

Take a moment to think about the one grandmother whom you know or knew best. Visualize her face, her hair, her hands. Think about what she means or meant to you. Does she spoil you with food and gifts? Was she the life of the party or the lady who sat quietly in the back holding your hand? Did she play with you, read to you, tell you stories?

Now think about what she might mean or might have meant to other members of your family, including your brothers and sisters, your parents, your aunts and uncles, your cousins. Your grandmother probably has or had many different relationships with these relatives, and her meanings to them are or were as varied as those relationships.

Researchers who study grandparents have determined that their meaning to family members is indeed varied. This finding is not surprising given that people are living longer than ever before and grandparents now have a chance of being a grand-parent for up to four decades and of being a great- and even great-great-grandparent. Researchers have found that grandparents play many roles, including surrogate parents, caregivers, teachers, mentors, mediators, nurturers, playmates, distant figures, and many others. When compared to grandfathers, grandmothers tend to have higher levels of satisfaction as grandparents and tend to be more nurturing and more interactive with their grandchildren.

This book is about my search for the many meanings of my grandmother's life and death. When Naunny died in 1994 at age eighty-six, she was survived by two sons, eleven grandchildren, fourteen great-grandchildren, three great-great-grandchildren, and numerous nieces and nephews (and grandnieces and grandnephews), cousins, and in-laws. I spent the last several years interviewing many of these relatives to find out what Naunny meant to them. I already knew most of them, but I also tracked down other relatives whom I did not know directly or had not seen since I was a little kid. Whether I knew them or not, when I told them what I was doing they welcomed me with open arms. I interviewed over fifty of Naunny's relatives who live in four states, and they all shared their homes, their food, and, most important, their stories of Naunny.

Many of Naunny's relatives still live in southern California, where Naunny lived from the 1920s when she moved there from Trinidad, Colorado, with her first husband until her death. I made several trips from my home in Sacramento, California, to visit with these relatives. On one memorable trip to Los Angeles, Uncle Chuck gave me a driving tour of Naunny's adult life, showing me where she lived, where she worked, where she played, and where she died. This tour was wonderful because it contextualized the information that I was gathering about Naunny and stimulated my uncle's memories about his mother.

I also traveled to Las Vegas, Nevada, to interview members of my immediate family as well as to Colorado and New Mexico to visit Naunny's birthplace near Trinidad, Colorado, to do genealogical research on her family history, and to interview relatives who live in that part of the country. Then it was back to California, where I conducted additional interviews and library research and worked on this book.

It was very gratifying to reconnect with so many family members and to hear so many stories about my grandmother. I learned much about her and realized that she had a richer life than I ever imagined. I also learned much about the meaning of the concept "grandmother" in American culture and realized that it is a richer concept than I had considered. Finally, I learned much about myself and about how our own biographies intersect with our grandmothers, grandfathers, and other members of our extended families.

Tim drove into the main entrance of Calvary Cemetery in East L.A., a sprawling urban graveyard with over two hundred thousand plots. Former movie stars of Hollywood's "Golden Era" such as Lionel Barrymore, Lou Costello, and Irene Dunne are buried there, along with Ronald Reagan's parents, John and Nellie. Uncle Chuck, Tim, and I instantly recalled how the place looked on the day of Naunny's funeral. It was early January when she died, and Christmas decorations were still covering family graves throughout the cemetery. Most were plastic trees and other paper decorations that might have looked tacky in isolation, but in combination they shimmered with elegance in the sunlight. The sight of those Christmas decorations shining in that cemetery is one of my most cherished life memories.

Even though we recalled the general area where Naunny was buried, I went into the information office and obtained a map of the vast complex. An elderly man at the desk circled the large section where we could find Naunny's grave.

Tim parked his truck near the area, and we piled out and started walking toward the spot where we thought her grave was located. Lance giggled as he jumped over various markers.

"If you step on somebody's grave and you don't know who's in there," Lance said, "you'll have dreams about that person."

Uncle Chuck, Tim, Lance, and I scanned the various graveyard markers. The first one we recognized was the grave of Charles Trujillo, Naunny's first husband and Uncle Chuck's father. Charley Sr. died in a car accident in 1934 at age thirty-two, when Uncle Chuck was seven years old and my father, Bill, was just four.

Uncle Chuck looked at the tombstone and recalled the day he found out about his father's death.

"My mother was in bed, still recovering from diphtheria," he said.

"Your dad and I had the Sunday funnies on the floor and we were listening to a guy on the radio who would read the funnies. He was really dramatic. We were following along when the doorbell rang. I answered the door, and a plainclothes policeman was there. He said, 'Is your mother home?'

"I said, 'Yeah,' and went to get her. I was standing in the doorway with my mother when the policeman said, 'Are you Mrs. Trujillo?' She said yes, and he said, 'I hate to tell you this, but your husband was killed.'

"Well, you know your grandmother. She couldn't stand bad news. She immediately passed out. So, Jeez, here I am, seven years old, and I just found out that my father was killed, and now it looked like my mother had just dropped dead, too. I remember I fell on the floor crying. I'll never forget that."

Uncle Chuck smiled softly.

"It was the middle of the depression, 1934, your grandmother was recovering from a life-threatening illness, and now she's a widow with two kids. But we survived, and, in fact, we landed on our feet running, which was amazing. And I don't ever remember feeling that I was poor or in a terrible situation. I don't know how your grandmother did it. I mean, other people would have fallen apart."

"She had to deal with traumatic things her whole life," Tim added, looking at the grave of the grandfather he never met.

"Oh, yeah," Uncle Chuck said. "Several of her brothers and sisters died very young. Her father suffered a stroke when she was a little kid, and they lost their ranch. It was rough times back then. Practically everybody in the family at one time or another had some illegitimate child or something. But their home was always open to all of them—wayward daughters, children, anyone and everyone."

Monday, December 24th, 1984

Dearest Nicky Jito—

We got here Friday at 6 PM. Stayed downtown for 2 hours, played a few games of Keno and some slots. Didn't do much. I hit a 25 cent slot for $15.00 and a couple of 4 dollar ones, but that's all. So we called your Dad to come after us. Saturday we went shopping with Lisa to Alpha Beta, and Pete hit a quarter machine for 80 bucks! So we made up for our losses! Your Dad, Bob, Todd and Jerry have been playing tennis every day. . . .

Your Mom has been cooking and baking goodies, as usual. We all miss you and are all anxious to meet Leah! Last night we went to a Church festival at the Station Palace, out by Sam's Town. Your Dad played with George Valdez, Howard Agster, Norm Prentiss and two others I didn't know. They sounded terrific! Norm taped it all and is going to let me have one, so God willing you'll be able to hear it when you come out next summer!

Guess that's all for now. Tonight we open our goodies. Wish you were here.

Bye now. I'll write again when we get back home.

Love and Blessings,
Naunny
xxxxx

Most granddaughters that I've met describe a feeling of calm and peace in their grandmother's presence, a sense that the daily pressures of home and school no longer exist.
—HOPE EDELMAN, *Mother of My Mother*

I don't think your Grandma ever understood why you and your dad didn't get along.
—SON

I think I was a pretty typical teenager in high school. I played sports, I had zits, I experimented with drugs and alcohol, and I was rebellious at home, especially whenever my father ordered me to do something, which was quite often. My dad has threatened to write a book titled *Take Out the Trash,* an amusingly painful reference to the fights that we reenacted almost every day when he ordered me to take out the trash.

"Take out the trash," he would demand in his autocratic tone.

"Say please," I would counter, knowing that he rarely said please to anyone.

"I don't have to say please!" he would respond, raising his voice.

"If you don't say please, then I don't have to take out the trash!"

"Then you don't have to stay in my house!"

"Then I'll leave!"

"Then go ahead!"

"OK, I will!"

I would leave the house, slam the door, and drive around in the 1960 Rambler station wagon that I inherited on my sixteenth birthday. After cooling down, I would come home, and my dad and I would apologize to each other. Then we would repeat the same performance the next day for the sequels *Clean Your Room, Give Me the Salt, Turn the Channel,* and others.

Ironically, or perhaps fittingly, I learned to be so defiant to autocratic authority from my father. He hated his brief stint in the military because officers ordered him around. He also was fired by Wayne Newton when the Las Vegas entertainer demanded that my dad laugh at his jokes between songs and my dad responded, "The only thing that's funny about you is your singing."

Although my dad resisted the demands of others, he readily made them of me, and when I did not automatically comply, he became defensive and angry, which prompted more defiance from me. And the dysfunctional pattern continued to cycle.

I'm sure that I would have experimented with drugs anyway, since many of my friends used them on and off during high school. But I have no doubt that the constant battles with my father provided even more motivation for me to use drugs, especially marijuana. My dad never hit me or abused me, yet the ongoing conflicts with him wore me down psychologically, as I'm sure they did to him as well. At that point in my life, I just wanted to not feel so stressed out all the time or, better yet, to be left alone, and smoking pot definitely facilitated that goal. So I smoked pot—a lot of pot—and I smoked it as often as I could.

However, I found that I did not usually smoke marijuana when my grandmother visited or when we visited her in Los Angeles. I wasn't afraid that Naunny would catch me with drugs. Rather, I felt completely at peace whenever she was around and really did not feel the need to get high. I only wished that she lived in Las Vegas so that I could have gone to her place whenever I was kicked out of my house for not taking out the trash.

After high school, I attended the University of Southern California in Los Angeles. I was so happy to leave Las Vegas and to leave behind the continued conflicts with my father.

Within a few months, however, I was, much to my surprise, homesick. Not surprisingly, I turned to Naunny. I drove over to her house in East L.A. at least once or twice each week, especially during my freshman year. Naunny would feed me, do my laundry, give me money, and scratch or tickle my back as we sat on the couch visiting. Sometimes I would even go to Naunny's house to study at night, since the dorm was very noisy, and Naunny made really strong coffee. I remember pulling an all-nighter once in her kitchen to write a paper, assuring Naunny that I was fine every hour or so when she checked on me.

I continued to go to Naunny's house for the rest of my undergraduate years, though not as often as I did during that first year. I was proud to take my friends and my girlfriends to her house as well, because she treated all of them as if they were her own grandchildren.

Those undergraduate years were my favorite times with my grandmother because I saw her on a regular basis. She helped me overcome my early homesickness, and her love remained unconditional in good times and bad times.

One of my favorite memories from this period is of the spring break when my girlfriend, two friends, and I painted the inside of Naunny's house. My friends and I bought all of the materials, and we took two days to paint the living room and the kitchen. Although the off-white color was too bright for Naunny's tastes, she thanked us and told us how much she loved it. I remember feeling that I had repaid her for her love, at least in a small way.

We continued to search for Naunny's grave, but next came across the grave of Naunny's mother, Catalina Maldonado Martinez.

"Grammy was a quiet little woman," Uncle Chuck recalled as he looked at the marker. "She had her hair in a bun and always wore

black. She took care of us while our mother was at work. She was always there for us. Your dad and I would get up in the morning, go to the bathroom, brush our teeth, have breakfast, and go to school, and we didn't have to worry about anything. The breakfast was always ready, and when we came home from school, our clothes were picked up, washed, folded, and put away, and our bed was made. As soon as we got home, she'd start making food. It was the perfect childhood. Your grandma was just like that, too."

He smiled, remembering his grandmother.

"When we were kids we used to come home from school and enter the house through the back door," he said. "Grammy would be sitting in the kitchen, which faced the backyard. She could see me come in from the gate there, and I used to see her get up from the table and crumple up some papers and throw them in the trash. At first, I didn't think anything about it. Then I started to wonder: What's my grandmother doing, drawing dirty pictures or something? One day she went into the other room for something, so I went over to the trash and opened it up. Well, she didn't know how to read or write. My mother would always sign her Social Security checks for her, and my grandmother would just put an X underneath. It turns out that what she was doing each day was practicing writing her name. That was the only thing she ever learned how to write. Finally she got to where she could sign her own checks. She was so proud of that."

June 5, 1983

Dear Naunny:

This is a very hard letter to write, so I think I'll get right to the bad news. I know I haven't written very much this past year, and I guess that's because it has not been a very good year with Sally. We have had some very serious marital problems and have recently decided to get a divorce. It's really hard to say what "caused" us to have problems—it's been a very stressful year with the move to the Midwest, finishing the dissertations, and adjusting to new positions, places, and people. And, unfortunately, we did not seek marital counseling until recently—a bit too late. I don't know what else I can tell you. It's still pretty hard adjusting to it, even though I was the one who "officially" asked for a divorce. We've seen one lawyer and will be seeing another one tomorrow morning. There is a 60-day "cooling off" period in Indiana, so we won't actually be divorced until August.

I start teaching summer classes at Purdue this week. Sally is going to Pat and Roger's this Wednesday. She may be calling you. I've told my folks. You can tell any of the relatives in southern Cal if you feel like it.

Sorry to have to tell you the bad news, but I think we'll be better off in the long run. I'll try to write more soon.

Love,

Nick

After I graduated from USC in 1977, I left Los Angeles to earn my master's and Ph.D. degrees and then to start my career as a professor. Naunny came to all of my graduations and to Las Vegas for her yearly Christmas visit, but I no longer saw her on a regular basis. I was too busy with my own life as a struggling graduate student and then as an overworked and underpaid professor to realize how much of a loss it was not to see her more often. I would write to her and call her on occasion, but my grandmother was no longer a central part of my life.

Soon after I took my first professor job at Purdue University in 1982, I got divorced. My marriage to Sally, who also had completed a Ph.D., was a casualty of our respective doctoral programs. We postponed working on our relationship so that we could finish our dissertations, but when we finally returned to our marriage, it was beyond repair.

Naunny was absolutely crushed when she learned about our divorce. Sally had been my college sweetheart, and Naunny loved her as a granddaughter. Naunny never said anything to me directly about the divorce, but when she found out about it, she stopped writing in the family history journal that I had asked her to start several years earlier.

"Now I know why you haven't written! And I'm heart-broken," her last entry read. *"What could have happened to break you apart. You had so ——— much going for you."*

A couple of years later, I married Leah Vande Berg, who had been a professor at Northwestern University when I was at Purdue. The following Christmas, Leah and I went to my parents' house in Las Vegas. Naunny would meet Leah for the first time, and I was a little apprehensive about their meeting because Naunny had loved Sally so much.

Whatever apprehensiveness I felt disappeared the moment we walked into the house. Naunny gave Leah a big hug and kiss as if she had known her for decades. She accepted Leah into the family as her granddaughter immediately and without reservation.

Time certainly does fly, and soon it was the 1990s. Leah and I moved to California to teach at Sacramento State University in northern California, several hundred miles from Los Angeles. I made a couple of trips to Los Angeles to visit Naunny and saw her at Christmas, but she still was not a central part of my life. Leah and I had classes to teach, articles and books to write, and bills to pay, and I am sad to admit that I did not expend much energy to make Naunny a more meaningful part of my life.

The last time I saw Naunny was in Sacramento in the spring of 1993. Uncle Chuck had taken her to northern California to visit various relatives who had migrated from southern California to Santa Cruz, Lake Tahoe, Napa Valley, and other areas. I was happy when he called and said that they would stop by our house in Sacramento for a visit.

When they pulled up, I ran out to greet them. I was surprised to see how frail Naunny had become, even more so than she was the previous Christmas. She could not have weighed more than ninety pounds and she seemed so weak. When I hugged her, I felt her bones and worried that I might actually hurt her.

I was especially happy that she would finally meet my beloved golden retriever, Wrigley, who at nine years of age was also relatively old and frail. Leah and I never had any kids, so our dogs have always served as our surrogate children, and I wanted Naunny to meet her "grand-dogs." But Naunny was so fragile that Wrigley almost knocked her over when he leaned into her for a scratch. We had to put him and Ragbrai, our young Airedale terrier, outside while we visited with Naunny in the living room.

Even though Naunny was frail, when we said good-bye I assumed that I would see her later that year when she made her annual trip to Las Vegas for Christmas. It never occurred to me that this might be the last time I would see my grandmother alive. But Naunny caught pneumonia that winter and died in early January.

I don't know how our visit that spring might have been different if I knew that it would be our last, but I sure wish that I could relive that moment. In fact, I wish that I could relive many of the moments that I shared with her. In some ways, though, my search for Naunny's meaning allowed me to vicariously relive some of those moments. Perhaps at some subconscious level, that is why I decided to conduct this search in the first place.

Uncle Chuck, Tim, Lance, and I still had not found Naunny's grave, so we decided to walk to an area that we had avoided because the sprinklers had been, and still were, running. As we read the markers on the wet grass, Tim recalled, "I remember Grandma used to say, 'When I die, I want to be buried with my mother.' I said, 'How come you don't want to get buried back in Trinidad [Colorado] with your father?' She said, 'Trinidad? All the teenagers drive by and throw their empty beer cans in that graveyard.'"

We laughed, remembering Naunny's unique sense of humor and her ability to laugh at just about anything. My thoughts flashed back to the time I drove from Indiana in 1984 to visit Naunny and Pete in their one-bedroom apartment. By then, Pete was a mess. He had emphysema and other ailments, and he was wearing a colostomy bag. We had just finished eating dinner and were watching one of Pete's television shows when his intestines started to rumble. He struggled to get up from his chair and then rushed toward the bathroom. He made it to the hallway before his colostomy bag exploded.

"Sheeeeeeeet!" Pete yelled as the content of the bag splattered on the floor.

"Yep, that's what it is," Naunny said, without missing a beat.

"When it looked like she wasn't going to make it, I called your dad," Uncle Chuck said. "I told him to get on a plane that afternoon. Then I went back and stayed with her for a while, and then told her that I was going to the airport to pick up Bill. She took off her oxygen mask and said, 'Ooh, that sounds ominous.'"

We laughed again.

"I think laughing at everything was an important part of her personality," Tim said. "She even laughed in the face of death. She wasn't freaked out about dying. It was like, hurry up, get me out of here." Tim paused. "That's the way she died. She was strong. She wasn't gasping, just trying to breathe. I guess her heart stopped or something, because she just grimaced, and that was it. Just a little grimace, and then perfectly still."

"What did you feel when she died?" I asked Uncle Chuck, who was in the room with Tim at the moment of her death.

"I guess I felt a combination of things," he said. "I was sorry to see her go, because I'd never get a chance to talk to her again. But I didn't want to see her suffer, either, so there was kind of a feeling of relief." He paused. "Not that it all happened at exactly the same time."

We continued to search for Naunny's grave until Tim finally found it.

"Here it is!" he yelled out.

My stomach tightened, and I felt upset with my dad for not calling me when Naunny's illness turned for the worse. "It happened so quickly," he had told me, but how long does it take to make a phone call? As I headed toward where Tim was standing, though, I realized, once again, that it was my own damn fault for not calling her more often when she was at the nursing home. I knew ultimately that I was the one responsible for making the naive assumption that she would recover from the flu, get out of that nursing home, and be back to feeling "peachy keen," as she always used to describe how she felt, even when everyone in the family knew that she was suffering.

As I walked toward Naunny's grave, I started to dread what I might feel when I saw her tombstone. Would it be guilt for not calling her more often? Shame for writing so infrequently? Sorrow for not making her eat more during the last few years of her life as her health deteriorated? Self-pity for not getting to see her one last time?

Would I need to confess to her? Ask her for forgiveness?

I arrived, took a deep breath, and looked down at the marker. It read, simply, "In Memory of Elsie Trujillo Alcaraz, 1907–1994." And instead of guilt or shame or pity or sorrow, all I felt was pure joy, for having known, and having been loved by, this wonderful woman.

"Her name was Eloysa," Uncle Chuck said, "but nobody knew her by that name. Everybody knew her as Elsie."

Uncle Chuck, Tim, and I stared at that marker in silence for several minutes, while Lance continued to run through the sprinklers. Each of us remembered, no doubt very differently, what a loving, unselfish, proud, funny, sensual, frail lady was buried there, one who had graced—and who had helped to produce—our lives.

And so the search for her grave had been successful, but the search for the meaning of her life—and for the meaning of the grandmother in American culture—continued.

August 20, 1985

Dearest Jito Lindo—

Your Dad called and said you were going to East Lansing. He didn't say when. So I guess this will be my last letter until or if I hear from you. I won't know where to send it! He said he'll be playing the Jerry Lewis Telethon from 2 AM to 10 AM, our time. Everyone is OK.

Timmy called. He'd just finished roofing Clint Eastwood's former home, now owned by his friend and partner. They've become good friends, and he told Tim that they're building a big set in Idaho, near Sun Valley, for a new flick, and they asked Tim to go along and hang out with them and they'd get him some extra parts in their new movie. He said he's going! Isn't that great! By the way, he got 14 thousand for the roofing job!

Last Saturday, my nephew Joe Jr. drove me to Hemet to visit my brother (his Dad) Joe. We were there on Feb 5th to help him celebrate his 85th birthday, and he looked good then. But now, just six months later, he doesn't look too good.

Chuck is on vacation, again, and I guess you know that Terese is getting married on Nov. 24th. They were married in Reno, but now they want a church wedding.

Pete and I are OK, in case you'd like to know. Everyone else is fine.

Oh well, Bye now.

Love and Blessings always,
Naunny

THE SEARCH BEGINS

All too often we have looked at grandparenthood in isolation, not taking into account how it is embedded in a web of relationships and lives.
    —GUNHILD HAGESTAD and LINDA BURTON,
      "Grandparenthood"

She was a grandmother for a long time. —GRANDSON

The following chapters reveal the results of my search for the many meanings of my grandmother and of the concept "grandmother." Naunny was "Mom" to her two sons, and "Aunt Elsie" or "Tia Eloysa" to her many nieces and nephews. She was "Naunny" to me and my two sisters, and "Grandma" or "Black Grandma" to my cousins because, as one of them told me, "she had black hair and our other grandma who had gray hair we called 'Gray Grandma'—well, we were little kids, and life was a lot less complicated back then." She was "Chubby Grandma" to her great- and great-great-grandchildren because of the cat named Chubby that lived with her and Pete for almost twenty years. And she was "Naunny Grapes" to my sisters' kids because, as my twelve-year-old niece said, "What I remember most about Naunny Grapes is that we ate grapes."

Just as Naunny had different names and nicknames to these many relatives, she also had many meanings for them. As I interviewed these relatives, they reconstructed a grandmother that I knew very well: one who was incredibly generous even though she was very poor, one who loved to serve people in every way, one who worked hard as a widow during the Depression to support her two kids, one who was very devout and read her Bible every day for much of her life, and one who loved being a grandmother but hated getting old. Much to my surprise, some of these relatives also reconstructed a grandmother whom I never knew: one who loved to hear and tell dirty jokes, one who had an active romantic life between her two marriages including a relationship with a married man, one who was anorexic for much of her life, and one who may have had an abortion during the Depression.

While talking to many friends and relatives about this book, I have recognized that my grandmother's life also reflects the lives of many grandmothers in American society. Like numerous women her age, my grandmother was born and raised in a poor rural area. Her father was a self-made man who made it big then lost everything. She worked hard as a child to help the family and then escaped by getting married and moving to a big city. She worked in menial jobs to make ends meet as a widow with two kids during the Depression and later made good money in the aircraft industry during World War II with thousands of other women until they were fired when the men came home. She enjoyed life as a single woman after getting over the tragic death of her first husband, then many years later married a happy, but hopeless, alcoholic. She spent most of her adult life serving and giving to others, and, in the process, denied her own needs. In the end, she struggled with dementia for several months before she caught pneumonia and died in a nursing home.

I also realize that the ways in which my relatives have reconstructed Naunny's meaning reflect the ways in which other families reconstruct the meanings of their grandmothers. After all, we remember our grandmothers and reconstruct their meaning in the stories that we tell about them. Scholars have argued that family stories are vital to our families, because they define the values and beliefs that make families unique to members. Family stories about our grandmothers, then, define the values and beliefs that make grandmothers unique as grandmothers, and they reveal our own beliefs about what a "grandmother" should be. For example, I recognize that in my own stories about Naunny, I had been stereotyping her—and in some ways, stereotyping every grandmother—as a nice old lady who gave presents, served food, and spoiled her grandchildren in almost every way. Naunny was all that, certainly, but what I failed to realize is that my grandmother, like all grandmothers, had a far more meaningful life. Fortunately, several of my relatives told stories that reconstructed her meaning with greater depth and richness.

In this book, I discuss some of the meanings of my grandmother that were revealed in family stories about her. My analysis of these stories was guided by cultural and critical perspectives. Cultural perspectives focus on the symbolic aspects of human experience and on how people interpret their everyday reality, so I analyzed family stories to find out how family members interpreted the meaning of my grandmother. Critical perspectives focus on the ideological aspects of human experience and on how people privilege certain meanings over others, so I also critiqued how family stories about Naunny privileged certain meanings of the grandmother over others, especially those in which gender, class, race, and age were used to reinforce beliefs about what a grandmother should be in our culture. (For an elaborated discussion, see the appendix.)

I use different forms of writing to tell the story of my search. I report what relatives told me about Naunny and critique how their stories privileged certain meanings over others. I weave in my own memories and feelings about Naunny and critique how I, too, marginalized her meaning. I narrate impressionistic fragments of Naunny's life, based on stories from her relatives and my own imagination. I give a "voice" to Naunny as well, by including passages from her family history journal, from the diary she kept for the last few months of her life, and from letters that she wrote to family members.

I hope that this book encourages readers to remember your own grandmothers—"Grammy," "Gagi," "Nana," or "Nonna." I also hope that this book motivates you to understand your grandmothers in a broader context, recognizing how gender, race, class, and age have influenced who they are or were as well as who you are and will become. Finally, I hope that this book urges you to reflect critically on how you and other relatives assign meaning to the lives of your grandmothers and other family women through your stories. As series editors Arthur Bochner and Carolyn Ellis have concluded, one of the uses of this kind of writing "is to allow another person's world of experience to inspire critical reflection on your own."

The Family Historian

Many analysts argue that children benefit immensely from hearing narratives about family history that only grandparents can tell. . . . Thus, intergenerational narratives not only inform present generations about the past but also link them through personal storytelling. —LAURIE ARLISS, *Contemporary Family Communication*

My mother's mother was Barbarita Pacheco Maldonado. After my grandfather passed away, all the children went to her for advice. She ruled our community of San Miguel. It was quite a pretty good-sized town, with nothing but relatives living there. When my grandmother died (I think in 1917), she left 13 acres to each of her kids. My mother wasn't there for the reading of the will, and she got what no one else wanted: the 13 acres of family bones. The cemetery!

—from Naunny's journal

Catalina Maldonado Martinez was in labor, lying uncomfortably in the small bed of what had become the birthing room of the house. At thirty years of age, Catalina was a tiny woman, not quite five feet tall, but she was incredibly strong and sturdy as any woman who was about to deliver her tenth child in the early 1900s had to be.

Of the nine children that she had delivered, four died at birth, and there was no guarantee that this one would survive. Any number of things could go wrong: the baby could be stillborn, it could be a breech, or there could be other complications. But, as usual, no doctors were present, and she was in a bedroom of a house, not the maternity ward of a hospital. Only the partera—the midwife—was there to assist, but this partera was a new one. Catalina had insisted on a new midwife, not because the previous one did anything wrong but because Catalina was a superstitious woman who desperately wanted this baby to survive.

Catalina's sister and oldest daughter were in the room to assist. Men were never allowed in a birthing room, so her husband, José Julio Martinez, was at the saloon he owned at the bottom of the hill from their house, getting drunk with his brothers and flirting with the barmaid.

With one last push, the baby, a girl, finally came out. The midwife cut the umbilical cord and cleaned the baby with the moist towels that Catalina's sister had prepared. Everyone in the room could see that this baby was a beautiful one, and Catalina had a feeling in her heart that her little girl would turn out to be very special.

Catalina named her new baby Juanita Eloysa Martinez. One week later, on November 27, 1907, in her birthplace of San Miguel, Colorado, Eloysa was baptized to wash away her original sin.

A few summers ago, I traveled to New Mexico and Colorado to visit the birthplace of my grandmother, to do genealogical research on her family history, and to interview relatives who live in that part of the country. My cousin Tim and his wife Sandra, who goes by the nickname "Jimmie," also joined me on this trek from their home north of Albuquerque, New Mexico. Tim had moved his roofing company from Los Angeles to New Mexico a couple of years earlier, tired of living in smog-ridden and fast-paced L.A. and wanting to spend the rest of his life in the clear and expansive land of his ancestors.

We drove from Albuquerque, through Taos and Santa Fe, to Trinidad, Colorado, roughly paralleling the old Santa Fe Trail that our Martinez and Trujillo ancestors had taken when they traveled with other Conquistadores from the Spanish "New World." Of course, we were going seventy-five miles per hour on well-paved roads with pit stops in clean rest areas, while our ancestors traveled in horse-drawn caravans, pulling supplies, herding sheep, and relieving themselves on the dusty trail and wiping themselves with corn cobs.

Even though I am half Polish and do not speak more than a few words in Spanish, I felt completely at home in this part of the country. Everywhere I looked I saw tanned people with thick dark hair, people who looked like—and in some distant way undoubtedly were—my cousins on my father's side. We ate authentic "Spanish American" food, including the beans and tortillas that Naunny had always cooked, as well as the tamales and empanadas that she would make for Christmas. With every bite, we remembered our grandmother: her face, her laugh, her smell, and her stories.

We arrived in Trinidad and drove to the place where the little town of San Miguel used to exist near the northern base of Fisher's Peak, a mountain ridge called Flat-top that rises to an elevation of 9,600 feet. In 1862, Hispanic settlers from an area known as Guadalupita in what is now New Mexico founded plazas in several nearby areas, including the one at San Miguel, which they named after St. Michael. San Miguel plaza grew into a small town that stood for many years until it died from neglect in the mid-1900s.

Although little is known about the history of San Miguel, the site where this town used to exist is on private property, owned by a crusty cattle rancher whose ancestors founded the plaza of Sandoval just a few miles from San Miguel. I had contacted the owner before my trip, and he graciously agreed to let us walk around the ruins of Naunny's birthplace. We met him at his house, and he pointed us in the direction of what was left of San Miguel. He asked us to visit the cemetery up there and lift the fallen gravestone of his grandmother, who we thought was the wife of the uncle of my grandmother's mother, though we could not quite untangle those obscure familial lines.

We drove as far as we could on the gravel road to the site, until we had to park the car and walk the last couple of miles. It was early June, and the hills were lush green.

"No wonder our great-grandfather started out as a sheepherder," Tim said. "This land is perfect for grazing."

We finally arrived at the site but found only two partial structures, one very old and crumbling brick house that the owner had identified as the former elementary school and a smaller but more "modern" building that had been the home of the schoolteacher. We walked around the area, gazing at the crumbling structures and at several other decaying foundations, wondering whether they might have supported the house in which Naunny was born.

We spent a few hours looking around the ruins and then searched for the cemetery. It took us almost an hour to find it because the trees and bushes surrounding the graveyard had hidden it from view. As we looked for it, we remembered the story that Naunny used to tell us about how her mother forgot to show up for the reading of the will when her grandmother died and ended up inheriting the cemetery.

We finally found that very cemetery. It was quite disheveled, and the small fence that once protected it had fallen. Cattle were using the area for grazing, indicated by the hoof prints that had cracked many of the old sandstone markers and by the massive cow droppings that seemed to be everywhere. Many of the tombstones were over one hundred years old, with death dates in the late 1800s. Several of the graves were those of children, some of babies, reminding us that our grandmother could have easily suffered the same fate as four of her siblings who died at birth or as many youngsters who died of influenza and other ailments, especially in the brutally cold winters. It was a depressing reminder of the hard life endured by the people in this forgotten little town.

We also found the fallen tombstone of the owner's grandmother, which likely had been knocked over by a not-so-sacred cow. We could not lift the solid marble slab by ourselves, so we used a fallen tree limb as a lever. After several attempts, we were able to prop it up and restore one tiny bit of dignity to this forsaken graveyard.

The next day, Tim and Jimmie headed back to Albuquerque. I stayed in Trinidad and interviewed some relatives who still live in the area, including Naunny's eighty-one-year-old cousin, Dolores Maldonado, who regaled me with stories about the little town of San Miguel where she, too, was born. I also spent time in local libraries, doing historical and genealogical research, and then drove to Denver to interview other relatives and conduct more library research.

Having spent time in the land of Naunny's ancestors, I was inspired to get to work. I was especially determined to write the story of my grandmother's family history, so that Naunny's descendants would always remember her—and our own—family roots.

Chapter 1

GRANDPARENTS AND FAMILY HISTORY

The family is not a "container" for stories . . . but rather stories formulate the family.
—KRISTEN LANGELLIER, "Personal Narratives"

I went to Colorado in 1936 when I was about nine years old. We went back there on a Pullman train. It was the middle of the Depression, and the only reason my mom could afford it was that she had just collected the insurance money after my father's death. My uncle Chris was still living there, in Cokedale, and he showed us all the coal-mining camps and the big coke ovens. He also told us stories about how awful it was working the mines. I was from L.A., so it seemed very strange.
—SON

Grandparents who tell family stories play an important role. They have been called the "oral historians" of the family who connect several generations of relatives through their stories. Social scientists point out that such family stories do not objectively represent events from the past because our memories are always subjective and context-dependent. Critical scholars would add that our family memories are also *political*, because family stories privilege certain aspects of family history and influence the way in which family history is interpreted.

Many of the relatives whom I interviewed recalled stories that Naunny had told them about her family history. As they retold these stories, they reconstructed Naunny's meaning as a family historian and reinforced certain aspects of our family history. I include these stories throughout the book but here focus on four commonly told sets of stories about Naunny's family history.

"Ay viene su padre!" Catalina yelled, announcing to Eloysa's brothers and sisters that their father was coming up the dirt road to San Miguel. It was a very special day for the Martinez family, since José Julio had just purchased a Model T in nearby Trinidad. This would be the first vehicle of its kind in San Miguel, and the entire town came out to see it.

~24~

José Julio sat regally at the wheel, waving to all of his friends and neighbors in town, many of whom were related to him as cousins and in-laws. He was one of the most successful men in the small community, having gone from a young boy who homesteaded there with his poor family from New Mexico in the late 1800s to a wealthy and respected businessman who owned one of the largest flocks of sheep in the area and several stores and homes in San Miguel, Gray Creek, Sopris, Trinidad, and other nearby towns.

As the strange-looking vehicle chugged up the dirt road, Catalina picked up Eloysa from her crib and carried her to the front door of their small house.

"Ay esta su papa," she said proudly and kissed her young daughter on the forehead. José Julio smiled at his wife, and the ends of his long handlebar moustache curled up, just as they always did when he smiled.

When I was a little boy, Naunny told me stories about when she was a little girl. I don't remember much about these stories, at least about the stories she told me when I was very young. I vaguely remember her telling me about how her father once was very wealthy, but then he lost everything. Naunny also said that as a young girl she had to go to work to help support the family.

These stories sounded so foreign to a young boy living in a middle-class neighborhood in Las Vegas. I never knew whether she was telling me the truth or just making up these stories to get me to work harder in school and/or to appreciate how hard my dad was working for the family.

It didn't really matter to me either way, because I didn't really pay much attention to Naunny's stories. At point in my life, I just wanted to play 500 Rummy with her.

THE RISE AND FALL OF JOSÉ JULIO MARTINEZ AND HIS FAMILY

My father had worked in coal mines in Gray Creek, Colorado. He started very young. Every payday, he'd buy a ram, ewe, or lamb, and keep it with his brother's flock, until he acquired a sizable flock of his own. By the time I came along, he was 34 years old and doing very well with his sheep ranches and other properties.

His wool was bringing in top money, and young J.J., as he was
known, was wealthy and respected by all.

Then in 1909, William Howard Taft became our 27th president.
He only served one term, but he ruined the sheep owners by
importing wool from Australia. My father lost everything, and
landed at San Rafael Hospital in Trinidad with a stroke. He was
there for a full year.

He still owned a grocery store in Sopris, Colorado, and my
mother had to move there with her six children. The children were
all too young to take care of the store, and my mother was busy
with the children. So she had one of her brother-in-laws help out.
He helped himself so well, that by the time my father came home
from the hospital, my uncle had opened up his own grocery store
and post office, and my father was forced to move his family to
Trinidad, and onto the last property he owned: a four-room house
on 1019 Boulevard Street.

—from Naunny's journal

It seems that almost everyone in my extended family has heard
the story of the rise and fall of Naunny's father, José Julio Martinez. Naunny emphasized this story in her family history journal, and she told it to so many relatives that it has become a
family legend.

It is not surprising that Naunny's father may have enjoyed
many years of success raising sheep. Historians have noted that
sheep had many advantages over cattle in the late 1800s and
early 1900s. Sheep needed far less pastureland for grazing than
did cattle, and their flocking instinct was far more pronounced
so they would not scatter as much as cattle during storms or
raids by predatory animals or rustlers.

For a variety of reasons, most of which will never be known,
Naunny's father lost his large sheep ranch as well as the stores
and houses he owned. Virtually everyone in the family who retold this story emphasized its *tragic* nature, presenting it as a
tale of a man from humble beginnings who made it rich then
lost everything. Naunny's eighty-one-year-old cousin, José
Julio's niece, told the story this way:

Tio [Uncle] José Julio's father, Sotero, was very poor, so I don't
know exactly how my tio got his money. I know he had a lot of

sheep. Mom used to say he was rich since all of his kids dressed so nice. But then they lost it all. Mom used to say his brother stole everything from him when Tio José Julio got sick. And after going through all that wealth, it must be sad, you know, to lose it all. If you don't have nothing, you don't know nothing and you don't miss it. That's true with me, anyway. I never had nothing, so I never missed nothing. But it must have been very hard for Tio José Julio and his family.

After telling the same story, one of Naunny's granddaughters said that Naunny had told her that the only thing her father saved after he lost everything was a big red velvet chair. "It was like his throne," she said. "Naunny told me it was his chair and that only he could sit in it. That chair reminded him that he had once been this proud wealthy man."

Other relatives offered explanations as to why this family tragedy occurred. Some relatives blamed José Julio's demise on the brother who had embezzled from him.

"The way I heard it was that José Julio had a lot of sheep and other businesses," Naunny's cousin-in-law said. "But then he got sick, and the family started stealing from him, and he lost everything. How awful. Can you imagine your own family doing that?"

Other relatives attributed broader sociocultural and political motives to the story. One grandson placed part of the blame on the *racism* of the time, framing the story in this way:

> José Julio's father homesteaded up there from Taos with his family before all the mining companies were there. It was free land and they made the best of their opportunity. Grandma said her dad had a bunch of sheepherders working for him and he owned about seven stores. Then he had that stroke, and the brother-in-law ripped him off, and he lost everything. But I think there was a lot of discrimination involved, too. You know, Manifest Destiny. . . . I mean, he went from owning all that property and a large herd to a complete nobody. That kind of thing doesn't just happen by accident.

Although it would be misleading to say that "Manifest Destiny" *caused* José Julio's demise, it is clear that the native Hispanics in the area were discriminated against by the Anglos who occupied the area in the late 1800s and early 1900s. Referring specifically to Hispanic sheep owners, historian Sarah Deutsch notes that as Anglo railroad and mining companies were built in southern Colorado in the late 1800s and very early 1900s, the range land available to Hispanic sheepherders became very limited and far more expensive. When this occurred, most of the residents of the Hispanic villages, including San Miguel, were forced to move away and became dependent on the American economy as laborers.

The story of Naunny's father's rise and fall, then, is a classic tragedy that is common in form to many family sagas and reflects historic changes that affected many families. The story emphasizes the humble beginnings of the father, his rise as a successful businessman, and his fall back into poverty as a pathetic figure who keeps only his "throne" to remind him of his past glory. It is a tale laden with class, race, and gender implications, as the wealthy Hispanic patriarch loses everything because of forces inside and outside the family and ends up in the hospital a destitute and debilitated man.

As retold by relatives, the story also presents Naunny as a victim. She is the defenseless little girl who suddenly finds herself in a poor family with an ill father and a corrupt uncle and in a changing society that had displaced her family and most of the native Hispanics of New Mexico and Colorado. Some relatives even suggested that this story was a guiding influence for Naunny throughout her life.

"Naunny always told me that people who steal from their own families are the worst kind of people," one granddaughter said after telling the story. "I think that's why she was so loyal to the family, even when family members might have been wrong about something."

WHEN I WAS in college in Los Angeles, I often visited Naunny and Pete, especially during my first year. After Naunny fixed a plate of beans and tortillas for me, I would join her on the couch in their small living room. As usual, Pete was on his pink Naugahyde recliner. And, as usual, we watched Pete's favorite television shows, including *The Rockford Files*, *The F.B.I.*, and any boxing match that was on.

During commercials, Naunny chatted with me. On many occasions, she would start to tell me a story about her father or about her life in Colorado before she moved to Los Angeles. The minute Pete's show would return, however, he would silence her with a "shhhhushhh," so Naunny finished very few of the stories she started.

Frankly, I was usually relieved when Pete quieted Naunny. As a homesick freshman, I just wanted to eat a home-cooked meal, get my laundry done, and have Naunny scratch my back while we watched TV.

Eloysa, or "Elsie," as she was called, squeezed the hand of her twenty-two-year-old sister Julia as they walked on the cobblestone streets of downtown Trinidad, Colorado. Julia had taken her six-year-old sister to join a parade of women and children who were marching in support of Mother Jones, the famous labor leader. Mother Jones had come to Trinidad to help the striking coal miners in the area, but she was being detained against her will in San Rafael Hospital, the same hospital where Julia and Elsie's father had recovered from a stroke a few years earlier. Julia wanted to be there to show her support for the cause because her husband and two of her brothers-in-law had been killed in a mine explosion in nearby Dawson, New Mexico, just three months earlier, in October 1913.

As Elsie and Julia headed north on Main Street with hundreds of other women and children, they could see dozens of National Guard troopers on horseback ahead, blocking the parade route. An imposing man with a thick white handlebar moustache sat calmly on his black stallion in front of the troops. Julia recognized him as General John Chase, the leader of the National Guard militia sent by Colorado governor Elias Ammons to protect the interests of the coal companies. Julia knew that the miners thought Chase was a villain in their struggle against the coal companies. He was the one who had arrested Mother Jones in Trinidad ten days earlier. Julia, still grasping Elsie's hand, dropped back in the crowd, sensing trouble.

The women leading the parade marched on toward General Chase. He ordered them to stop, but they continued. He inched his horse toward them and tried with his spurred boot to nudge away a teenage girl who had walked right up to his horse. He did not kick her forcefully, but the girl fell back, causing the horse to buck, and General Chase fell onto the street. As the general picked himself off the ground, the women in the crowd ridiculed and laughed at him.

His face now flushed with embarrassment and anger, General Chase jumped back on his horse.

"Ride down the women!" he screamed, to the amazement of the women and children as well as his own men. He pulled out his saber, kicked his horse with his spur, and surged into the crowd.

Panic erupted. Julia picked Elsie up and ran behind a buggy. They watched in horror as General Chase and his men knocked down several women and children. One of the troopers slashed a woman's face with a sword. Another one bloodied a woman's hands as she tried to protect her face from the onslaught.

Julia pulled Elsie into a feed store on Main Street, and they huddled behind some barrels, looking out the window at the chaos. Elsie cried uncontrollably, and Julia hugged her and stroked her long black hair. As Julia tried to console her little sister, she prayed, asking God why He had forsaken her family. She also wondered what Elsie might remember about this awful day and about the awful turn of events that seemed to have cursed her family for the last several years.

THE LABORS OF FAMILY MEN AND WOMEN

Dad was paralyzed on his whole right side. My mother took care of the house, the washing and cleaning, and the feeding of my brother Lou, me, Bun, Bita, my nephews Lee and Tito, and Johnny and Winifred. I don't know how she managed to keep the house running. My two sisters worked at the Columbian Hotel in Trinidad for 12 dollars a week, and that's what we lived on—the twelve of us. . . .

My oldest sister Margaret married Felix Montoya in 1908. In October 1913, Felix was killed in a coal mine explosion in Dawson, New Mexico. Two other brothers of his died at the same time. So Margaret had to move in with us because they wouldn't let her live in the company-owned houses anymore. The houses were for the miners and their families only!

We lived in Trinidad until 1917. My brothers Joe and Chris moved

to Dawson to work in the coal mines, and then sent for us. We lived there until 1922. But then Joe and Chris got married and moved away, and we had to move again because we had no miners in the family. So my sisters Julia and Margaret and I worked in a Greek Boarding House to support the family.
—from Naunny's journal

Another set of stories my grandmother told relatives had to do with the hard work that she and her family performed to support the family after the demise of her father. In retelling them, relatives emphasized the *class* implications of these stories, noting how poor the family was during this time. A few relatives even told stories about how Naunny and her siblings had to go to work as children to help support the family. Yet, relatives never told these narratives as horror stories about child exploitation but instead as courageous sagas in which everyone, regardless of age, sacrificed for the family.

Relatives also emphasized the division of labor between men's work and women's work in their stories. Although a few relatives referred to the fact that some female ancestors worked in hotels and boardinghouses, most relatives emphasized the *housework* of Naunny's mother, Catalina. Many of these relatives—both male and female—simply mentioned the fact that Catalina did the housework, but they did not narrate any stories about this housework. In her family history journal, Naunny herself merely stated, without much fanfare, that during this period her mother "was busy with the children" and that she "took care of the house, the washing and cleaning, and the feeding of [relatives]."

Only two relatives—both relatively older women who also were born and raised in Trinidad—elaborated on the housework performed by Catalina during this period. As one of them told me:

Your grandma and I would always tell each other stories about our mom. Just like my mom, your grandma's mom worked very hard in the house. They'd make our food and sew our shoes and make our clothes. And, of course, every year they were pregnant, so they'd make the diapers and the bands that they used to put around a baby's navel where they cut the cord. They also scrubbed floors on their hands and knees and washed windows once a week. They kept the house immaculate. I wonder where they found the time.

Although relatives shared few family stories about the working women of that era, they retold several stories about how the men worked in the coal mines. Most of them emphasized the fact that this work was unbelievably dangerous, and some said that a few ancestors had died in accidents and explosions. In the passage from her journal, Naunny mentioned one of those accidents, noting that it was October 1913 when her brother-in-law and two of his brothers were killed in a mining accident in Dawson, New Mexico. That accident killed more than 250 men and was one of the deadliest of what one historian called an American "holocaust."

"Working in the coal mines in Dawson was hard work, and it was very dangerous," said a niece, who like Naunny also had spent part of her childhood in Dawson. "I don't remember this, but your grandma said they used to ring a bell when there was an explosion in the mines. All the men in town would go out there to help the victims, and all the women would line the streets to see if their husbands were coming home or if they were killed. It was absolutely horrible."

Naunny also told a few relatives about how the union tried to help the miners. A niece said that Naunny had once told her about "some protests" that supporters of the miners participated in when she was a little girl. One of those protests, called "the Mother Jones riot," occurred in Trinidad in the fall of 1913 when my grandmother was six years old and resulted in injuries to several women and children when the National Guard broke up the demonstration.

That protest paled in comparison to what happened a few months later during the so-called Ludlow Massacre. On April 20, 1914, just hours after the miners had played a baseball game, the National Guard approached the tent colony at Ludlow where the miners and their families were living. After gunfire was exchanged, the guard set fire to the tent colony, and several men, women, and children were killed. The author of a report to the U.S. Commission on Industrial Relations in 1915 indicated that five men and one boy were killed by machine gun and two women and eleven children were burned to death or suffocated.

Several days of violence followed the Ludlow Massacre as miners set fire to several mines and other company property and continued to battle with militiamen. President Woodrow Wilson ultimately dispatched more than 1,500 troops to southern Colorado, and order was restored. The strike itself officially ended in December of that year, with the miners' union being denied bargaining rights and the coal companies creating a "company union" that ensured somewhat better working conditions and slightly higher wages.

When I read historical accounts of the Mother Jones Riot and the Ludlow Massacre during the research for this book, I was stunned. This was *the* Mother Jones, inspiring protests from the same hospital where my great-grandfather recovered from his stroke. This was the same Ludlow Massacre I read about in a Sociology of Labor course when I was an undergraduate student in the 1970s, and the same Ludlow Massacre that was featured in a Bill Moyers's special on PBS that I showed to my public relations students at Southern Methodist University in the 1980s because it included a story on Ivy Lee, one of the founders of public relations, who was hired by John D. Rockefeller after the incident to sway public opinion in favor of the mining companies. Yet I never knew that these historic events took place near my grandmother's hometown when she was a young girl. I don't remember Naunny ever talking about them with me, and relatives said that she had only vaguely mentioned that there had been "some protests" between the miners and the coal companies when she was a little girl.

Perhaps Naunny didn't want to burden family members with details about the horrific events experienced by her family during this period in American history. Perhaps, as she suggested in her own journal, she forgot about these events because they were so appalling. Or, perhaps I just wasn't listening to her when she told me stories about these events.

Whatever the case, I am embarrassed to admit that I was completely unaware that these important historical events occurred in my grandmother's hometown when she was a young girl. The fact that most of my relatives shared my ignorance about these events is not at all comforting. As Naunny's descendants, I believe that all of us should know about these important historical events that, at least in some small way, shaped her life.

August 23, 1984

Dear Naunny & Pete—

Sorry it's been a while. My vacation lasted until the middle of August—I stayed in Chicago until then. Long live the Cubs (especially since the Dodgers seem to be out of it this year).

Vacation was great. Best summer in my life! Too bad school had to start again (it started on the 23rd of August).

Saw Johnny & Emma at Naunny Chicago's on Sunday. Had a big Polish feast. Pretty fun (and fattening). Emma said they're going to Trinidad. I had fun there in July. Met Dolores Maldonado and her daughter and grandkids. She's a nice lady. It was fun roaming around the hills where San Miguel used to be. I camped out the night before in Taos (actually in the mountains near Taos). A great trip all in all. Didn't get much family info though.

No I'm not married again. Won't be for quite a while. I have been seeing the lady in Chicago for some time though. Her name is Leah.

I'll move to East Lansing in January and live there until June. It's a visiting professor position at Michigan State. The offer was too good.

I'll write more later. Take care,
Nick

CATALINA GETS HER GUN

I don't know if you know this story, but Aunt Elsie's dad, José Julio, had a saloon and a grocery store. I guess he was a pretty big party boy. Aunt Elsie said Grandma Catalina saw him going by with some floozy, heading toward the saloon. Grandma Catalina used to have this black shawl—in fact, my sister Margie has Grandma's shawl—and she put it on, over her shoulders, then hid a big revolver and went after him. Then her brother—I don't remember his name—but he stopped her from going in. He said, "No, no.

Nice women don't go in there." But she was going to go in there
and take a shot at José Julio for cheating on her.
    —NIECE

Naunny did not write down this particular story in her family
journal, but she told it to several relatives. Naunny told it to me
when I was in college, though I remember her saying that
Catalina actually fired a shot at her womanizing husband. Other
relatives also remembered different details: Some thought
Catalina had a shotgun, while others thought she had a long
Colt .45; some said it happened at the saloon, while others
thought it happened in an alley outside their home.

Like most family stories, the details of this story are far less
important than its overall meaning to family members. Some
relatives emphasized the actions of José Julio, though, surprisingly, not a single relative criticized his actions. After retelling
the story, one of Naunny's daughters-in-law said this: "Naunny
also talked about how her father would go into town and
whoop-de-do with ladies of the evening. He'd even drive past
their home in a carriage with his women while Grammy was at
home taking care of kids. But Naunny never criticized him for
doing this."

One of Naunny's nieces, who had also grown up in southern
Colorado, even described José Julio's actions as "normal" for the
time: "It wasn't the fact that he was cheating on her that bothered Grandma Catalina. All the men did that back then. It was
the fact that he was with some floozy that bothered her."

Whether adultery was or was not prevalent at the time, I was
surprised that Naunny's relatives, especially her female relatives,
did not criticize her father for his infidelity. Perhaps these relatives did not want to criticize a long-deceased ancestor. I was
more surprised that some of Naunny's relatives characterized his
infidelity as "normal" for that period in history.

Other relatives emphasized the actions of Grandma Catalina,
presenting her as an eccentric personality. When I asked one
grandson about the story after he told it, he laughed and said,
"That just goes to show you what a character Grammy was.
Here's this little woman who hardly ever said anything bad, and
she grabs a big Colt .45 and goes after her husband."

In their stories about this incident, relatives naturalized the actions of José Julio by presenting his adulterous behavior as normal for the time, and they trivialized the actions of Grandma Catalina by presenting her not as a strong woman who challenged her cheating husband but as a tiny, eccentric character. As a reviewer of an article based on this chapter put it, the story "is funny because it depicts little [Catalina] with her big gun, not because it depicts José [Julio] with his pants down." Of course, as another reviewer suggested, at least Catalina gains a little symbolic power in the story because she takes a gun—a symbol of phallic power—and goes after her husband.

ELSIE GETS A HUSBAND

It all started for me in September of 1923. I met Charley Sr. at a dance in Berwind, Colorado. His folks were from Delagua, Colorado, but had moved out to Los Angeles two years before. He'd come to Trinidad from Los Angeles to marry a girl named Lorraine McCauly Reeves, a divorcee. But they broke up and I got him on the rebound (I think).

Then two months later, on my 16th birthday, he gave me a beautiful ruby ring, and we became engaged. We'd planned on getting married as soon as he got a steady job. He was a movie projectionist. He worked at the Strand in the afternoons and the Palace at night, but he was only the relief man so he didn't work all the time. Then on or about the first week in March of 1924, he received a wire from his brother Joe, in California, that his mother was very ill. So we got married on St. Patrick's Day, and then two days later we took a train to Los Angeles.

—from Naunny's journal

The final set of stories that relatives told about Naunny's history in southern Colorado dealt with how she met, courted, and married her first husband.

According to historians, dances were very important leisure activities at the time, and Naunny met Charley Trujillo at one of these dances.

"I remember Naunny talked about when she met Charles," one granddaughter told me. "They were at some dance. Naunny went with her girlfriend. So when Charles started walking over to the table, Naunny's girlfriend thought that he was going to ask her to dance. But he came and asked Naunny to dance, and, of course, Naunny almost peed her pants, because he was such a good dancer and she was a lot younger than he was. She said he was really good-looking, suave, and everything."

I find it especially ironic that this dance occurred in Berwind, Colorado, just a few miles east of Ludlow, where the Ludlow Massacre had occurred years earlier.

At that time these dances were one of the few legitimate means of contact between unmarried men and women. These dances often led to a courtship, and Naunny told relatives that she and Charley had got engaged just a month or two after their first dance. One granddaughter said that Naunny had agreed to get married quickly so that she could "get out of a bad situation," though it appears that one situation that was not improved with marriage was her financial situation. As another granddaughter told me:

Naunny said they had to get married really early in the morning because they were so poor that they had holes in their shoes. And so they go to the church at like five in the morning, so that when they knelt down on the kneelers, their feet would face out and nobody would see the holes in their shoes. So they get there, and the priest started doing the Mass, and the Catholic school kids came in for the Mass, and she's sitting there with holes in her shoes, and the whole Catholic class is watching. She said she was totally embarrassed, because she thought everybody was looking at the holes in their shoes.

Even though Naunny's new husband seemed to be as poor as she was, relatives still framed the story of her marriage in terms of how she had improved her lot in life. One granddaughter said that Naunny told her that she married Charley to get out of her hometown, while another grandson wondered, "Who knows how worse it would have been for her if she didn't get married and get the hell out of there?" As Naunny's niece concluded, "When you married a guy back then, you stayed with him even if he beat you up, because you had no place to go. You couldn't go to your parents because they were poor and probably glad to get rid of you anyway. So what did you do? You stuck it out with [him]."

Of course, through his marriage to Naunny, Charley, too, improved his lot in life, because he was able to leave his own poor family and start a poor family of his own.

As retold by relatives, these stories about my grandmother's first date, courtship, and marriage to my grandfather reconstruct an image of Naunny as a teenage girl who was constrained by poverty and patriarchy. She is presented as virtually powerless to control her circumstances yet so very desperate to do so. Charley asks Naunny to dance, José Julio gives her permission to marry him, and Charley rescues Naunny from poverty and desperation, even though he was just as poor as she was and perhaps even more desperate since, according to Naunny, he was "on the rebound."

Whether it was out of desperation, love, or some combination of the two, Naunny did marry Charley, and they moved from the poverty-stricken place of their ancestors to the Promised Land of California to begin a new life, living initially with Charley's parents. A few years later, however, Naunny's father died, and when she returned to Colorado with her brother for the funeral, she did not wish to return to California. As she wrote in her journal:

> In July, 1926, my Dad had his final stroke. My brother Joe and I were able to take the trip [back to Colorado], by train. . . . My brother Joe returned to Los Angeles, right after the funeral. But I didn't want to come back. I'd been sooooo lonely and homesick and miserable, living with my mother-in-law. . . . Finally, Charley sent me a wire that read, "Don't forget. You're still married!" I had to come back.

Being the "good wife," Naunny returned to Los Angeles and stayed there for the rest of her life. That, however, is another story. . . .

"We have to go now," Charley told Elsie for the third time as the conductor made the last call for passengers to board the train that was leaving downtown Trinidad for southern California.

Elsie ignored Charley as well as the conductor and continued to hug her mother and father. She knew that this was probably the last time she would see her father alive, as his health had seriously deteriorated the last few years.

"Yo lo quiero, Papa," she said, expressing her love for her father as she wiped the tears from her dark eyes. She looked at him one final time, then turned around and boarded the train with the new husband she had married just two days earlier.

Elsie and Charley could not afford a sleeper car, so they spent the long trip sitting in a crowded passenger cabin, gazing out the window. A spring storm had blanketed Colorado with snow, and Elsie stared at the bleak landscape, thinking about the sad situation she was leaving. So many bad things had happened in the sixteen-plus years she lived there: Her father had lost all of his wealth and was now a poor old man with failing health, her family members had moved around many times as they struggled to find work, and several of her relatives had died of disease or were killed in mining accidents. Yet as the train crawled its way out of southern Colorado, she was already feeling homesick.

"At least there won't be snow in California," Charley said, smiling softly.

Two days later, the train finally pulled into Union Station in Los Angeles, California. Elsie rubbed her bloodshot eyes and looked over at Charley. Although he had not slept during the trip either, he looked incredibly handsome to her. She clutched his hand, feeling excitement about the prospects for their new life in California.

Charley's brother was waiting for them when they got off the train. Charley rushed over and gave him a hug. Elsie extended her arms to hug her new brother-in-law, but he stepped back and looked over at Charley.

"Where's Lorraine?" he asked, referring to the woman Charley originally had gone back to Colorado to marry and bring back to Los Angeles.

"Welcome to California," Elsie mumbled to herself.

I am embarrassed to admit that I did not pay attention to Naunny's stories about her family history until I was in graduate school. I completed my Ph.D. at the University of Utah in Salt Lake City, a city that is dominated by members of the Church of

Jesus Christ and Latter-Day Saints (LDS), known by most people as Mormons.

Although I am oversimplifying their theology, Mormons believe that relatives will rejoin each other in the afterlife. Not surprisingly, then, genealogy is very important to Mormons so that they will know as many relatives as possible who might join them in the afterlife. Thus, the LDS church houses an unbelievable repository of family records for *all* families, not just Mormon ones, because members of any given family could become converts, and then their relatives would have the possibility of joining them in the afterlife. And converting as many families as possible is a definite goal of the Mormon Church, since adult males are sent on two-year missions to proselytize throughout the world.

One day, out of curiosity, I went to the LDS office building in downtown Salt Lake City to look up information about my family history. I tried to look up records on Naunny's ancestors, but I couldn't even remember her maiden name. I vaguely remembered some of the stories she had told me about her family when I was in college, but I realized that I had retained very little information from those stories because I had not really listened to Naunny when she was telling them to me.

Later that year, I decided to write a paper on family history and genealogy for a graduate class. I purchased a University of Utah spiral notebook, sent it to Naunny, and asked her to write about her family history. I planned to use her journal entries as "data" for the paper, and, knowing that I would take an "incomplete" in the class, I told Naunny that I would pick up her journal in a couple months at my parents' house in Las Vegas when Naunny made her annual Christmas visit.

When I arrived in Vegas that Christmas, I immediately made a copy of the notes that Naunny had taken in her journal. I also conducted a tape-recorded interview with her about her family history. I returned home to Salt Lake, finished the paper and completed the class, and then never did anything else with that "data."

I suppose my lack of interest in family history for most of my life was not that unusual. Like many other people at that age, I was mostly oriented to the present, sometimes to the future, but rarely if ever to the past.

However, when Naunny died, I longed for the past. I wanted so much to hear her voice on that tape. I searched for hours to find it, to no avail. I must have misplaced it or thrown it away with other items that I thought I would never use.

Fortunately, I kept the copy of her journal, and after her death, I read the family stories that I had essentially ignored for much of my life. I only wish that Naunny were still alive, so that I could listen—this time *really* listen—to her tell those stories again.

Family stories are one of the cornerstones of family culture.
—ELIZABETH STONE, *Black Sheep and Kissing Cousins*

Grandma was a great storyteller.
—GRANDDAUGHTER

One of the most important roles that our grandparents play is to tell us stories about our family histories. Although the specific characters in Naunny's family stories are unique, the stories themselves are common in form to the stories of many family histories in that they are about family struggles and sacrifice, and they involve issues related to class, gender, and ethnicity.

These stories about Naunny's family history reinforce certain meanings over others. Like many family stories, these stories reinforce the ideal of the family unit itself. Although Naunny and her ancestors are presented as victims of various sociocultural forces, *the family survives*. Naunny's family endures, even after the patriarch loses everything. The men, women, and children sacrifice to maintain the family by working for low wages in terrible conditions. The mother stays with the father even though he commits adultery. And Naunny finds a husband and forms another family union, ensuring the family's continued survival.

These stories also reinforce gender ideology in family relations. Relatives emphasized the gendered division of labor—men had jobs outside the home while women were housewives—and presented men's work as more significant to the family—men were paid for their work while women were not. Relatives also portrayed men as far more powerful than women—men had harder jobs and were more involved in making decisions—and women as far more dependent on men—for money and for courtship and marriage. It is more accurate and far more empowering to say that the family was dependent on the men and women (and children) for survival.

I am not suggesting that distinctions between men and women did not exist at that time in history, nor am I suggesting that Hispanic family culture is not patriarchal in many respects. Clearly, there were (and still are) many differences between men and women. However, while historical and/or contemporary divisions between men and women may frame family storytelling, family storytelling also reinforces those very divisions. When family stories are told in the context of patriarchal family structures, those stories can also reproduce those very structures, especially when men and women retell these stories to their relatives.

Finally, these stories of my grandmother's family history, like all stories of family history, present the family *in history*. All family histories occur in a particular time and place and are influenced by greater sociocultural and political forces. For example, the stories about my grandmother's family history provide insight into how gender, class, and ethnicity were experienced by people who lived in northern New Mexico and southern Colorado in the late 1800s and early 1900s. Native Hispanics who settled the area in the 1800s were displaced from their villages during the American expansion of the late 1800s and early 1900s. These Hispanics lost their herds and other businesses, and they were transformed into a class of workers that were dependent on coal companies and other industries and subjected to horrific working conditions. Hispanic women went from community leaders in their villages to housewives in company-owned homes.

This historical shift is represented eloquently in Naunny's family history journal, as her overall narrative moves from her grandmother, Barbarita, who "ruled our community of San Miguel," to her mother, Catalina, who "was busy with the children" and "took care of the house." Sadly, most of the relatives I interviewed knew very little about Naunny's grandmother's role as community leader but much more about Naunny's mother's role as housekeeper. In the process of retelling stories about Catalina's housework but not about Barbarita's community leadership, relatives unintentionally minimize the true influence that women of Barbarita's generation had on our family and on history, and they unintentionally ignore the historical changes that limited women of Catalina's generation to domestic roles.

I never listened closely to my grandmother's stories about our family history, and I only became interested in this history after Naunny's death when I decided to write this book. I suppose that we never truly appreciate history until it is much harder to reconstruct. Very few of my relatives knew much about our family history, either, especially Naunny's great- and great-great-grandchildren. For members of these younger generations, family history is virtually nonexistent, a situation to be expected in a visual, media-oriented culture where the oral tradition of storytelling has been displaced by CDs and DVDs.

However, there may be hope for younger generations to recoup their family histories. In recent years, genealogy has become a big industry and a significant presence on the Internet. It is easier than ever before to trace your family roots using various websites. Unfortunately, although these genealogical sites offer lists of family names, they do not provide the *stories* associated with those names.

The best sources for those stories continue to be our grandparents. But once our grandparents are gone, stories about our family history are buried with them. I wish that I had asked my grandmother to tell me more stories about our family history, and I encourage readers whose grandparents are still alive to ask them to tell their stories.

A Lifetime of Work, a Lifetime of Poverty

Virtually all life experiences are mediated or influenced by social class.
—MARY ANN LAMANNA and AGNES RIEDMANN,
   Marriages and Families

Grandma worked her whole life but never had much to show for it.
—GRANDSON

Elsie was now working full-time at the boardinghouse for the Greek immigrants who worked in the coal mines near Trinidad, Colorado. She had just finished the sixth grade, and her father thought that would be more than enough education for a girl who just needed to know how to cook and clean so she could land a husband. And working at the Greek boardinghouse would certainly teach her those skills.

Elsie arrived early in the morning to serve breakfast to the miners before they started their shifts. Then she would help clean the tables and put away dishes. In the late morning she changed sheets and cleaned the rooms. Then it was back to the dining area to serve lunch to the miners. She spent the afternoon cleaning dishes, doing laundry, cleaning more rooms, and getting ready for the dinner rush. After dinner, she helped with the cleanup and then went home for the evening. It was a lot of work, but she was making ten whole cents a day.

Elsie was proud to contribute to the family. She knew that her father had never quite recovered from the stroke he suffered years before, and all of her brothers and sisters were working for the family.

One night after saying her prayers, she promised God that she would always work to help her family.

Every summer, my family would take our summer vacation from Las Vegas to see Naunny and Pete in their tiny rental house in East Los Angeles. Naunny worked for a commercial laundry company, owned by a man named Cecil, where she would sew and repair uniforms before they were cleaned. Sometimes she took off from work during our family visits, but on other occasions she simply could not afford to take any time off.

As a boy, I couldn't understand why Naunny had to work. She was a grandmother in her late fifties and early sixties, and it just didn't seem right to me. One time, when I was about ten years old, I asked her why she had to go to work.

"So I can buy presents for you at Christmas," she said.

I don't remember what I said, but I do know that I felt torn. I didn't think it was right that my grandmother had to work, but I really liked getting presents from her every Christmas.

A LIFETIME OF WORK

From the earliest days of manufacturing, women have entered occupations that cannot attract male laborers because wages are too low, opportunities for advancement are insufficient, or working conditions are less attractive than other available work.
—MAUREEN HONEY, *Creating Rosie the Riveter*

Your grandma was a hard worker. Everybody wanted to hire her.
—SON

Like many grandmothers, Naunny worked throughout her entire life. Relatives said that she started working when she was a child and continued to work until she retired in her late sixties. Since she became a grandmother in her late thirties, all of her grandchildren, and even some of her great-grandchildren, knew firsthand that she had a job because we saw her leaving for work whenever we visited; some of her grandkids even accompanied Naunny to work on a few occasions. Accordingly, for her relatives, one of Naunny's identities is as a worker who made money to help support the family.

Even though she was employed for most of her life, relatives said that she did not really have a "career." Like most working-class women, she had very limited choices about the kind of work available to her. So she was employed in a variety of low-paying, blue-collar jobs and remained poor throughout her life.

Naunny's Childhood Labors

Dad was paralyzed on his whole right side. . . . My brothers Joe and Chris moved to Dawson to work in the coal mines, and then sent for us. We lived there until 1922. But then Joe and Chris got married and moved away, and we had to move again because we had no miners in the family. So my sisters Julia and Margaret and I worked in a Greek Boarding House to support the family.
—from Naunny's journal

Naunny started working as early as nine years old, after her father lost his sheep ranch and other businesses. One of her daughters-in-law told me about Naunny's early work:

Naunny always talked about how she had to go to work at nine years old, because they were so poor. She worked for a family, taking care of a girl who wasn't much younger than she was. She also worked in a place, a boardinghouse, where she helped serve the food, and at a hotel. She didn't really have a childhood. Like my mom and dad, she started work so early.

Relatives did not know how much money Naunny earned for these various jobs when she was a young girl, but I am confident that it was a pittance. And although she joked in her journal that she could not recall too many "happy times" from her childhood, relatives said that Naunny never complained about it. Her daughter-in-law said that Naunny always talked fondly about her work as a child. In addition, neither Naunny nor her relatives ever suggested that she was a victim of child exploitation. Relatives who knew about Naunny's early work reinforced the idea that all family members, even children, were expected to help the family during hard times.

Some family members also suggested that her early work experiences instilled in Naunny a strong work ethic and a belief that every family member should work to help the family in difficult times. According to relatives, Naunny brought this work ethic with her when she moved to California with her husband Charley.

California, Here They Came . . . to Work

Charley had been a movie projectionist in Trinidad. When we first arrived in Los Angeles, he went to register at the union hall. But he was told that in order to qualify, he'd have to attend Western Electric Sound System, as the talking pictures were coming. It would cost $300 cash for the complete course, and hardly anyone, at least in our family, had that much cash. So he had to go out and find any old job.

We moved in with his folks. That was a bad move. There, in that house were Joseph, his wife Margaret, Joe Jr., and Margie. Then there were Bill and Alice, Charley and I, Fidel and Charley's mother and stepfather. Well, to make a short story long, the old adage still goes: no roof is large enough to cover two women. Imagine what it was like, with four women sharing the same kitchen!

—from Naunny's journal

Naunny and Charley moved from Trinidad, Colorado, to Los Angeles, California, in March 1924, just a couple days after getting married. According to relatives, they moved in with Charley's mother and several other family members, and they lived there for a couple of years until they had enough money to rent a place of their own.

When Naunny and Charley were finally able to rent a place of their own, they also decided to start a family of their own. Naunny's first child, a girl, either was stillborn or died very shortly after birth, a fact I never knew about until I conducted interviews for this book. They even named the child Mary or Maria and supposedly had the newborn buried in a cemetery, though I could not find any record of her burial.

After that tragedy, they tried again, and in 1927 they had their first son, whom they named Charles, after his father. Three years later, in 1930, another son arrived, whom they named William, after his uncle.

Unfortunately, the Great Depression also arrived in the 1930s. Naunny asked her mother, Catalina, who was still living in Colorado following the death of her husband, to come to California to help with the kids so that Naunny could work to bring in extra money. Naunny wrote about this decision in her journal:

We sent for my mother. She took care of the two boys, and I went to work at Cubbison's Cracker Company across the street from where we lived at 3430 Pasadena Avenue. Charley worked at Welch's laundry as a distributor, and that was across the street also. I started at 19 cents an hour.

My father said that Naunny never complained about her job at Cubbison's, adding that he loved that job because Naunny would bring home bags of broken cookies that were called "washboard cookies."

Like millions of other married couples during this period, Naunny and Charley also decided not to have any additional children. Two relatives also told me that Naunny had an abortion during this period. I do not know for certain that Naunny actually had an abortion, and no other relatives could confirm it. But if she did have such a procedure, it would not have been unusual for the 1930s. During the Depression, *many* women— even married Catholic women who loved children such as Naunny—had abortions. In her book *When Abortion Was a Crime*, Leslie Reagan estimates that tens of thousands of women had abortions during the Depression, indicating that women had abortions "on a massive scale" such that it "was not extraordinary, but ordinary."

Most of these women had abortions because they could not afford to have additional children and/or because they wanted to keep their jobs or save their marriages. Both of Naunny's relatives who told me about her abortion said that Naunny did not believe in abortion but she had it done because they didn't have much money and did not think that they could afford another child.

Both relatives also said they were told that Naunny's abortion was performed badly and that she hemorrhaged. Reagan writes that such postabortion emergencies were relatively common during this period as women endured septic infections, perforations of the uterus, hemorrhages, and damages to other organs.

Elsie walked slowly, considering what she was about to do with every step. Her destination was over a mile away from her home, but Elsie had decided to walk there, so she would have ample time to think about her decision. She would take the bus back after the procedure. But now she was just two blocks away from the clinic, and time was finally running out on her to follow through on her decision.

Of course, she didn't really feel that it was her decision. Charley was the one who said they couldn't afford another baby, and he was the one who insisted that Elsie have it done. Charley wanted Elsie to do it herself like the lady next door had done, until Elsie reminded him that she had almost died after her failed attempt with a crochet needle. Another lady in the next neighborhood had died after trying to induce a miscarriage by drinking a lethal cocktail of whiskey and gunpowder.

Charley reluctantly agreed that they would pay the forty dollars to the practitioner to perform the procedure. It was a lot of money, about one month's pay for Elsie, but it would be a lot less than paying for another baby for the next sixteen or so years. Charley had taken the money they had saved in their mattress and had borrowed additional money from some of his friends to pay for it. He even hawked his watch at a pawnshop. He had to work that day as well, so Elsie went by herself. She couldn't take her mother with her because she had decided not to tell her mother.

Elsie finally arrived at the clinic. The practitioner was a pharmacist, but the illegal abortion trade was so good during the Depression that he had developed a lucrative side business that was now taking most of his time. Several of the women in Elsie's neighborhood had gone to him in the past year, and all of them were back home just a couple hours after the procedure, except for the one that had to be hospitalized because of a perforated uterus.

She opened the front door very slowly and then walked into the clinic. The waiting room was very small and had drab wallpaper and dark drapes that blocked the sunshine from coming through the window. Elsie thought it looked more like a loan shark's office than a medical clinic.

A receptionist greeted Elsie and told her to take a seat. Elsie grabbed a Saturday Evening Post from the table and froze when she saw the cover. It was a Norman Rockwell family scene, with a mother, father, and three children. She put down the magazine and caressed her belly.

After almost thirty minutes, the practitioner finally came out.

"You must be Elsie," he said, matter-of-factly.

She nodded yes.

"You know that it's sixty-five dollars, right?"

"Sixty-five?" Elsie said. "My friends said it was forty."

"Our prices have gone up," he said.

"I only brought forty," she said.

"Well, then, I'm sorry," he said and turned around.

"All right, then," Elsie said and stood up. She started to walk toward the door.

"All right," he said, just as Elsie got to the door. "I'll do it for forty."

He led Elsie to a small room containing a large examination table covered with a sheet, a sink, a few cabinets, and a smaller table near the larger table. Two stirrups were protruding from the front of the examination table. A nurse looked up at Elsie and smiled, and then continued to line up various instruments on the smaller table.

"Take off your skirt and undergarments, lie on the table, and put your feet in the stirrups," he said.

Elsie did as he ordered. She said a few Hail Marys, as he moved the instruments around. She thought about saying an Our Father, but she thought Mary would understand her situation much better, especially since she would have named the baby Mary if the baby had been a girl.

He handed Elsie a leather rope.

"This is going to sting a little," he said. "You should bite down on this if you need to."

"It's going to be all right," the nurse said, though not in a particularly comforting voice.

He dilated Elsie's cervix with a metal dilator, the first step in a procedure known as a dilation and curettage, or "D and C," as it was usually called.

The metal felt cold, and Elsie said another quick Hail Mary.

He then took a curette, a spoon-shaped instrument, and started to scrape fetal and placental tissue out of her uterus.

The pain was intense, and Elsie bit down on the rope.

"Damn," he said, just as Elsie felt an excruciating pain. The nurse scrambled to get something off the table.

"You've got a little bleeding here," he said, soaking up blood with gauze. "But don't worry—it'll be fine."

He continued with the procedure. It was the longest thirty minutes of Elsie's life. Afterward, the nurse gave Elsie a skimpy robe to wear and helped Elsie to a bed in another small room.

"Just lie down here until you feel better," she said.

Elsie collapsed onto the bed, dazed. She ached down below.

After an hour, she got up and put on her clothes. She opened the door just as the nurse came in to check on her.

"You sure you're ready to go home?" the nurse asked.

"Yeah," Elsie said. "I feel peachy keen."

Elsie walked slowly out of the clinic. She headed for the nearby bus stop, but after taking just a few steps, she felt more dampness where the practitioner had performed the procedure. She stepped into an alley and turned around to make sure no one was looking. Before she could check on herself, she saw a drop of blood hit the asphalt.

She started to head back toward the clinic but felt woozy.

A man making deliveries to a corner grocery store saw Elsie stagger toward him.

"Ma'am?" he asked.

Before she could say anything, she fell into his arms.

He placed her on the ground and saw the blood.

"Oh, no," he said. "We gotta get you to the hospital."

He yelled for the grocer to call an ambulance. The ambulance arrived within fifteen minutes and took Elsie to the hospital.

A nurse came out to meet the ambulance attendants. She saw the all-too-familiar blood on Elsie's skirt and immediately knew the problem.

"We've got another abortion," she yelled out.

The attendants placed Elsie on a hospital gurney, and the nurse wheeled her to a receiving room. A few minutes later, a doctor came in and determined that Elsie had suffered a perforated uterus. The nurse hooked up an IV to her arm as the doctor worked on her.

An hour later, Elsie woke up and asked the nurse where she was.

"You're in the hospital, ma'am," she said. "We almost lost you."

Elsie closed her eyes and sighed. She wondered how much this was going to cost and how she would explain it to Charley when he got there.

When I first heard that Naunny might have had an abortion, I did not believe it. Only one female relative seemed to know about it, and no one else could confirm it. In fact, several other relatives criticized the relative in question for "making something up like that" about Naunny. I personally did not think that this relative was lying to me about what seemed to be such a surprising revelation, but I thought that maybe Naunny herself had made up the story to serve as a cautionary tale for this relative when she got pregnant at a young age.

But then another relative, who also was a trusted confidant of Naunny, told me the abortion story months later. I had to confront the possibility that Naunny might have actually had an abortion, though I still had trouble believing that a devout Catholic who loved children could actually abort one of her own. I did, however, believe that if her husband wanted Naunny to have the procedure, she would have done so to save her marriage and her family.

Like many men, I knew very little about abortion, so I read several books about the subject, especially about abortions performed during the Depression. I learned that tens of thousands of women had abortions during those years in order to keep their jobs and/or their marriages and to feed and clothe the children they already had. Like Naunny, thousands of women also suffered injuries from their illegal abortions.

I then agonized over whether to include a reference to Naunny's abortion in this book, because I did not feel comfortable about revealing her family secret, and I did not want to dishonor her memory. I also did not want to upset relatives who might be angry or disappointed about this disclosure.

I ultimately decided to write about it because my grandmother was one of many poor, working-class women during the Depression who had to make very tough decisions that may have gone against their beliefs. During this horrendous period of American history, getting pregnant was not merely an inconvenience; it was a threat to the very survival of the family. Whether Naunny had an abortion or not, thousands of grandmothers and great-grandmothers did have them during the Depression and later, even though their choices may, in retrospect, seem so uncharacteristic of them. I also believe that a majority of the women who have had abortions probably kept their decisions secret from most of their children and grandchildren.

I hope that this disclosure about my grandmother's alleged abortion encourages readers to think about the difficult choices that their own mothers, grandmothers, and great-grandmothers had to make during their lifetimes. Most important, I hope that my relatives understand my reasons for writing about Naunny's family secret.

A Widow with Two Children

On September 9, 1934, Charley was killed in an auto accident by Westlake Park. I'd just come home from the hospital. I had diphtheria.

   —from Naunny's journal

Naunny's economic situation became even more problematic a few years later when, in 1934, her husband was killed in an automobile accident. Details of that accident are unclear, and it remains a mystery to Naunny's relatives, even to this day. In a very brief story published the day after the accident, the *Los Angeles Times* reported that Charles "Trejil" had died when he was thrown through the windshield of his car and suffered a severed jugular vein.

The problem with this newspaper account, according to relatives, is that my grandfather did not own a car, and he did not drive. Some relatives said that Naunny believed Charley was riding in the front passenger seat and was killed when he went through the windshield on that side of the vehicle. Naunny believed that his friends pulled his body from the windshield and placed him in the driver's seat, so that they would not get in trouble for driving under the influence of alcohol. One of Naunny's granddaughters said that Naunny had told her that Charley and his friends had been playing poker and drinking that night and that after the accident they put Charley's body in the driver's seat to make it look like he was driving.

When I was in college, Naunny also told me that she had not done laundry in several days and that Charley was actually wearing a pair of her bloomers instead of his own underwear under his trousers. She always joked about that, telling me to wear clean underwear in case I was ever killed in a car crash.

Charley's death was never investigated, and Naunny, now a widow with two young boys and very little money, did not pursue any legal recourse.

At the time of the accident, Naunny was in bed recovering from diphtheria, a relatively common but serious respiratory ailment at the time. After she recovered from the disease and the shock, it was back to work, now as a single parent to support her two young boys and her mother. To make ends meet, Naunny almost always held multiple jobs to bring in money to support her mother, her two boys, and herself. As Naunny's son recalled:

It was the middle of the Depression, 1934, your grandmother was recovering from a life-threatening illness, and now she's a widow with two kids. But we survived, and, in fact, we landed on our feet running, which was amazing. . . . I've heard people say that my mom didn't know how to handle money. But she did whatever it took. She always had a lot of part-time jobs. If she needed extra money, she got a part-time job to pay off bills or buy something.

Ironically, Naunny's status as a widow actually might have helped her maintain employment during the Depression, since married women were subjected to intense pressure to stay at home. Some states even passed legislation preventing married women from working.

Even though relatives said that Naunny was earning very little money, they all commended her for managing to fulfill the pact that she and her husband had made regarding their boys. As Naunny wrote in her journal:

Charley Sr. and I always discussed giving our boys a musical education. We both loved music and dancing. We won a dance contest in 1926. Two months after he died, I rented a trumpet and clarinet from Hillside School for $2 a semester. And I hired a music student from Lincoln High School for 50 cents a week to teach the boys the basics. I was still working for Mrs. Cubbison at the time, but now I was earning big money—27 cents an hour. When school closed at the end of the semester, I had to return the instruments. So I bought second-hand ones from American Music for $24 each.

Naunny continued to work throughout the 1930s in low-paying, blue-collar positions as a waitress, laundress, and other jobs. She never told relatives that she ever suffered from discrimination, but it is likely that she experienced some because she was Hispanic. According to one scholar, the "Mexican Expert" for the Los Angeles Chamber of Commerce in the 1920s and

1930s said that a "Mexican is an Indian and must be considered so," adding that "to pay him a living wage and add to his future comforts seemed to be the only way in which to handle him."

Naunny continued to work in these types of occupations until 1941. World War II was under way in Europe and about to break out in the South Pacific.

She's Working for the Army Now

In 1941, I went to work for Douglas Aircraft punching out parts for the DC6 and DC7 on a 71-ton Minster Punch Press! I started at $1.20 an hour and I was able to buy Bill his first sax and Chuck his first new trumpet.

    —from Naunny's journal

World War II was the best thing that ever happened during Naunny's working life, because she was able to get a better job working at the aircraft plants that were built to serve the war effort. Historians have written about the war years, and they concur that the negative attitudes about working women that characterized the Depression quickly changed when war was declared. There simply were not enough men to fill the jobs that had been created to win the war, since many men were in the military. In fact, by 1943, up to 40 percent of people employed in the aircraft industry were women. Naunny also benefited by living in Los Angeles, since many of the aircraft manufacturers were based there because the good weather allowed companies to produce and test aircraft year-round.

One fact that I was surprised to learn about as I read about the war years is that most of the women employed in the war industries were not housewives who had never worked but were already in the labor force. I had always thought that most of the women were housewives who went to work for the first time when their husbands went to war, a misconception fostered by mediated images of "Rosie the Riveter"—the fictional woman portrayed in songs and paintings of the era who symbolized housewives that went to work for their country. Women that had been waitresses, seamstresses, and other similar jobs were happy to work for the war industries because they earned more money and learned new skills.

Several of Naunny's relatives told me stories about her

wartime employment. Her oldest son said that Naunny first worked for Lockheed Aircraft in Burbank and later for Douglas Aircraft in Santa Monica. He said that those were the best jobs that Naunny ever had.

"Auntie used to wear her hair like Rosie the Riveter," one of Naunny's nieces remembered about her Aunt Elsie during that period. "She was a driller or something in an aircraft plant. She always said that she loved that job."

Even though the women working in the war industries were doing jobs previously held by men, they were still women. Not surprisingly, they continued to be marginalized and objectified, as I discovered when I read magazine articles from this period. Some representative titles from *Douglas Airview*, the magazine of Douglas Aircraft, include "Pretty Is as Pretty Does," "Hard Work-Soft Complexion," "Heads Up for Victory," "Best Face Forward," "Designs for Duty," and "Glamour Girls of 1942." These articles instructed women on how they could maintain their feminine appeal even though they were doing "men's work."

I suppose it is only fair to remember that these articles were written in the 1940s. Even so, they are compelling reminders that women were objectified sexually even as they performed "men's work" for a country at war.

The working women of the war industries not only worked hard; many of them, including my grandmother, *played* hard as well. According to relatives, Naunny frequently went to dances at the Palomar Ballroom and joined a bowling league with some of her coworkers. Her oldest son recalled that Naunny was a very good bowler who had a bracelet with charms for all of her 200-games.

"I think those war years were the best time in your grandma's life," he said. "She had a great job, and she was dancing and bowling and having fun with her friends." He laughed and added, "It's too bad the war had to end."

But the war did indeed end. And when our nation won the war, most of the women working for the war industries lost their jobs. These women were considered to be temporary workers in these industries, even though they had performed their work very well and most of them wanted to keep their jobs. Historians have reported that in the Los Angeles aircraft industry, the proportion of women workers dropped from 40 percent during the war to less than 18 percent by 1946.

Naunny was one of the many casualties of winning the war. She was fired from Douglas Aircraft along with thousands of other women.

It was 1946 and the U.S. of A. was celebrating. We had won World War II, "the war to end all wars." We had defeated the Nazis in Europe and the "Japs" in the South Pacific, and our boys were coming home.

But for Elsie and thousands of women that worked for Douglas, Lockheed, and other aircraft plants, it was a bittersweet time. And today would be far more bitter than sweet.

When Elsie went to work at Douglas that morning, she knew it was going to be her last day at the plant. She had received her pink termination notice two weeks earlier, and her D-Day had finally come.

Naunny and hundreds of her female coworkers were told to meet in one of the large hangars at the plant. There was to be a "celebration" of their contribution to the war effort.

As the women gathered, there were lots of hugs, lots of tears, and lots of promises to keep in touch. Elsie wrote down the addresses of several friends and promised to write.

"Write?" one of her friends said. "You won't need to write to me, Elsie, 'cause we'll still be going to lunch together."

"But you live in Santa Monica, and I live in Lincoln Heights,"Elsie said.

"That's why they have trolleys," her friend said. "So don't think you're getting rid of me that easy." A tear trickled down into her smile.

The head of the plant walked up the platform and approached the microphone.

"Testing," he said, tapping the microphone. "Testing. May I have your attention?"

The crowd of women quieted to a murmur.

"I just wanted to say how proud we at Douglas are of you ladies," he said. "Nobody thought you could do it, but you sure showed them!"

The crowd applauded. Several cheered.

"But now the war is over and our boys are gonna need jobs," he said.

The crowd became hushed again.

"And Uncle Sam needs you to go back to your homes and your husbands," he said.

"I don't have a husband," Elsie mumbled.

The plant manager paused for dramatic effect. "So it's time to put down your punch presses and pick up your baby baskets!" he said with excitement, pleased at the last line of the speech that he had written the night before.

A few women in the crowd cheered, but most of them just applauded politely.

"It's time to start picking up plates at the cafeteria," Elsie said.

"And cleaning rooms at the motel," a coworker added.

"And sewing buttons at the laundry," another said.

Before they left the hangar, the women had to turn in their badges. Then they left the premises, never to return.

As Elsie walked to the trolley station to go home, she asked God why the war had to end.

I traveled to Boeing Aircraft in Long Beach, California, in 1999 to do research on Naunny's work during World War II. Boeing purchased Douglas Aircraft many years ago and holds most of the Douglas archives at the Long Beach operations. I received permission to search those archives, including the Douglas magazines and newsletters from the 1940s.

I spent an entire day at the company, reading through magazines, newsletters, and other materials. I had hoped to find some mention or picture of Naunny in the company publications from the war years when she worked for Douglas.

I read countless articles on the women workers of the era and scanned hundreds of photographs. I read hundreds of personals about company employees, ranging from company promotions to birthdays and bowling scores.

But I never found any reference to or picture of Elsie Trujillo.

I was disappointed that I could not find anything about Naunny in these archives. Nevertheless, I enjoyed reading through all of these materials, amazed at the gender and ethnic propaganda of the war years that emphasized women's glamour on the job and caricatures of the "Japs." Even though I didn't find anything about my grandmother, I learned a lot about what her job and her life must have been like during those years.

Back to the Blue Collar

I lost my job at Douglas. And I went to work at Thompson Sprinkler Co. . . . I'd never taken a vacation. I thought only rich people took vacations. I'd work right through mine, and collect double pay. And I could pay off some of my bills.
—from Naunny's journal

For the remainder of her working life, Naunny was employed in a variety of low-paying jobs. She was a machine operator for a sprinkler company, a waitress for at least two coffee shops, and a seamstress for at least two laundry companies. And since she was making less money than when she worked at Douglas Aircraft, she usually had two jobs at once. My father said that when he came back from the army in 1949 and lived with his mother for a brief time, she was a waitress at the Greyhound Depot in downtown L.A. and also worked at Thompson's Sprinklers. Several of her grandchildren also remembered Naunny's various jobs, as a waitress at Louise's Café and as a seamstress at Welch's Laundry. As one grandson concluded, "She always had a couple of jobs. She never just had one job."

In 1954, twenty years after her first husband died, Naunny finally remarried when she wed Pete Alcaraz. Pete was a talented musician, but he also was a hopeless yet happy alcoholic who only worked a few nights per week. So Naunny continued to work. At that point, Naunny was employed as a seamstress for a man named Cecil who had started his own laundry company. A granddaughter said that Naunny worked for Cecil for up to twenty years, even though it was "kind of a sweatshop."

Naunny had always taken the bus to work before she took the job with Cecil. It was only a ten-minute drive to Cecil's shop by car but took over an hour to get there on the bus because of transfers. So in 1964, at age fifty-seven, Naunny learned how to drive and bought her first and only car: a little blue Corvair.

Almost everyone remembered Naunny and her little blue car.

However, relatives disagreed about the quality of Naunny's driving abilities.

"I'd go visit Grandma on a Saturday and go to work with her in her little blue Corvair," one granddaughter told me. "She'd put on her gloves, adjust this mirror, adjust that mirror, sit there, adjust the seat, adjust her gloves. Uncle Pete told her she looked like a chicken trying to lay an egg. After about ten minutes we'd get going. She'd look this way and that way. She was so funny. She was really cautious. She had her little route all planned out. There was a certain bridge we'd go over. Side streets, *never* the freeway. We'd go all around town in that little car. She was a very safe driver."

"She was a terrible driver," a grandson said. "She called one day and told me to come over to her house because she wasn't sure how to get to my mom's house. I said, 'You just get on the freeway,' but she said, 'No, I'm afraid of the freeways.' So I drove over there, and she got into her little blue Corvair and took off at about eighty miles an hour. She was running red lights. I had to work hard to keep up with her. I thought, 'What the hell is she afraid of freeways for—she drives like a bat out of hell.' She was real fast, real aggressive. I had a Volkswagen van, and I was doing my best to keep up with her."

Regardless of what kind of driver she was, relatives agreed that Naunny was very proud to get her driver's license, and we were all very proud of her for doing so. Although I never fully realized it at the time, Naunny's decision so late in life to learn how to drive and to purchase a car demonstrated incredible courage. Unfortunately, a teenager from the neighborhood crashed into Naunny's Corvair one night, and the insurance company would not fix it and gave her very little money in the settlement so she could not afford another car.

Naunny went back to the inconvenience of taking the bus to Cecil's until she finally retired in the 1970s. She was in her late sixties when she retired and had worked for over fifty years. Yet she had very little to show for this lifetime of work.

"One again, I'm sorry it took so long to get this to you," the man from the insurance company told Elsie. "I'm also sorry for your loss, ma'am. At least this will help you and your boys."

He handed Elsie the check for her deceased husband's insurance policy and left her house.

"All right, boys!" Elsie called out.

Charlie and William Lee ran into the living room and sat down next to their mom as she opened the envelope. Catalina stayed in the kitchen washing dishes.

"That's a lot of money," Elsie said, staring at the $4,000.00 amount on the check. "Look at all those zeroes," she said, handing it to her eight-year-old son.

Charlie stared at the check in silence.

"Lemme see," William Lee said.

"You're too young," Charlie said to his five-year-old brother. He gave the check back to his mother.

"So what should we do with it?" Elsie asked.

"Spend it!" Charlie shouted.

"Then go get the Sears catalogue."

Charlie ran to get the catalogue from a shelf in the kitchen and then sprinted back to the living room.

Elsie and Charlie went through the catalogue as William Lee watched. They picked everything they ever wanted to have and then a few more things.

The next day Elsie took a cab, not the bus, to Sears and bought some of the items they had selected. For the boys, she purchased Schwinn bicycles, baseball gloves, a football, and suits and top hats so that they would look like little gentlemen. For her mother, she bought a black dress, a black shawl, and some undergarments. For herself, she bought a dancing gown, shoes, a silk blouse, and some undergarments.

Later that summer, she took her boys on the Pullman train to Trinidad, Colorado, to show them where she grew up and to visit the relatives who still lived there.

After music instruments and lessons for the boys and another shopping spree that Christmas, all of the money was gone.

A LIFETIME OF POVERTY

A look at sex differences in poverty over a thirty-year period has provided strong evidence that the feminization of poverty is not a myth.
   —J. ROSS ESHLEMAN, *The Family*

I never realized how poor Grandma was.
   —GRANDSON

Relatives agreed that Naunny had never made enough money to purchase a house, and she had never had any significant investments. I do not know what her net worth was in any given year, but I am confident that it was close to or below the poverty line for much of her life. As such, Naunny was one of thousands of women that represent the "feminization of poverty," an expression used by some researchers to indicate that far more women than men live at or below the poverty line during their lives. Researchers estimate that families headed by women are six times more likely than two-parent families to have incomes below the poverty line.

Other scholars have criticized the feminization of poverty argument, saying that it ignores the impacts of class and race. Some sociologists also criticize what has been called the "add-and-stir" approach, in which class and race impacts are simply "added onto" gender as an afterthought. These scholars maintain that oppression is not an additive phenomenon and that black and Hispanic women experience racism and sexism that make their situations *qualitatively*, not quantitatively, different from white women.

As a working-class Hispanic woman, Naunny had an experience of poverty that was, no doubt, unique. But some relatives insisted that although Naunny was poor, she never really *experienced* "poverty."

I don't ever remember feeling that I was poor or in a terrible situation. I don't know how your grandmother did it. I mean, other people would have fallen apart. But we always had nice clothes, food on the table, toys. She got them on credit or whatever, and she always paid her bills.
   —SON

Despite Naunny's low income, most relatives said that they never really knew she was poor. Naunny herself never complained about her financial situation, and she managed to provide very well for her two boys.

"My mother didn't have any money, but she always got us everything," my dad said when describing his childhood during the Depression with a single mother. "I don't know how she did it. I guess she'd pay something like fifty cents a week. I had a Schwinn bike, all the best gloves, footballs, everything. She would always say, 'We're not poor; we just don't have any money.'"

Other relatives also said that they did not know Naunny was poor, and some of them even told me that they thought she was rich. One of Naunny's nieces recalled the time when she visited her Aunt Elsie as a young girl and thought that she was rich because the storage area underneath a window seat in the living room was filled with toys.

After talking with relatives, I am not surprised that family members thought that Naunny was rich. Naunny would spend whatever money she had at any given time on things for her two boys and for visiting relatives. For Naunny, this shopping and spending may have constituted the "cultural capital," as Pierre Bourdieu called it, through which she could influence other people's perceptions of her family's economic situation and social class.

One niece in her sixties remembered the time when she was fourteen years old and stayed with her Aunt Elsie and Grandma Catalina all summer. Naunny spent so much money on her that she felt that she was "living like a movie star," but later she found out that Naunny had cashed a war bond so that she could treat her niece.

Even on the very rare occasions when Naunny acquired money, she spent it quickly. Her former daughter-in-law talked about the time when Naunny's husband died and left her and her two young boys with a $4,000 insurance policy:

> To have that kind of money back in those days was considerable. But your grandmother was funny about it. She once told me, "Well, I probably should have bought a house or something, but what the heck, I didn't want to." So she blew the whole darn

(margin, handwritten) This is me — "Bobby Martiny" (female), daughter of my dad, Joe, Julio (called "J.J" and "Joe".)

thing. . . . The guys also had tap-dancing lessons and music lessons, and they were dressed like little gentlemen. Then they went back to Trinidad. They had a great time for a while, until she had spent it all. That was your grandmother.

As Naunny got older, she continued to spend money on her many grandchildren and to influence their perceptions of her social class. As one grandson in his fifties recalled, "I remember when I was growing up, she dressed like a sophisticate. When we went somewhere, it was always in a cab, never in a bus. I loved the smell of the red leather seats in Yellow cabs. She always gave a big tip, too. We'd eat downtown, not in a little local joint."

Naunny continued to spend money on others into her old age, even when she and Pete lived in a government-subsidized complex for the poor elderly. Although she no longer dressed "like a sophisticate," she continued to max out her credit cards to buy presents for her many grandchildren and great-grandchildren. And when Pete died in the mid-1980s, Naunny joined the large category of single elderly women who represent the poorest segment of society.

June 7th, 1982

Dearest Jitos Lindos—

Sorry I hadn't written. It seems that nothing has gone well for me for a couple of months, and I don't like to write when I feel down. But I must write to let you know I love you and that you're always on my mind and heart. (You know that, huh!) So here goes. . . .

Pete quit smoking, and he's nervous as a dog full of fleas! Tuesday the 3rd, I was figuring out the bills, as that's the day we get our Social Security checks. He reached over and took a couple of the bills, from May Co. and Broadway, and he hit the ceiling. He said, "What the hell are these bills for?" I said I keep them (the charge plates) in case there's a birthday or something. One bill was for $174, the other was close to $200. Then we waited for the mailman, in silence. Finally at 4 PM I called the postmaster, and he said the mailman's truck had been ripped off and all the checks and mail were stolen. So I called the S.S. office and told them. They said they'd take down the information, mail us some forms, then send us substitute checks in 3 weeks or a month. So I borrowed $200 from my friend Faith. She loaned me the 200, along with a lecture. Why can't you save? What do you do with your money? And stuff like that.

Pete was still bitching. He never gave a gift in his life. He can't understand that with me, it's part of living!

I finally started packing a bag. He'd unpack it, and I ran out. I took a bus to town, had dinner, all by myself. I nibbled, I couldn't eat. I finally had to come home.

Things are a bit better. Penny is going to pay off my bills and I cut up my charge plates. I'll pay her so much a month. And for birthdays and Christmas, if I don't have the money, I'll go into hibernation, until after the holidays. Good thing I already have your Dad's gift. I found a sliver of a snapshot of Grammy, had it enlarged, tinted, and framed for him. That cost a lot. Pete would probably strangle me if he knew!

The doctor was amazed that I went 4 days with a broken rib. The X-rays also show gallstones the size of quarters! He said the rib would fuse back together in 6 weeks, then I'll have my rocks removed, the ones in my gallbladder. The ones in my head will just have to stay there!

Now you know why I hadn't written. Hopefully my next letter will be Happy. I'll probably be in Denver if things don't improve here. I'll stay there, God willing.

> God Bless. I love you,
> Naunny
> Xxxxx

For all of my childhood and most of my adolescence, I also thought that Naunny and Pete were doing fine financially. I knew that they were not rich because they lived in a tiny, one-bedroom house, but I never thought that they were *poor*. Pete was a part-time musician who wore a tuxedo to his job, and Naunny worked full-time at Cecil's laundry business. They always had enough food to eat and more than enough beer for Pete to drink, and Naunny always seemed to wear nice clothes and buy us great presents for Christmas. And whenever I visited them in the 1970s when I was in college, Naunny would almost always slip me a $10 or $20 bill. I just assumed they were making enough money and had saved enough money to live comfortably in their cozy house.

I was in my midtwenties when I finally realized how poor Naunny and Pete really were. By that time, they both had retired, and I assumed that they had adequate pensions from their previous jobs. Then I learned that they had been asked to leave the house that they had rented for almost twenty years, because the owner's adult children wanted to live there.

I called Naunny and asked her where they were thinking of living. Naunny told me that they could not afford to rent an apartment and said that they were hoping to move into a one-bedroom unit in a government-subsidized complex for poor elderly residents. When I asked about her savings and pensions, she laughed and told me that they were completely dependent on Social Security as well as Medicare and Medicaid.

I remember saying something insensitive like, "I had no idea you were so poor."

"We're not poor," she said and laughed again. "We just don't have any money."

In retrospect, I can't believe how naive I was to Naunny's financial situation. The signs had always been there. I can understand my naiveté as a child, but I should have realized how poor she was when I was in college. But I was too preoccupied by my own financial limitations and my own life to recognize, let alone empathize with, my grandmother's situation.

Even when I finally recognized her poor situation, however, I really didn't do much about it except give her nice presents for her birthday and Christmas. I was a struggling graduate student, then a struggling assistant professor, and then a not-quite-struggling associate professor with a mortgage, car payments, and other bills. I was always too preoccupied with my own economic situation to really worry about Naunny. Besides, I assumed that Naunny's two sons would help her—which they did in various ways—just as I assume that I will help my own parents when they are elderly and in need of financial support.

I don't punish myself with guilt for my inattentiveness to Naunny's economic woes, but I do wish that I had paid for her to go to southern Colorado one last time before she went into the nursing home.

I also feel very lucky to have been born two generations after Naunny and to have been raised in a middle-class environment. My father made a good wage as a musician in Las Vegas, and my mother took part-time jobs from time to time to bring in extra money for the family. Like most children, I took the privilege of our middle-class existence for granted, but with age I have come to realize how fortunate I was and how thankful I am that my parents worked so hard for the family.

I feel even more privileged now as a full professor who is married to another full professor. We make good money, live in a modest but nice house, and have purchased coastal property where we will build our dream house when we retire. We also have nearly total autonomy in our jobs and careers. I can't complain, but, as the saying goes, sometimes I still do. Whenever I get the urge to complain about my job or my salary or my life, I just think about how Naunny struggled to make ends meet, and I realize how lucky I truly am.

> October 3, 1962 [from Las Vegas when Uncle Chuck and his kids lived there for a very short time after he got divorced]

Dearest Mom,
I hope and pray that you're feeling "fit as a fiddle" when you get this (and from now on!). We're all fine up here. I guess Pete will have you up to date on everything, but just in case he hasn't, here goes.

Today I received a very good break. The pit boss called me over to the side as we were about to finish our shift. He told me that there is an opening on the day shift for a dealer, and he thought I was ready to take a stab at it. The action on days is pretty thick and fast, but I'm going to give it all I've got. So keep your fingers crossed! It means a raise and a cull cut on "tokes." The hours will be the same as Timmy's (11–7). It will also mean that I can be home at night with the kids, and when we get our own place, it will work out much better. So I've really got something to work for. But the pit boss, Tommy Musso (I think he thinks I'm a wop too) said not to worry, that I could always go back to my old shift if things didn't work out yet. I wish you would call Robyn and tell her. . . .

If good wishes were money, I'd be a millionaire, because everybody I know or have come in contact with has wished me good luck. You may have failed to impress upon me the value of money or how to be practical, but the things you did teach me (mostly by example) I think are the most important, and will pay off in the long run. The world would be a wonderful place to live if everybody were like you, Mom. At least it would be the most happy place.

I could be happier tonight if the Dodgers hadn't blown that game today, though. Wasn't that sickening? That poor Maury Wills tried to win it all by himself today, didn't he? Well, that's the way it goes sometimes.

And now I have to go, so I will write soon and tell you how I'm doing. In the meantime, take it easy, Mom, and keep those wonderful letters coming to your number one son. Okay?
Love, Chuck

Older Chicanas have experienced the repercussions of an economic system that has only been concerned with their labor output and has had very little regard for their immediate and future quality of life. . . . They are . . . dependent on government safety nets such as Medicaid and SSI.
—ELISA FACIO, *Understanding Older Chicanas*

I felt sorry for her every time I visited her at that little apartment.
—GRANDDAUGHTER

Although some of our grandmothers came from wealthy families, a vast majority of them did not and had to work during their lives, whether on a full-time or part-time basis. Virtually all of them also worked at home as housewives and homemakers. In their stories, my relatives reconstructed a working-class grandmother who held many low-paying jobs throughout her life, except for the short period during World War II when she worked for the aircraft industry. These relatives also presented her as a woman who spent whatever money she had to provide everything possible for her two sons and visiting relatives and to prove to the world that she had "made it," even though she was very poor.

Relatives also presented Naunny as a woman who remained poor despite a lifetime of work. My grandmother, like so many grandmothers, had very little to show for her lifetime of work at the end of her life. Sadly, poverty is still a problem for *millions* of elderly people, and the poverty rates for elderly blacks and Hispanics are two to three times higher than those for whites. Even more distressing is the fact that the problem of poverty among the elderly may get worse as mortality rates continue to decline. Predictably, elderly women continue to suffer the most, and so the number of poor, working-class grandmothers will continue to rise.

Sex and the Single Grandma

Sexual identity is not a reflection of a natural state of being but a matter of representation.
—CHRIS BARKER, *Cultural Studies*

She was a sensual, sexy little grandmother who loved pretty clothes, good dance music, and especially her family.
—GRANDSON

Elsie was celebrating her twenty-ninth birthday with a few lady friends from work at a neighborhood bar near the Palomar Ballroom where she and her friends danced after work. And she was having a great time.

Her husband had been killed in a car accident more than a year earlier, and Elsie was enjoying life again. The Depression was still in full force, but Elsie herself was not at all depressed. She was not making much money, but it was enough to keep her two young boys fed and clothed. Her mother, Catalina, was living with her and taking care of the boys when she was at work. Elsie had met some new friends at work who loved to dance as much as she did, and they often went to the ballroom after work.

At the bar, Elsie had just finished her second glass of wine, and she was, as she used to say, "feeling no pain."

A cocktail waitress brought out a small cake with a single candle on it, and her lady friends started to sing "Happy Birthday." Soon, everyone in the bar joined in. Elsie beamed.

One of her friends reached down and picked up a gift-wrapped box from out of a shopping bag. She placed the package in front of Elsie on the bar.

"We all pitched in and got you a little something," she said.

Elsie feigned surprise and then quickly unwrapped the present.

She pulled out a lovely cream-colored slip. She lifted it out of the box and held it up against her body. She swayed her hips to the rhythm of a jitterbug tune that was playing on the jukebox.

"Try it on, Elsie!" one of her friends yelled.

Elsie did a little dance holding the slip against her body. Everybody in the bar started to clap and cheer.

The song ended, and Elsie went off to the rest room.

A few minutes later, she came back out, wearing only the slip. She started to dance in the middle of the floor to the sound of another big band swing.

"Oh, my gosh," one of her friends whispered through her hands.

A man from across the room joined Elsie on the dance floor. Everyone clapped as they jitterbugged on the dance floor.

After the song ended, the crowd cheered. Elsie curtsied, holding the ends of her slip out, and joined her friends at the bar.

"I can't believe you did that, Elsie!" said one of them, still laughing.

Elsie just smiled and took another sip of wine. Then she went back to the rest room and put her dress back on.

THE GRANDMOTHER AS SEX OBJECT

My grandmother was beautiful and cultured. She was not "Grandma," but "Grammy," a child's version of "Grandmère." . . . Grammy used little makeup, and said she'd never gotten a blemish in her life. She loved bathing in the tub and always looked tan and rosy.
—TARA MASIH, "Scrim-Shaw"

P.S. Pete said, "Maybe Nicky got married." I hope not. Enjoy yourself for a couple of years before you tie another knot. Love you forever!
—from Naunny letter, 1985

The words *sex* and *grandmother* are not used in the same sentence very often, at least not by most grandchildren. Obviously, our grandmothers had sex, or we would not be alive, but research reported by the American Association of Retired Persons indicates that grandmothers and grandfathers enjoy "senior romance" well into their later years. According to these studies, 50 percent of married people in their sixties and up to 35 percent in their seventies have sex at least once a month. These statistics notwithstanding, the sexy—and sexually active—grandmother does not correspond to the image that many grandchildren have of their grandmothers.

Although grandchildren and other family members may not think of the grandmother as a sex object, feminist critics argue that women of all ages are objectified sexually in American society. As the term suggests, *objectification* is the process of representation in which women are treated as objects; in the case of sexual objectification, women are treated as sex objects.

Feminist critics tell us that such objectification occurs in societies in which women are judged by their appearance more than anything else and in which certain kinds of appearances—those viewed as "feminine"—are preferred over others. In her book *The Beauty Myth*, Naomi Wolf argues that even though certain images of "beauty" for women are presumed to exist universally, these images are politically defined in a culture and change over time.

Several relatives, especially older ones who remembered Naunny as a young woman—and a relatively young grandmother—reinforced this beauty myth by describing how "pretty" she was in her prime.

"Aunt Elsie came to Denver with a boyfriend during World War II," a niece in her sixties remembered. "She was kind of a glamorous type. Her hair was black, and she used to wear it in a pompadour in front and curly down the back. I remember her in the kitchen, sitting on her boyfriend's lap. I was only about six years old, so I don't know who he was. I just remember thinking how pretty she is."

One grandson, now in his mid-50s, described Naunny's beauty in this way:

I remember the time Grandma and Uncle Pete moved back to L.A. from Denver into an apartment across from Lincoln Park. As soon as they got into town, I ran down to see her after school. The door was slightly ajar, and she was standing in that dark little place wearing a beautiful dark suit with long, dark gloves and had this hat on with a veil. She looked so beautiful! I ran over and gave her a big hug and just soaked it all up, her voice, the smell of her perfume, and powder.

This grandson added that he uses a hair care product called "Improve-Hair-so-Thick" that smells just like our grandmother. "Every morning I rub a little onto my hands and into my hair," he said, "and there's Grandma—that distinct voice, the little dark house, the scent of cigarettes, the perfume, and the powder."

In these and other ways, relatives objectified Naunny sexually, and they constructed an image of the grandmother that reinforced the beauty myth in American culture. These relatives meant to pay tribute to Naunny by representing her as an attractive young and middle-aged woman, yet by doing so, they suggested that Naunny had indeed met our society's cultural expectations of beauty, at least at some point in her life. She was "pretty," "sensual," "glamorous," and "sexy." If Naunny never had these qualities—or was not represented as having had these qualities—would she have been the ideal woman that we all remembered?

Family members also said that Naunny objectified herself (and others) sexually. Some critics have argued that women are always conscious of their image of themselves and of the way in which others watch them. According to relatives, Naunny did pay a lot of attention to her image of herself as a woman. Some of them described Naunny as a "party girl" and a "good time girl" who liked to show off her thin figure.

"She loved to dress up," her oldest son said, remembering his mother when she was a widow in the 1940s. "She'd work all day long, whether it was at the bakery or the laundry or Douglas Aircraft, then come home, take a bath, have dinner, put her gown on, and go out to dance. She would come in and ask, 'How do I look?' And she looked great."

Naunny also objectified herself and others sexually through her humor. Some relatives told me that she loved to hear and tell dirty jokes. She especially liked dirty limericks, and relatives were able to rattle off several of their favorites. Her former daughter-in-law told me the earliest one she could remember from Naunny:

Here's to the girl who wears red shoes,
She'll smoke your cigarettes and drink your booze,
She's lost her cherry,
but that's no sin,
She still has the box the cherry came in.

One of her granddaughters also remembered that Naunny liked jokes that used plays on words, and she said that this joke was one of Naunny's favorites:

An elderly woman met a fellow at a bar. The fellow looked at her, and she said, "I may have winter in my hair, but I have summer in my heart." Well, one thing led to another and they went back to a motel. Finally the guy tells her, "Lady, you may have winter in your hair and summer in your heart, but if you don't get a little spring in your ass we'll be here 'til next fall.

Naunny's great-granddaughter remembered when Naunny, or "Chubby Grandma," as she used to call her because of the cat named Chubby that Naunny had for many years, gave her some advice about boys:

When I was about fourteen, we were talking about my boyfriend. Chubby Grandma looks over at me, and she says, "Let me give you a little advice that my mother shared with me." So I was waiting to hear some deep thoughts or wisdom passed through the generations. And she says, "My mother told me, and you remember this, 'If you can see a guy that you think you love and want to marry taking a crap under a tree, and you can still kiss him and want to marry him, then he's the one for you.'" I was, like, horrified, and I thought, I'm never getting married.

Naunny's former daughter-in-law told me that Naunny's bawdy sense of humor even continued when she was an elderly woman in the nursing home:

When your grandma had her broken hip at the convalescent home, she couldn't get out of bed because it was very painful. This adorable physical therapist came in and was cajoling her. He said, "Can I help you Mrs. Alcaraz? We'll put on your pajama bottoms." I said, "Mom, you're not appreciating this physician here." Without missing a beat, her response was, "What, you want to see an old snatch?" He got kind of flustered, and that just delighted her to no end. I'm sure the idea that at her ancient age and in pain she was flirting with this young guy appealed to her sense of humor.

A granddaughter concluded that toward the end of her life Naunny couldn't remember what happened ten minutes ago, "but she remembered every dirty joke and limerick she ever heard."

I have to admit that I never recognized my grandmother's sexual identity, and I was surprised when relatives described her as "sexy" and "glamorous" and as a "party girl" and "good time girl." Naunny was forty-eight years older than I, and by the time my adolescent hormones kicked in she was in her late fifties. And those adolescent hormones did not permit me at that time to see a woman at that age, let alone my own grandmother, as a sexual or even sensual being. Of course, it wasn't the hormones that prevented me from seeing Naunny's sexual identity but cultural definitions of beauty that emphasize youth. In this way, I also reinforced the "beauty myth," not by remembering a grandmother who used to be beautiful but by refusing to see beauty in someone who was so much older than I was.

If I was surprised to hear relatives describe Naunny's beauty, I was shocked to learn that she loved to hear and to tell dirty jokes. This was a grandmother that I never knew. She never told me a dirty joke, even when I was in college and old enough to appreciate one. The closest thing to a dirty joke that I ever heard from Naunny was the story about her blind grandfather who had twenty-two children. As she wrote in her journal, "He had a terrific sense of humor. He overheard someone say once, 'I wonder how Mariano has produced 22 children when he's blind!' And he answered, 'Do you light a candle?'"

Naunny never told any dirty jokes to my father, her youngest son, either. Perhaps she wanted to "protect" us because he was her youngest son and I was her youngest grandson. But she certainly told dirty jokes to other relatives.

I was also surprised to hear stories about how she objectified the boyfriends she dated between marriages.

Auggie arrived at Elsie's house in Lincoln Heights several minutes late, as usual, and knocked on the door.

Elsie's twelve-year-old son, Charlie, answered the door and scanned Auggie's outfit. He was wearing a baggy suit with pinstripes that seemed too wide and two-toned spats that were way too shiny. His jet-black hair was slicked back, and Charlie thought his pencil moustache looked like a baby caterpillar that had been pasted on with black shoe polish.

"Hey, Chuckie," Auggie said, pinching Charlie's cheek as he walked into the small living room. "Whatcha think of my new dancing shoes?"

"I'll get Mom," Charlie said, turned around and went to get his mother.

Charlie didn't like Auggie. He seemed so phony. But he did make his mother happy, and for that, Charlie could tolerate him.

Charlie knocked on the faded door of the back bedroom.

"Auggie's here," he said.

His mom opened the door. She was wearing an elegant black ballroom gown, and her hair was pinned with a tortoise shell comb. She looked absolutely beautiful.

"How do I look?" she asked, twirling around to let the lacy ends of her gown swing in the air.

"Fine," Charlie mumbled, then went back to his room.

Elsie knew that Charlie did not like Auggie, but she was not in love with him so she was not overly concerned about it. Auggie was a great dancer, and Elsie loved to dance. And that was the extent of their relationship.

That night Auggie and Elsie took a cab to the Palomar Ballroom. The Palomar was having a dance contest that night, and one hundred couples had signed up. The winners would get a free pass to the Palomar for an entire year.

Elsie and Auggie danced all night long to the sounds of Clyde McCoy and his Sugar Blues. They made it to the top five, but then one of the judges tapped them on the shoulders to sit down.

Elsie was disappointed, but she was happy to have made it so far and to have been able to dance for so long. She was mildly upset with the judges because she thought the couple who won the contest was all flash and no substance.

After the contest, Auggie took Elsie to a nearby tavern for a glass of sherry, and then they took a cab back to Elsie's house.

Auggie walked Elsie to the door, holding her hand. She could feel the moisture on his hand, and she prepared herself for the impending kiss. Elsie did not like the way Auggie kissed. He was too active with his tongue and with his hands. But she felt she had to kiss him because he had taken her out.

"I had a nice time tonight, Elsie," he said, leaning in for the kiss. Immediately his hand started to reach up toward her. . . .

ROMANCING THE GRANDMOTHER

I remember she used to say, "I've been married twice. I was faithful to both, but, oh, the fun I had in-between."
—Niece

Several relatives were old enough to remember the twenty-year period between her marriages when Naunny was dating. In their stories, these relatives reconstructed a grandmother with an active romantic life.

"She was never unladylike," her former daughter-in-law said. "But she definitely enjoyed leading a single woman's life. Her mother was living with her, so the baby-sitting was covered. She enjoyed dating, and she broke the hearts of several men who fell madly in love with her."

One of the men whose heart Naunny may have broken in the 1940s was a coworker at Douglas Aircraft named Auggie. "I took one look at him," her oldest son recalled, "and I thought, 'If this isn't a gigolo, I've never seen one.' But Auggie liked to dance and your grandmother loved to dance, so they had some fun for a while."

Relatives said that Naunny also dated a foreman at Douglas whose nickname was "Okie," though no one could remember his real name. Okie was in my grandmother's life for a much longer time than was Auggie, and relatives have very fond memories of him. They described him as an amiable man who stood about five foot, eight inches tall, with a big round face and a large bald spot on the top of his big round head about which Naunny used to joke. Naunny's two oldest grandsons remembered that Okie used to do magic tricks for them when they were little kids. Two older nieces recalled that Okie would take my grandmother and her mother to the movies and bowling, since he had a car and my grandmother did not have one.

Some relatives think that my grandmother might have married Okie, except for one small problem: *he was already married.* "I think Okie loved my aunt very much," a niece recalled. "But he had a family, and his family even knew about Aunt Elsie. I don't know what arrangement they had, but it was discreet. She might have married him, but he was tied up with his own family. But he was there so often it was like he had two families."

Relatives said that Naunny also had a relationship with a man named Eldon, though some relatives thought they were lovers, while others thought they were just good friends. Eldon lived near Naunny's house in L.A. in the Lincoln Heights area and later rented a room from her in the house that she was renting. According to relatives who remembered him, Eldon was a decent guy with a good heart, but he was also an alcoholic and a diabetic with a bad liver. And alcoholism and diabetes were not a good combination for Eldon.

"Mom would always tell me how he'd drink and then give himself a big shot of insulin, which would counteract it," her former daughter-in-law said. "Sometimes he'd make a big mistake, and he'd have to drink some orange juice or something. So he was kind of teetering on the brink of death at all times."

One night, Eldon did indeed have one drink too many and died. Relatives said that he had been so taken with Naunny that he made her the beneficiary of his life insurance policy. She received a check for a few thousand dollars, a very large sum of money in the 1940s, especially for a poor widow with two kids. However, Eldon's surviving family members were upset that they were left out of the settlement, and they insinuated that Naunny had developed a relationship with him just to get his money. Relatives said that Naunny would rather remain poor than to have people question her character, so she spent the entire sum on Eldon's funeral. Supposedly, it was a great funeral!

Finally, there was Vernon. He was a lieutenant in the army who, according to my jazz musician father, looked like Harry James, a trumpet player from the 1940s and 1950s. Vernon and my grandmother had a very serious relationship, and Naunny had even taken him to meet her relatives in Denver. They had also talked about getting married, and some relatives thought that they were engaged. That was until Vernon revealed his plans to discipline Naunny's two boys after becoming their step-father. My uncle Chuck remembered the story this way:

> One Sunday afternoon Vernon and my mom were having dinner with some other couple. It was in the early 1940s. Your dad and I were sitting at the table, too, and I went to reach for something. Vernon said, "If you want something, ask for it and say please." I looked at my mother kind of funny and thought, "Who the heck is this guy?" You know how your grandmother was—we didn't have any rules or regulations. Well, Vernon tells the other couple at the table, "As soon as Elsie and I get married, I'll straighten out the boys." Then later he tells us to go to bed, and it was like 8 o'clock. Your dad and I looked at each other and laughed. We were young teenagers by then, and we went to bed whenever we wanted. But your dad and I went to bed, and we called Mom and asked her to come see us for a second. She comes up and I say, "You're not gonna marry that creep are you?" She says, "Not if you don't want me to, honey." We said, "No, we don't want you to!" Well, that was the end of Vernon!

Vernon and Naunny broke up shortly after that incident, and no one is really sure whether she had any second thoughts about not marrying him. If she did, she kept them to herself.

My aunt also remembered something else Naunny said about Vernon. "Years later," she said and laughed, "your grandma told me she didn't mind not marrying Vernon because he had a little pee-pee."

Naunny might have had other boyfriends or suitors, but no one could remember anyone specific. According to relatives, it was not until both of her boys had moved out of the house and were married that she became serious with another man. That was in the early 1950s, and this time it would be the man she would marry.

My father said he played a role in getting them together, though it was a role he would regret. My dad was playing in a Latin jazz band led by Lalo Guerrero, and Pete Alcaraz was the piano player. He remembered the story this way:

My mom used to make me beautiful Argyle socks with little musical notes on them. I used to wear those socks to play, and Pete asked me, "Hey, man, where'd you get those crazy socks?" I told him my mother makes them, and I think she made some for Pete. Then I went on the road with another band, but Pete stayed with Lalo, and I guess they started dating.

My dad remembers calling his mother from Chicago one night and learning that she wanted to marry Pete. "I was very upset," my dad admitted on the tape recording that he sent to me. "I told her, 'Mom, he's the nicest guy in the world, but he's a total lush.' He was a sweetheart of a guy and an incredible piano player, but he was always drunk. So I told my mother, 'Do you want my advice? Don't marry him. He's a drunk, and I don't think he can take care of you.' Well, she didn't heed my advice and married Pete anyway."

Fortunately, Pete, whom Naunny called "Poppy," was a happy drunk. So although he didn't work very often and rarely left his pink Naugahyde recliner when he was at home, he was never abusive to Naunny. And some of Naunny's female relatives said that unlike Vernon, Pete did *not* have a "little pee-pee." Naunny's older nieces said that she used to share an inside joke with them about the large organ on her piano player. But since Pete was usually inebriated, they said that Naunny would often tell them that Pete was "too drunk to get it up."

> July 4th, 1984, 6:00 A.M.
> (from Las Vegas)
>
> Dearest Poppy—
> Went out gambling with Don and Margie last night. Don and I didn't do beans, but Margie came home with 140 bucks more than when she started! They're leaving this morning. I'll hate to see them leave, especially my Bita! God alone knows when or if we'll see each other again. I'm not being morbid. I always say that, every time we part!
> I don't know what's on the agenda for today. Guess we'll play it by ear! Not too much more to report, so I'll write more mañana. . . .
> Love,
> Elsie, your better half!

July 5th, 6:15 A.M.

Dearest Poppy—

Claudia, Jennifer and I went to a barbeque yesterday, at Barbara's, and we watched the glorious fireworks display from Cashman Field from their back yard. It cooled off, and it was nice! We got home at 11:30 PM. Bill was home from his gig, where he played the Engelbert Humperdink show. We talked for an hour, had a glass of wine, and went to bed. I got up at 5, made my bed, had my shower, made coffee, and here I sit, with my little cup, waiting for the family to get up. I'll probably take a nap, after I put this letter out for the mailman! I wrote you a letter yesterday, so you'll probably get two letters at the same time!

Don't know what's planned for today, but whatever, it will be different. . . .

Have you had any more flak from our bitchy manager? Oh well.

> Lotza love!
> From your better 1/3
> El

July 6th

Dearest Poppy—

It's overcast today. Claudia says it looks like rain. I said maybe it will cool off. It's been 116 every day since I've been here. She said, "No way, it will only rain enough to make it muggy." Oh well, at least it's nice and cool in the house. Thank God for air conditioning.

Bill and Claudia play tennis every day, then go in the pool. I just sit and watch them for a while, then I come in the house and read. I haven't watched any T.V. to speak of. Tomorrow is the Big Day. Claudia and the kids are buying Bill a new work suit. He needs one badly. The old one is getting pretty shiny. Bye for now.

> Will write more mañana.
> Love and Blessings,
> Elsie

Chapter 3

July 7th—Bill's Apio
Verde

Dearest Poppy—

I won't be able to mail this today, but it's 5:30 A.M. I've said my morning prayers, and no one else is up, so I'll write!

I met the nicest lady next door. She has two lovely little girls, and they come over to play with Jennifer. She came after her little girls, and she sat and had a glass of wine with us. She told me I was beautiful (she made my day) and asked if I'd ever eaten tempura. I said "No." so yesterday she called over the back fence, and handed Claudia a plate of fried shrimp and tempura. It's little round disks as big as a chocolate chip cookie. It's yams, dipped in a delicious batter. We really enjoyed them!

I don't suppose I'll be able to go to Mass today, as Claudia has to bake the cake for the birthday boy. Do you think God will forgive me? Claudia asked Bill what he'd like for his birthday dinner and he said beans and torts. But since he couldn't have that, he told her he didn't want her to knock herself out cooking (it's their 31st anniversary too), so we're having hamburgers and potato salad, and cake!

I'll write more mañana, God willing.

Love and Blessings,

E.

Naunny shared jokes about the body parts of her boyfriends only with her female relatives, such as her daughters-in-law, sisters, and older nieces and granddaughters. Even though Naunny never shared this inside joke about Pete with me, I confirmed the large size of his organ on at least two occasions. The first time occurred on a visit to L.A. when I was about eight years old. I needed to use the bathroom, which meant that I had to go through the bedroom because they rented a tiny one-bedroom house, and the only bathroom was adjacent to the bedroom. When I walked in, Pete was taking his usual afternoon nap, lying naked on top of the sheet and snoring away. I saw his large penis flopped over and thought to myself, "God, I hope mine never gets that big."

Several years later when I was in college and happened to see it again under the same circumstances, my attitude had, of course, changed. I remember thinking to myself, "Man, can I borrow that thing on Friday night if you're not using it?"

I have to admit that when I first learned about how Naunny made jokes about her boyfriends' body parts, I was stunned. It is one thing to tell a few limericks and quite another to joke about the privates of her sexual partners. However, knowing that my grandmother had such a bawdy sense of humor adds more color and character to my memories of her, even if it changes my boyish feelings for her as the nice old lady who played 500 Rummy with me.

I also recognize that I had been stereotyping my grandmother as an elderly, asexual woman, even though she, like many women, actually became a grandmother when she was in her late thirties, younger then than my wife is today. I also realize that I failed to recognize that grandmothers, even elderly ones, are sensual, sexual women.

Elsie stood naked on the scale in her bathroom. Her boyfriend had broken up with her the night before, and now there was more bad news. The scale read 106 pounds, two more than it had read the previous morning.

She could not understand how she could have gained two entire pounds when all she ate yesterday was coffee for breakfast, a half sandwich for lunch, and a cup of soup for dinner. She decided to go on one of her coffee fasts to lose the extra pounds. She would have a cup of coffee for breakfast and one for lunch and then treat herself to a piece of toast and a glass of wine for dinner.

She put on a slip and walked over to the full-length mirror that was attached to the back of her bedroom door. She gazed up and down her body from various angles, but all she could see were the puffy areas where she was fat. She adjusted her slip, sucked in her belly, and tightened her buttocks.

"I'll show him," she said, determined to get back down to 100 pounds, buy a new dress, and glide past her former boyfriend at the ballroom where they danced.

THE ANOREXIC GRANDMOTHER

Anorexia is not a philosophical attitude; it is a debilitating affliction. Yet, quite often a highly conscious and articulate scheme of images and associations—virtually a metaphysics—is presented by these women.
—SUSAN BORDO, *Unbearable Weight*

Grandma would not eat. She still had this thing about how thin she was. I think she was anorexic her whole life.
—GRANDDAUGHTER-IN-LAW

Just as the words *sex* and *grandmother* are not used very often in the same sentence, the words *anorexia* and *grandmother* do not seem to fit together either. Some of our grandmothers, like my maternal grandmother, are rather portly, especially as they get older. But Naunny was probably anorexic for most of her adulthood.

I did not know much about anorexia, so again I turned to the literature. I read that anorexia nervosa was first diagnosed in the late 1800s as a form of "hysteria" that affected mostly middle-class females between fifteen and twenty. Today it is considered one of several eating disorders that affect people of all ages. Although men also have anorexia, it is still an overwhelmingly female experience, with women making up 90 to 95 percent of the sufferers. No one knows exactly how many women are afflicted, but researchers estimate that one in every 200 to 250 women between age thirteen and thirty-two and one in five female college students develop anorexia.

Feminist critics have focused much attention on anorexia and other eating disorders. Although theories about the disease vary widely, many of these critics argue that anorexia is ultimately not about food but about control. Drawing on the work of Michel Foucault, Carol Spitzack argues that anorexia is one way in which women discipline their bodies in an effort to conform to a narrowly (and thinly) defined ideal of feminine beauty. For anorexic women, thinness symbolizes their power to control their bodies.

Despite this emphasis on control over their bodies, anorexic women, ironically, seem to lose the very control they seek. For example, Kim Chernin writes that anorexia does not result in a triumph over one's body but an "alienation from the body," noting the irony that the typical anorectic is submissive.

Although anorexia usually begins early in a young woman's life, it can remain a problem for some older women as well, especially in Western societies where old women are not valued as wise mentors but as "old maids." Not surprisingly, then, some middle-aged and older women come to despise their womanly form, preferring a girlish (or even boyish) body that reminds them of their adolescence.

Naunny's relatives suggested that she might have lived most of her life under what Chernin calls the "tyranny of slenderness." Her daughter-in-law recalled that when Naunny was a younger woman, she would often starve herself. "Every now and then, you could tell that some boyfriends had treated her mean or something," she said. "She'd drink coffee, smoke cigarettes, and get herself really skinny. But then she'd always pop herself back up again."

A niece also remembered that every time Naunny visited her relatives in Denver, she would gain about ten pounds and complain that her butt was too big, even though her niece thought she looked much better.

It seems that as Naunny aged, she longed to keep her slim body and continued to starve herself. A granddaughter told me that Naunny often showed her pictures of herself in a bathing suit from when she was younger. As she got older, however, it became difficult—and ultimately impossible—to maintain her "girlish figure."

A granddaughter-in-law remembered a time when she visited Naunny in the hospital when Naunny was in her late sixties. "She was in the hospital, and she wouldn't eat," she said. "So I told my husband, 'Make her eat,' because he could always make her do anything. She did, but then afterward she said, 'God, I feel like throwing up.' And I thought, 'I wonder how long that has been going on.'"

Other relatives talked about how Naunny would make jokes and sarcastic comments about the weight of family members. "She would always say that so-and-so was four axe-handles wide," one grandson recalled. A granddaughter shared a similar story about how Naunny would make fun of one of Pete's relatives whom she thought was overweight: "Grandma used to make fun of her, saying that she would walk in with this tight skirt and this fat butt and these little feet with high spiked heels and make dent marks in her linoleum."

My mom recalled how Naunny would eat very little when she visited my parents' home in Las Vegas. She said that she would also find Naunny's food wrapped up in a napkin and hidden behind a pillow on the couch or in the trash.

In her personal journals, Naunny made critical comments about her own body and the bodies of others. She was seventy-four years of age when she wrote this entry:

> Today, Pete and I will go on a diet to try to lose some of the pounds we put on over the Christmas holidays. Pete weighs 202, me 108. All my life I've had a 24-inch waist. Now in my old age, I'm getting middle age spread. . . . I look like an avocado!

Even during the last few months of her life at a nursing home, she was still concerned with how her frail eighty-six-year-old body looked. As Naunny wrote in her diary: "I love taking my bath at home, where I can soak. But I don't like these young chicks with their cute solid bodies staring at my bones. I too had a nice body a long time ago!"

I wonder whether Naunny's relatives used the fact that she lived to be eighty-six to rationalize our choices not to intervene more forcefully with regard to her eating disorder. As one grandson put it, "It's ironic in this day of diet and health food that Grandma lived one of the unhealthiest lives. She was a chain smoker, she drank wine or cough syrup everyday, and had a diet of a few jelly beans and coffee. And she lived to be in her late eighties."

Whatever the case, her "girlish" figure and our reluctance and/or inability to motivate her to change her eating habits no doubt caused additional deterioration to her body, especially when she was older.

I also remember that Naunny seemed to be obsessed with how thin she was. When my sisters and I were little kids, Naunny would let us play with the flab under her arms. She'd put her arms straight out, and we would flip her flab back and forth. Naunny always made self-deprecating jokes about this flab, but it seems that for her entire life she tried to lose that flab by not eating. Paradoxically, the more she starved herself in an effort to lose that flab, the skinnier *and* the flabbier her arms became.

During my lifetime, Naunny usually weighed close to one hundred pounds, and I remember many years, especially late in her life, when she weighed in the nineties and maybe even in the eighties. When she was an older woman, she smoked cigarettes, drank coffee and wine, and ate crumbs. Yet she would proudly display her waif-thin body in her skimpy bathrobe every time I visited and ask, "Don't I have a girlish figure?"

Like most relatives in my family, I would always say, "Yes, Naunny," even though I thought she looked pathetically frail. Susan Bordo notes that "the emaciated body of the anorectic . . . represents itself as a caricature of the contemporary ideal of hyper-slenderness for women," and in that skimpy bathrobe, Naunny certainly fit this caricature. I wonder whether our affirming responses reinforced her continued anorexia. If we all had answered, "No, Naunny, you look frail and sick and you need to eat," might she have eaten more and enjoyed better health? I doubt it, but the feeling that we might have been able to make more of a difference still lingers in my mind.

Naunny was in Las Vegas, enjoying another one of her yearly Christmas visits to see Bill and his family. All of the family members were sitting at the dinner table, eating another amazing feast prepared by Claudia. Everyone thought the meal—which consisted of chicken Marsala, green beans with bacon bits, rice, fruit salad, and fresh rye bread—was incredible. Everyone, that is, except Naunny.

Family members had wolfed down their food and were helping themselves to seconds. Naunny picked at her food, but ultimately it appeared that she had finished her first serving.

"Would you like seconds?" Claudia asked Naunny.

"No, honey," Naunny said. "I don't want to go back to L.A. looking like an avocado. Pete won't recognize me."

"Oh, Mom," Claudia said and sighed. "You don't look like an avocado. You're skinny."

"We need to fatten you up!" Bill said and laughed. "You'll need to

lose weight when you start looking like this," he added, lifting up his shirt to reveal his massive belly.

Naunny smiled politely then excused herself to go to the rest room. No one at the table noticed that Naunny had taken her napkin with her as she left the dining room.

Once Naunny was in the rest room, she opened up the napkin. More than half of her meal was crammed into a ball in that napkin. She dropped the food into the bowl and flushed the toilet.

"There goes five pounds worth," she said as she watched the food twirl around the bowl before disappearing. She threw the paper napkin in the trash, washed her hands, and went back to the dining room.

"You OK, Mom?" Claudia asked.

"Oh, I'm fine, sweetie," Naunny said. "I was just making some room for dessert."

Unfortunately, Naunny is not the only member of my family preoccupied with weight. I believe that her legacies of body obsessions and eating disorders have been passed on to members of my immediate family.

My younger sister Michelle, or "Mishe," as we call her, suffered the most from this dysfunction. Mishe was bulimic during her adolescence and young adulthood, and she was addicted to laxatives for a time. Now in her forties, she no longer has an eating disorder but remains very conscious of her weight.

My father also has been fixated on weight for most of his life as a parent. Curiously, however, he has never been obsessed with his own weight, even though he has weighed over two hundred pounds for most of his adult life. Instead, he has been obsessed with *my* weight. Almost every time that I have seen him during my visits to Las Vegas in the last twenty-five years, his first question, often before he says hello, has been, "How much do you weigh?" Yet he never asks my sisters or anyone else how much they weigh when he sees them.

Over the years, I have asked him to stop asking me that question and have told him how rude he is for asking it, but he continues to do so.

I was never concerned about my weight when I was growing

up. I was fairly thin as an active young boy, and I developed an athletic build as an adolescent and young adult due to regular participation in organized sports. I was especially proud of my muscular thighs, which only thickened as I continued to run sprints and work out with weights for strength and stamina. These thighs helped me to excel in baseball as a pitcher, because, contrary to common thinking, the power in pitching is generated from the legs rather than the arm. These thighs pushed my weight up and forced me to buy pants that were one or two sizes larger than the size of my waist, especially in the days before loose-fitting jeans. As I continued to develop athletically as a college pitcher at USC, I continued to buy pants that accommodated my power thighs. I was not quite 5'11" tall with a 32-inch waist, and I weighed about 185 pounds.

After my college athletic career ended, I began a rather sedentary two-year master's program. I jogged and played tennis, but I did not participate in regular regimented workouts. Not surprisingly, I gained weight. I did not consider myself to be "fat," nor did I experience any eating disorders, but I became more conscious of the results of my occasional trips to the bathroom scale. And the very thighs and hips that were once the source of my athletic power became a disconcerting reminder of my need for an even larger pant size. My dad's constant question, "How much do you weigh?" started to weigh on my psyche.

During my Ph.D. program, I took up distance running. I started this new activity mostly because I missed the rigors of athletic training, but once I got into it, I loved the endorphin buzz that occurs during a ten- to twenty-mile run. Yet I must admit that I was quite pleased when I lost over twenty pounds and could comfortably fit into pants with a thirty-two-inch waist. My thighs were still thick, but they were thinner than they had been since my freshman year of high school. I even started to take pride in answering my father's ever-present question, since I had gone below the 180-pound mark for the first time since high school.

I continued to run into my early thirties until a back injury forced me to stop. Within a month of the injury, I gained ten pounds and moved up a pant size. I also stopped weighing myself regularly. My dad kept asking his question on every visit, but I ignored him.

When I moved into my forties, however, I became heavier, past the dreaded two-hundred–pound-mark. But I was less concerned with my weight and more concerned with my cholesterol levels, which went up for three consecutive years. Although I did not have high blood pressure, a family history of heart attacks, or other indicators of potential health problems, my doctor told me that I should make an effort to lower my cholesterol. I heeded his advice and changed my diet, eliminating red meat and other fatty foods. I took longer walks with my dog and played tennis on a regular basis.

As I had hoped, I lowered my cholesterol considerably, and, much to my surprise, I lost almost twenty-five pounds in the process. I have maintained that cholesterol level and my weight, more or less, for the last few years and plan to continue to do so.

The Christmas before finishing this book, my wife and I went to Las Vegas to my parents' house for the first time in several years. As is all too common around the holidays, I put on about ten pounds from Thanksgiving leftovers and holiday parties before we went to Vegas. So I was not surprised when I walked into the house and my dad greeted me with a hug, then stood back, scanned me up and down with his eyes, and said, "You're huskier than you were the last time I saw you. How much do you weigh?"

I just ignored him, but my mom responded immediately.

"Bill?" she asked, more forcefully than I expected. "Why are you so obsessed with Nicky's weight?"

My dad got defensive and left the room.

The more I have thought about it, I believe that my father's question is not really motivated by a concern with my weight but is the result of the strained relationship that we have had since I was a teenager. We fought with each other when I was in high school, college, and graduate school, and even since becoming a professor. We rendered some Christmas vacations legendary, with confrontations that were usually triggered by his demands and my resistance to those demands but also by games of Trivial Pursuit and even the wrong kind of eye contact.

Soon after I became a professor in the early 1980s, I came

home for Christmas. When I arrived, my mom and sisters pulled me aside.

"We don't want you to ruin another Christmas," my youngest sister Lisa told me directly. "So when Dad says, 'Give me the salt,' just give him the stinking salt."

"Why doesn't Dad ask for the salt?" I said. "At least he can say please."

"Dad is not going to change," Mom said. "So why don't you be the one to change?"

I swallowed my pride and put the chip that I had always carried on my shoulder in my suitcase. And that evening, when my father said, "Give me the salt," I took a deep breath and without saying a word, gave him the damn salt.

We have had relatively few fights since that day and no major blowouts. When he orders me to pass the salt or give him the newspaper, which he continues to do, often without asking or saying please, I bite my tongue and give it to him.

But in avoiding conflict with each other, we have mostly avoided communication with each other. At least when we were fighting, we were talking to—or, more accurately, yelling at—each other. I honestly believe that my father continues to ask me about my weight not because he is obsessed with thinness but because he wants to pick a fight with me. I refuse to take the bait, so although my feelings are hurt when he continues to ask his irritating question, I just walk away and interact with him as little as possible in order to avoid a scene so that we can maintain a veil of civility.

Of course, it very well could be that my father's apparent obsession with my weight is just part of the legacy of my grandmother's obsession with her weight. It is also possible that Naunny made comments about my weight after my sedentary master's program. But at least Naunny did not offer such comments or questions to your face.

A woman obsessed with the size of her body, wishing to make her breasts and thighs and hips and belly smaller and less apparent, may be expressing the fact that she feels uncomfortable being female in this culture.

—KIM CHERNIN, *The Obsession*

How much do you weigh?
—SON

In their stories, Naunny's relatives reconstructed a grand-mother who was beautiful and sexy, had many boyfriends, and loved to hear and tell dirty jokes. It was a grandmother whom I never knew in my lifetime, but I am happy that I have come to know this part of her through my relatives' stories.

As they reconstructed her sexual identity in their stories, rela-tives represented Naunny as one of many women living in a culture where people judge them by their physical appearance. Family members suggested that Naunny, like many other women, was influenced by these cultural expectations of beauty for her entire life, even when she was an elderly woman trying to maintain her "girlish" figure.

Perhaps most depressing to learn was that my grandmother may have suffered from anorexia for most of her adult life, even as an elderly woman. Very little is written about elderly women with eating disorders, except for studies indicating that some older women who are institutionalized fast in an effort to con-trol their deaths. That my grandmother—and other grandmoth-ers—suffered from eating disorders so late in life attests to the pervasive influence of cultural expectations about women's fe-male beauty.

The fact that Naunny's relatives did not criticize her anorec-tic lifestyle also attests to the power of our cultural expectations of thinness. In some of their stories about Naunny's sexual iden-tity, relatives may have even naturalized eating disorders as a typical, even "normal," way for women to maintain their weight. In this way, relatives may unintentionally reproduce eating disorders in the family and pass them on to subsequent generations.

In the final analysis, I have very mixed feelings about my grandmother's sexual identity. Even though it may reinforce a beauty myth, I am pleased to know that Naunny once was a beautiful woman who attracted many men, though I am disap-pointed that none of these men seemed to be the right man for her. I was initially shocked to hear that she told sexually ori-ented jokes to certain relatives, especially about the body parts of her partners, but this knowledge has added more color and character to my memories of her. I was, and still am, saddened to realize that she was probably anorexic for much of her life in an effort to maintain the thin body that made her more attractive as a young woman but even more frail as an elderly one. Ultimately, I can't help but feel some guilt about not complimenting her more often about how she looked and about not forcefully encouraging her to eat more so that she might have looked better and suffered less.

Serving Us Proudly and Giving Us Everything

My grandmother was a tall, beautiful, warm-hearted woman who devoted her entire life to other people.
—SIBYLLE BERGEMANN, "Luise Maria Liss"

Grandma would do anything for you.
—GRANDDAUGHTER

Naunny and Pete were sitting in the living room of their house watching television, as they did every night. Pete had settled into his recliner as usual, and Naunny was on the couch, secretly hoping that one of her many grandchildren would call or drop by for a visit. She would never call one of them when she and Pete were watching television because Pete did not like interruptions during his favorite programs.

"Change the channel, honey?" Pete asked in the whiney voice that he used anytime he wanted Naunny to do something for him.

"Yes, Poppy," Naunny said. She got up from the couch, walked to the television, and changed the channel in time for The Rockford Files, *one of Pete's favorite shows.*

"Would you get me a beer, honey?" Pete asked.

"Yes, Poppy," Naunny said, walking into the tiny kitchen. She returned with a can of Falstaff and gave it to Pete. "Anything else?" she said in a slightly sarcastic tone that Pete did not detect.

"No, honey," he said, and popped open his can of beer.

They watched Rockford *in complete silence. When the show was over, Pete broke the silence.*

"Change the channel, honey?" Pete asked again in his whiney voice.

"Yes, Poppy," Naunny said. She got up from the couch, walked to

the television, and changed the channel in time for The FBI," another one of Pete's favorite shows.

"Would you get me another beer, honey?" Pete asked.

"Yes, Poppy," Naunny said. She took his empty can and went back into the kitchen. She returned with another can of Falstaff. "Anything else?" she said, in a sarcastic tone that Pete still did not detect.

"No, honey," he said, and popped open his can of beer.

They watched The FBI in complete silence. When the show was over, Pete broke the silence again.

"Change the channel, honey?" Pete asked.

"Yes, Poppy," Naunny said. She got up from the couch, walked to the television, and changed the channel in time for Pete's favorite local news show, the one with celebrity weatherman Dr. Fishbeck to whom they always sent—and from whom they always received—a Christmas card.

"Would you get me another beer, honey?" Pete asked.

"Yes, Poppy," Naunny said. She took his empty can and went back into the kitchen. She returned with another can of Falstaff. "Anything else?" she said, in a sarcastic tone that Pete nearly detected.

"No, honey," he said, and he popped open his can of beer.

The next evening they would repeat the cycle, as they would almost every night from when they were married in 1954 until Pete died in the mid-1980s.

When we took our family vacations to Los Angeles to see Naunny and Pete, we always arrived at their little house early in the morning. Naunny would greet us with a big hug and then lead us into her tiny kitchen, where she fed us scrambled egg burritos.

After we finished eating, we would take naps. Mom and Dad slept in the bedroom, while my sisters and I slept on the couch bed in the living room. While we napped, Naunny took a walk up the big hill on 6th Street to Suzi's corner market, while Pete sat on the front porch drinking beer.

An hour or so later, Naunny would return, and she would wake me up by placing her hands gently on my face. Naunny always had very cold hands, but when she placed them on my face while I was sleeping, they were incredibly soothing, like the feel of the other side of the pillow at night. I would wake up slowly, and Naunny would gently scratch my back with her long fingernails until I was alert enough to get out of bed.

SERVING US PROUDLY

Serving others is a basic principle around which women's lives are organized.
—JEAN MILLER, *Toward a New Psychology of Women*

Whenever there were family get-togethers, she'd always be in the kitchen, cleaning up or making food. Everyone would try to get her to sit down, but next thing you know, she'd be there cleaning up again.
—GRANDSON

Women have served others, especially their family members, throughout history. Scholars point out that such service is not an inherent or a biologically driven function of women but rather is a cultural expectation.

This expectation has been especially prominent with respect to women's service to their *families*. In her book *Who Cares*, Julia Wood argues that the very essence of motherhood is defined by caring for others. Elisa Facio makes a similar claim about *grandmothers*, noting that because of their age and sex, grandmothers "are expected to primarily conform to a caregiving and nurturing role."

Relatives presented Naunny as the epitome of this cultural ideal for family women. In their stories, they reconstructed a grandmother who was more concerned with serving and caring for the family than with anything else.

Some relatives suggested that Naunny's devotion to serving her family was learned from her own mother. Catalina Maldonado Martinez was born and raised in a time and in a place where Hispanic women went from community leaders in their villages to housewives in Anglo communities when their husbands became dependent on American industries for work. Accordingly, many of my relatives, especially the older ones, told stories about how Catalina took care of the family and how she taught Naunny to do the same.

"Whatever clothes I was wearing on a certain day, after I retired that night, Grandma Catalina would wash them, by hand,

This was me. Most of the relatives called me "Bobby."

I was visiting Grandma & aunt Elsie the summer I was 14. My dad, JJ, was aunt Elsie's brother.

and iron them," one of Naunny's nieces in her sixties said about her grandmother. "When I got up the next morning, all those clothes were freshly pressed on a hanger in my bedroom. She passed that on to your grandmother, too."

Naunny's former son-in-law said that relatives had told him that Catalina would go to any lengths to serve family members. "Whenever relatives were staying with Naunny and the two boys, Catalina would give them her bed, and she would sleep in a crib," he said. "*In a baby crib*! She was so small, she'd fit in a crib, and she didn't think anything about it. The family's needs always came before her own needs."

As Naunny's oldest son concluded about his grandmother:

> Grammy was a saint. She lived just for whatever she could do for the family. She used to cook, clean the house, and do the laundry, everything. She didn't ask for anything out of life. She just wanted to serve us. Everybody should have a grandmother like that. . . . Your grandma was just like that, too.

Naunny was indeed like that. Whether she learned it from her mother or not, Naunny always waited on, took care of, and looked after others. Family members told story after story about how Naunny had served them. One niece described her time with her Aunt Elsie in this way: "It was so pleasant just being there with her. I'd get up in the morning, and she would have breakfast ready. We'd eat, sleep, and talk. I didn't have to do anything."

Commenting on how Naunny served her husband Pete, one granddaughter went so far as to say that Naunny "would wipe the sweat off Pete's brow," which was often, since Pete sweated profusely, especially when he ate. Pete always sweat when he ate, regardless of whether he ate spicy chili or an unseasoned salad, though he rarely ate salad because he always said that lettuce made him sleepy.

"I only had one gripe about visiting Naunny," my mother told me. "Your dad would always revert back to being a child. It was always, 'Mom, get me this or get me that.' He'd never get up and go get it for himself. He'd just let her serve him like she did when he was a kid. But Naunny loved it."

When I think of Naunny, the very first image that comes to mind is beans and tortillas. *Every* time I visited Naunny—as a boy with my parents and as an adult by myself or with friends—I would have a plate of pinto beans and fresh flour tortillas that Naunny would warm up over the gas burner. I would spray Squeeze Parkay margarine on the tortilla, plop a few spoonfuls of beans on it, and roll it up. Naunny watched with joy while I ate one end and bean-margarine juice oozed out of the other end.

After I finished eating my bean burritos, Naunny would make one of her famous banana splits with rich vanilla ice cream that was always soft because the tiny freezer compartment in her little refrigerator never could completely close due to a buildup of frost. She would squirt a pile of whipped cream from the can on top of the ice cream and place a cherry on the very top, and then watch me devour the entire thing.

Bean burritos are so synonymous with Naunny that even to this day I cannot eat one without thinking of her, though I refuse to put Squeeze Parkay on anything.

Serving Us Food

We're about to go to Las Vegas for Christmas. . . . We've got a dozen empanadas, a dozen tamales, three pounds of chorizo, and three dozen torties.
—from Naunny's journal

Although Naunny served in so many ways, virtually every relative I interviewed recalled how she served *food* to them. Serving food may be the quintessential activity of mothers and grandmothers. Susan Bordo discusses this cultural expectation of women, noting that preparing and serving food has long been interpreted as a way for women to demonstrate their love for others. As she concludes, "Food is equated with maternal and wifely love throughout our cultures."

One of Naunny's passions did indeed seem to be serving food to family members. A niece wrote that the first turkey dinner she ever had was at her Tia Eloysa's house. They had all the trimmings, including pumpkin pie.

A nephew and niece told me of a time when Naunny taught them how to make tamales. Her nephew started the story:

We went to visit your grandmother one time, and we got to taling about food and got to talking about tamales. We said, "We'd sure like to learn how to make tamales." Aunt Elsie said, "Well, you just get all the kids together, and you pick us up, and we'll come over and make tamales." And that's what we did. We spent all day long making tamales one Saturday. We picked them up early in the morning, and they were here until late in the evening.

His wife finished the story:

Your grandma told me what kind of meat to buy and how to cook it the night before, and the seasonings and spices. And she told me where to get this and where to get that. It cooked and cooked and cooked. We had all the kids over and we made tamales. And still to this day, when we're all here at Christmas time, the kids say, "Hey, let's make tamales." I say, "No, Aunt Elsie's not here. Forget it."

Most relatives, however, talked about the simple pinto beans and flour tortillas that were her signature dish. "She was famous for her beans and torts," one great-grandson remembered. "She had a special ladder for me to sit on at the table when I ate. I was her bean boy. I could just eat a bowl of beans. Nowadays I can't eat just a bowl of beans. It has to be beans and something else. But with her, I could just eat her beans."

One of her great-granddaughters thought it was amazing that Naunny always had beans and tortillas for relatives whenever they visited. "Unless you were expecting company," she said, "you would have to run to the store if somebody came over, but Chubby Grandma always had everything there. She always had beans, tortillas, and ice cream. It was like she was always ready, just waiting for us to come over."

Naunny continued to prepare and serve food to her two sons even after they moved out of the house and started families of their own. Her older son recalled that after he married his second wife in the 1960s, she used to bring a big pot of beans and freshly made tortillas every Saturday to his house.

Naunny's service is and always will be cherished by family members. But this commitment to service may have had some detrimental consequences for my grandmother as it has had for many women who are defined by their service to others.

As usual, Naunny was in the kitchen cleaning up while all of the cousins and guests talked and laughed in the spacious living room at Robyn's Spanish-style house in Long Beach. Robyn was hosting one of her regular family parties, and all of her children were there, along with their spouses, kids, and assorted friends. Even though Robyn and Chuck had divorced and remarried other people in the 1960s, they still maintained good relations for the seven children whom they had together, and Naunny always treated Robyn (and her husband Ed and their son Matty) as part of the family.

Naunny had brought a big pot of beans for the event, and she was hovering over the sink, cleaning the pot and other dishes.

Cathy, Robyn's oldest daughter, walked into the kitchen, looking for her grandmother. "I thought you'd be back here, Grandma," she said. "Why don't you leave this for Mom and come visit with us?"

"I'm fine, honey," Naunny said. "Just let me finish this one load."

"Did you have enough to eat?" Cathy asked.

"I wasn't really hungry," Naunny said. "I had a big breakfast with Poppy before we came over."

"But Uncle Pete had a huge plate of food," Cathy said.

"He can always eat," Naunny said. "That's why he's so fat. I'm trying to keep my girlish figure."

Cathy smiled politely and grabbed Naunny's hand.
"OK, Grandma, time to visit with your grandkids," she said.

Naunny resisted slightly but then yielded and walked with Cathy to the living room and sat down on the couch.

A few minutes later, Cathy went to check on her kids and Naunny sneaked back to the kitchen. She did another load of dishes by hand, as the rest of the family talked and laughed in the living room.

Subordination, Sacrifice, and Self-Denial

She would always wait for us to eat before she ate.

—GRANDSON

Several scholars have argued that women's commitment to serving others can have negative consequences, especially when others interpret serving as one of women's "natural" roles. When viewed in this way, women's commitment to serving others may be devalued, as are the women who perform such service.

The activity of serving *food* in particular has been used to subordinate or marginalize women in our culture, especially when serving food is considered as natural as breathing. Women who do not perform such expected service may be seen as not completely fulfilling their roles as women.

Women's commitment to serving others also can lead some women to engage in sacrifice and self-denial, because they pay so much attention to the needs of others that they ignore their own needs. In her book *Slaying the Mermaid*, Stephanie Golden argues that this self-sacrifice can have harmful effects, quoting one doctor who described it as the "burnt toast syndrome," an affliction that occurs when women always put others first and settle for what's left. Golden added that over the long term this syndrome may lead to health problems including breast cancer, uterine fibroids, and heart disease.

This cultural expectation of serving and self-sacrifice has also led many women to serve others while denying service—and food—for themselves and has led to eating disorders, aerobics obsessions, alcoholism, refusal to seek medical attention, and other self-destructive practices. As Julia Wood concludes eloquently, this cultural expectation of self-denial as an expectation of womanhood "leads to the paradox that many women can only affirm themselves by denying themselves!"

Sadly, my grandmother did suffer from excessive sacrifice and self-denial, and she did engage in some of these self-destructive practices. Naunny constantly denied herself food, causing her to have a frail body and a variety of illnesses and ailments, especially later in life.

However, even though she regularly suffered from these various pains and problems, Naunny rarely if ever complained to others. Several relatives fondly recalled her use of the expression "peachy keen" to describe her state of being, regardless of her ailments on a given day. A grandson-in-law wrote this about her, "When I think of Naunny, I think of someone who never complained. It was always, 'Peachy keen.' Did she ever have a bad day? If she did, she never showed it."

I recall one time in the early 1980s when Naunny cracked

her sternum from sneezing. I called her immediately to find out how she was doing. "Peachy keen," was her trademark response. When I asked how she could be "peachy keen" with a cracked sternum, she made some self-deprecating remark such as, "Oh, I'm just a bag of old bones anyway," and redirected the conversation to talk about how I was doing.

I still feel guilty that many of us in Naunny's family reinforced her sacrifice and self-denial during her life by accepting her service so willingly and by refusing to challenge her self-destructive practices more forcefully. Personally speaking, I always ate her beans and tortillas but rarely encouraged her to eat, even when I knew that she was not eating. I always let her do the dishes and make the bed whenever I stayed at her house or apartment. And I always let her "peachy keen" remark suffice, never insisting that she talk—truly talk—about how she was really feeling.

Family members have continued to reinforce Naunny's service and sacrifice even after her death, by sharing stories that glorify how she served us and sacrificed, and how she did so willingly and without complaint. I would never suggest that family members should not recall fondly how our grandmothers and other family women have served us. Naunny's service to her family was extraordinary, and all of her relatives, including me, are so very thankful for her service to us. However, as bell hooks has argued, we should honor women's history of service to their families without reifying such service as women's "natural" role. Despite suggestions to the contrary, Naunny and Grandma Catalina did *not* live only to serve us. To suggest that they did so grossly oversimplifies the importance of these women and also reproduces conditions under which other women in the family may choose to serve others and subordinate themselves, and do so without complaint, at least if they wish to be remembered in the same loving terms by their relatives.

Naunny climbed the stairs of the city bus that would take her from her house in East Los Angeles to downtown L.A., where she would go shopping in preparation for her annual trip to Las Vegas. As the bus crossed the bridge over the trickle of water that is called the Los Ange-

les River, she looked at the Christmas list she had written. Pete had told her not to spend more than $300 on gifts for everybody that year, but Naunny knew that was impossible. That amount might have been enough in 1960, she thought, but this was 1980. And she had to get something for her two sons, Bill and Chuck, for their wives Claudia and Penny, as well as for her former daughter-in-law Robyn and her husband Ed. Then there were all the grandkids and their families: Tim, his wife Jimmie, and their two kids Laura and Eric; Tom, his wife Kim, and their son Ethan; Cathy, her husband Luis, and her two kids Lisa and Mark; Terese; Chris and his wife Cathy; Pat; Nick and his wife Sally; Michelle and her husband Justin; Annie and her husband Mike; Matty; and Lisa. Then there were her sister Bita and her husband Willie; her cousin and close friend Alice; her best friend Faith; the landlords, Mr. and Mrs. Garcia; and, of course, her husband Pete.

She looked up and down the list one more time and sighed. Then she opened her wallet and stared at the $300 cash that Pete had given her.

"That's just not enough," she whispered to herself. Then she opened another compartment of her wallet to confirm that she had brought her credit cards from Sears, Broadway, and May Company.

"I can always pay them off later," she mumbled, and she thought about how she would hide the bills from Pete that would come next month.

My fondest memories of Naunny are of her annual visits to our home in Las Vegas for Christmas. Naunny came to Vegas *every* Christmas, a tradition she started very soon after my family moved there in 1960. Even though Naunny was very poor, she would always bring piles of presents with her on the Greyhound bus, most of which were for Mishe, Lisa, and me, especially when we were kids, but even when we were adults. I learned many years later that Naunny went into more debt every year to pay for those gifts, but that did not matter to her because she was determined to buy the nicest gifts for her grandchildren.

We opened our presents on Christmas Eve every year, immediately after the traditional meal that my Polish American mother had prepared. The meal symbolized the simple life into which Christ was born and included fish, pirogies (potato pancakes), lumpy mashed potatoes, and a vegetable dish. We also had to eat prunes, which were somehow supposed to remind us of the suffering that Christ experienced throughout his life. I always wondered whether Jesus had constipation.

Before dinner, we also had to endure the Polish ritual of sharing *opwatke* (blessed host), whereby every possible pair of individuals at the table would share a piece of the host with each other and say something meaningful to their partner. Eager to open our presents, my sisters and I would quickly rip off a piece and say, "I hope you like your presents," but Mom would deliver separate ten-minute speeches to each individual. We agonized as Mom went on and on and on, but finally the ritual was complete, and we wolfed down our food and rushed into the living room where the presents were piled under the Christmas tree.

Dad announced each individual present and handed them to me, his "Santa's helper," and I would pass them on to the appropriate person. Once all the presents were handed out and stacked into massive piles, we would rip them open with a frenzy. Naunny mostly watched us unwrap our presents, as Pete played jazzy renditions of Christmas carols on the piano. Naunny would ultimately open her presents, and when she got to the bottle of Emeraude perfume that I bought for her every year, she would say, with a surprised face, "Oh, you remembered my favorite," then give me a big hug and a kiss.

[Circa 1985]

Dear Naunny,
Thank you for letting us stay here. You and Pete are so sweet—you shouldn't have let us have your bed. We would have been fine on the couch! Thanks again. Here's a little something so you can get yourself a bottle of wine since we didn't have the time!

Thanks, Naunny!
Love,
Lisa

GIVING US EVERYTHING

The firmly ensconced cultural view of women as givers creates the injunction that women must be givers to be good women.
      — JULIA WOOD, *Who Cares?*

I've finished my Christmas shopping. At least all we can afford! This is one time I wish I'd been born rich, instead of poor. I'd love to give so much more. Pete says, "It's better to receive than to give." I always tell him, "You have to share, that's what living is all about. You know, Bread cast upon the water." He says, "For that, you get a soggy mess." Oh well, to each his own.
      —from Naunny's journal

Like serving, giving is another one of the defining acts of a grandmother. In her book on family and nostalgia, Stephanie Coontz notes that throughout history, both men and women have romanticized giving by mothers—and, by extension, by grandmothers—as an act of altruistic love and generosity. Most children expect their grandmothers to give them gifts for their birthdays and holidays, and cookies and candy or other treats when they visit them. Quite simply, most relatives interpret giving, like serving, as one of the idealized acts that define the essence of grandmothers and other women in the family.

Not surprisingly, then, many of the stories about my grandmother focused on her generosity to others. Family members made almost identical comments about how Naunny would give you virtually anything. Naunny's niece put it this way in a letter to me: "You never told Aunt Elsie you liked something she had, because the next thing you know she would give it to you or send it by mail to you. I have a Persian lamb jacket she sent me because I told her I liked it on her."

Other relatives told stories of when my grandmother gave money and/or gifts to them. My cousin Tim said that when he was a little kid Naunny once went door-to-door to borrow money so that he could buy a mask. His younger brother Tom told me that Naunny would buy him pancakes when he stopped by Louise's Café where she worked as a waitress.

Other family members recalled how she gave her *home* to all family members, especially relatives who were moving to or visiting California. One niece wrote this recollection:

Dad would tell us stories about how in the 1930s everyone in the family from Colorado who was going to California to look for work stayed first with Aunt Elsie and Grandma. Auntie and Grandma put everyone up, not just individuals but entire families! My mom, dad, and I lived with Auntie and Grandma for a short time until Dad found work.

My father shared a similar memory on a tape recording, recalling the time when he was a teenager and living with his mother, and Naunny slept on the couch so that he could have the bedroom.

Relatives also remembered how Naunny wrote letters to them, even though they rarely wrote back to her. Her niece said that Naunny wrote to her twice a week and once even wrote to her dog to see whether he would answer her letters. Naunny herself commented on not receiving return letters from all the relatives in a journal entry in 1981:

Pete always tells me, "You should write a book! Even if it didn't get published, you'd at least get a rejection letter, which is more than you get now, with all the letters you write." I wish you kids would write. I don't mind writing. In fact, I like to. It's given me something to do since my retirement. But when you write for three months to some very dear people, with no answers, it's very frustrating, and a very big worry! Please write! God Bless!

Finally, and most important, virtually all of the relatives I interviewed described how Naunny gave love and acceptance to literally everyone she met. One granddaughter put it this way: "Grandma was always there. Always very positive. She'd always tell you how beautiful you were." The husband of her former daughter-in-law admitted that he was surprised when Naunny accepted him into the family, even though he had married the woman who conceived seven of her grandchildren with her son:

Naunny's grandparents
Mariano Maldonado and
Barbara Pacheco Maldonado
circa 1864.

Jose Julio Martinez
and Catalina
Maldonado Martinez
and older brothers and
sisters, circa 1905.

With big sister Juliana and
baby brother Abundo,
circa 1912.

Naunny circa 1913.

With Charley circa 1924.

Catalina Maldonado Martinez circa 1927.

With Charley and Charlie Jr at Santa Monica, circa 1931.

In Lockheed Aircraft uniform, 1941.

With Charlie, circa 1943.

With first grandson Tim Catalina
and brother Lulu, 1946.

With Bill and grandson Ricky, 1956.

With sister Rita grandson
Tim and niece Linda on
their way to Catalina
Island 1962.

With Bill and daughter-in-law Claudia, 1963.

With granddaughters
Miahe and Lisa, 1965.

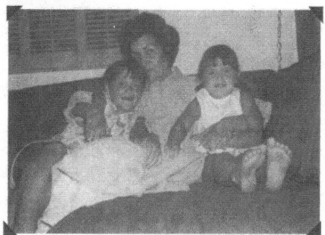

Circa 1970.

With Nicky at his college graduation, 1977.

With Peter, circa 1980.

At family reunion, circa 1981.

With great-grandson
Dominick, circa 1990.

With Chuck and Nick, 1992.

At funeral, 1994.

Naunny's grave.

All that remains of San Miguel, Colorado, 1999.

Your aunt told me that your grandmother would accept me as a son, which I thought was hard to believe. Normally you don't accept anyone until after you get to know them. But sure enough, the minute I met her she gave me a big hug, and we got along famously from then on. . . . She accepted me as part of the family, and then our son as the same. I always found that to be fantastic, because I lost my own mother and father many years earlier, and they basically were her age, just a little older. . . . I thought of her as a mom, and at the same time as a very good friend.

As one of Naunny's grandsons concluded, "What motivated Grandma to give so much to all of us was her love of family."

December 19th, 1984

Dearest My Nicky—

So surprised and happy to hear your voice last night. But sorry you won't be able to make the Christmas scene! Your gift will be late, as I'd already packed it for Vegas! I understand why you won't be able to make the trip out here. It took us two weeks to unpack, and put things up, when we moved here, besides the expense. You didn't say whether you received your small birthday gift. We're a bit short of funds around this time of the year. What with Greyhound fares going up. Almost a hundred for 2 round trip tickets. And a gift for each in Vegas. I've cut out giving to all. I only give to Chuck, Penny, Angela, Christine and Timmy's family! The family keeps growing and the income stays pretty much the same. By the way, send me Leah's size or what you think she'd enjoy getting from Naunny! She must be pretty *special*, since you plan on staying with her! How far is Lansing from Chicago? Pete says try for a job out here. He was stationed in Texas, and he says it's the hellhole of creation! I do pray you'll get a job at USC. Won't that be great! Besides seeing your friends, you can come over for beans and torts! Speaking of which, I wanted to send you some torts, and Pete said they'll spoil. Let me know.

God Bless. Love you a bundle. Merry Christmas and the best of everything in 1985.

Naunny

Xxxxxxoooooo

Chapter 4

GIVING TOO MUCH

If she had a fault, it was probably her generosity, and that would get her into trouble. She'd go into debt to buy things for people, then she couldn't handle it later.
—DAUGHTER-IN-LAW

Even though Naunny gave so much, it never seemed to be enough for her. "Women constantly confront themselves with questions about giving," Jean Miller writes. "Am I giving enough? Can I give enough? Why don't I give enough? They frequently have deep fears about what this must mean about them. They are upset if they feel they are not givers."

Some relatives suggested that Naunny may have been haunted by these questions, and perhaps that is why she spent above her means throughout her life. When she was older, she bought Christmas presents for all of her children and grandchildren, even though she could not afford to be so generous. Predictably, she would max out all of her credit cards every December, which caused additional financial strain on her and Pete.

"She would only pay the minimum, so the balance kept going higher and higher," her daughter-in-law said. "She didn't want Pete to know about it, so she asked if we could help her out. But she was wonderful. She would pay back every week whatever amount she had told me she would pay."

Paradoxically, the more she gave to enrich our lives, the more she needed to borrow, and the poorer she became. Yet she still yearned to give even more.

Her son, my father, continued this legacy of overspending in the family. As a jazz musician, he made a good middle-class wage, especially from the 1960s to the early 1980s when almost every hotel in Las Vegas had an orchestra for their nightly shows. My mom also held various secretarial positions from time to time to bring in additional money. But, like Naunny, they never seemed to save any money. Instead, they spent all of it, mostly on their kids. Every Christmas my sisters and I would get literally everything that we wanted, and they would usually be the most expensive brands.

"Nothing but the best," my dad would always say and then

later try to cope with the mounting bills that put him in constant debt.

I am very thankful that my parents spent so much on us, and I recognize how lucky we were to have such generous parents. I can't help but wonder, though, that if they had saved and invested back then they might have more money to spend on themselves now. They own a nice three-bedroom townhouse and have few expenses, but they are on a relatively fixed income and cannot afford many luxuries. Leah and I have helped out from time to time for special occasions like my father's seventieth birthday party, and we expect to pay much of the bill if they ever need to be placed in a nursing home in the future. If it comes to that, I will be pleased to do so because they have given me so much.

May 1, 1984

Dear Naunny—

Two weeks and I'm on the road! Hurray! Still don't know exactly when (and for how long) I'll be in Denver. I'm finalizing my plans next week. I'll write Auntie Bita and Uncle Willie this week (Johnny and Emma too).

Loaned my dad and mom $500 last month and was going to send another $500 this month. But Dad won't take the money. He says he's from the "old school" and doesn't want to borrow from his son. Oh well. I'd prefer it if you didn't tell him that I told you. (I didn't tell him that you asked me to loan them money). That's OK. Now I can buy the computer I want this summer.

Not much else is new. I'm grading papers, papers, and more papers this weekend. Then I'm DONE!

See you next month!

Love,

Nick

As my relatives told stories about my grandmother's giving, I recognized my own complicity in reinforcing the paradox created by her spending habits. Like most kids, I loved to get presents, and my enthusiasm every Christmas no doubt motivated Naunny to try to give even more the next year. But when I was a young adult and old enough to recognize my grandmother's poor financial situation, I continued to accept and reinforce her giving. When I was an undergraduate student living in Los Angeles, I continued to accept her monetary gifts, even though I knew she could have used the money for herself. I am embarrassed to admit that on at least a few occasions, I went to Naunny's house in East L.A. for a visit when I thought I needed an extra $10 or $20 for a date or a new eight-track tape or whatever. I relieved my guilt by never asking directly for the money, but I knew she would always give it to me whether I asked for it or not. Most of the time, she would just grab my hand, place the bill on my palm, and then squeeze my hand until I agreed to take it. But even when I refused, telling her that she should keep the money for herself, she found a way to give it to me, secretly placing it in my book bag or my laundry.

In retrospect, I could have saved or invested some of that money for her, but I was too focused on spending to satisfy my own desires rather than saving to satisfy my grandmother's needs. Of course, even if I had saved her monetary gifts to buy her something really nice or to invest it for her, she ultimately would have given the gift to or spent the money on some other family member. After all, that was my grandmother.

The more women are defined in terms of an ideal myth . . . the more possible it is for men to ignore or actively abuse women who do not meet that ideal.
  —STEPHANIE COONTZ, *The Way We Never Were*

Naunny was the perfect grandmother.
  —GRANDDAUGHTER

My grandmother was a server and a giver, two related identities that seem to define the ideal grandmother. The many stories from relatives that commended my grandmother's commitment to her service and giving attest to the power of this ideal.

There may be several limitations and potential costs for women who are idealized in this way. Women who perform excessive serving and giving sometimes engage in sacrifice and self-denial, which can result in eating disorders, alcoholism, refusal to seek medical attention, and other self-destructive practices, as illustrated by my grandmother. Women who are idealized as servers and givers also may be reduced to those roles and not valued in the context of their overall lives. Although my relatives intended to celebrate and honor my grandmother by discussing her service to the family, I believe that some of them—including me—unknowingly essentialized her role as server and giver, using these two acts to define her very essence. I may have reduced Naunny's meaning in this way before this project, but I realize now that she was so much more than someone who served me food and gave me gifts.

When women like my grandmother who serve and give so much are considered to be the ideal—or, even worse, the "norm"—then other women in the family who do not meet this standard may also be marginalized. Indeed, if my grandmother's level of service and giving is used as the basis against which other family women are judged, they clearly will never measure up. And when relatives define loving women in the family as those who sacrifice their own desires to buy and to do things for us, they reproduce conditions under which other family women may continue to sacrifice their desires, at least if they also want to be remembered as "loving" ones by their families.

Some scholars have argued for an alternative model of service and giving, one that does not glorify sacrifice and self-denial. For instance, some have called for an alternative model in which women care for themselves as much as they care for others. If this or a similar notion of serving and giving is used as a model, then my grandmother's role as server and giver may not represent an ideal identity to be emulated but a limited one to be avoided. We need to cherish our grandmothers' commitment to serving and giving while critiquing the limitations of that commitment.

I admit that I still have conflicting emotions about my grandmother's level of service and self-sacrifice to the family. Influenced by sociological writing on racial and gender equity in college, I came to be attracted to strong women and to believe in economic and domestic equality for married couples. I dated a collegiate athlete, and when we married, we hyphenated our last names. After getting divorced, I later married a college professor who studies feminist criticism and kept her family name.

I also learned to cook many years ago, and, although Leah and I might disagree on the exact percentages, I share in the cleaning and other housework.

As such, I realize that I have not had much respect for women who choose to be subservient housewives and even less respect for men who marry such women and expect them to adopt those roles. And I could never understand or appreciate why my mother was so willing to serve my father's every need, especially when he simply expected her to do so.

On the other hand, I recognize that I loved Naunny so much in part because she did serve me in every way. I realize that it is inconsistent to respect my grandmother's service but to think less of my mother for her service to my father. I need to recognize and honor my grandmother's *and* my mother's service. Thank you, Mom, for everything you have done for our family! And, Dad, I hope that one day you will truly honor your wife for her lifelong service to you and stop expecting everyone to serve you.

When Naunny Became a Mexican

Grandparents represent an especially important tie to ethnicity and religion where the middle generation has assimilated into mainstream culture.
—HOPE EDELMAN, *Mother of My Mother*

I was always a little confused about our ethnic heritage. I never knew if we were Spanish or Mexican, and I didn't know what the difference was.
—GRANDSON

When my sisters and I were little kids, my father, who was born in Los Angeles in 1930, usually referred to himself as "Mexican." Naunny, however, always told us that we were not Mexican but Spanish. She said that no one in our family was from Mexico, though no one seemed to be from Spain, either. Naunny herself was born in southern Colorado, and her ancestors had lived in New Mexico for generations. My sisters and I never really knew the difference between Mexican and Spanish, but "Spanish" sounded more exotic, so we used that label whenever classmates asked us what nationality we were.

NAUNNY WAS ONE of a growing number of elderly Hispanics, a group that is predicted to increase to 2.5 million by 2010 and to 5.6 million by 2050. Researchers who have studied Hispanic grandparents have confirmed the importance of the family among Hispanics and state that grandparents are considered close relatives in the family. Researchers have also found that Hispanic grandparents feel they have a declining influence on their grandchildren, especially with respect to using the Spanish language, and that Hispanic *grandmothers* carry out more expressive roles than grandfathers and have a stronger cultural influence on grandchildren.

Naunny definitely had a strong influence on her descen-

dants' sense of their Hispanic culture and identity. To truly understand this sense of ethnic identity, however, it is necessary to
place Naunny's life in the context of Hispanic history in the
United States, especially in southern Colorado and northern
New Mexico where she was born and raised.

---

*Elsie was walking home from school with several boys and girls
from her fifth-grade class in Trinidad.*

*"Let's take a shortcut over the tracks," said Roberto, one of the
more rambunctious kids in the class who seemed to have a crush on
Elsie. He tried to impress her by kicking rocks from the gravel road on
which they were walking.*

"No!" shouted the little girls, including Elsie, in unison.

"Why not?" asked Roberto.

*"'Cause that's where all the Spics live," said Margarita, Elsie's
best friend.*

*"Yeah," said Maria, another one of Elsie's classmates. "My papa
told me never to go over there. He said they're not very nice."*

"My daddy said they never take any baths," said Margarita.

*"My papa told me the same thing," Elsie said. "I'm glad we're not
Spics."*

*The kids rejected Roberto's suggestion and took the usual route
home to their section of town.*

THE HISPANOS OF NEW MEXICO

The facts that it [New Mexico] was occupied by Spanish
Conquistadores before the first English settlement at Jamestown
and that it did not become a part of the United States until 1846
are clearly of great importance. The stamp of Spanish culture was
firmly impressed upon the land during the intervening two-
hundred-odd years.

—NANCIE GONZÁLEZ, *The Spanish-Americans of New Mexico*

If you go to New Mexico and Colorado today, most people still
consider themselves Spanish. Grandma always used to say, "We're

Spanish." I've heard this in New Mexico a hundred times. They're obviously Mexicans. There's no doubt about it. But they all thought they were different from Mexicans. They say, "Nobody in my family has ever been born in Mexico." They were born in Colorado and New Mexico, not in Mexico, and their ancestors were from Colorado and New Mexico. But if you go back far enough, Colorado and New Mexico were part of Mexico. So, of course, they're Mexican. What's the difference, anyway? Mexicans are Spaniards and Indians mixed, and that's what we are.
—GRANDSON

With the birth name of Juanita Eloysa Martinez, my grandmother was a descendant of an extremely long line of Martinez people from New Mexico well before this area was part of the United States. It was quite frustrating to try to determine Naunny's exact Martinez lineage because the name Martinez is one of the most common Spanish surnames in the world. I was only able to trace her paternal lineage back four generations before being overwhelmed by the thousands of Martinez names I came across as I conducted my genealogical research.

Although I did not track down more than a few generations of Naunny's Martinez ancestors, it is likely that she was a descendant of Hernan Martin Serrano who came to the area of what is now New Mexico in 1598 with Juan de Oñate and his colonists. In his book on the origins of New Mexico families, Angelico Chavez writes that Martin Serrano was forty years old when he was a "Sargento" on the muster roll of the Oñate expedition. His wife, Juana Rodriguez, and two sons, Hernan II and Luis, accompanied him, along with their equipment and livestock. Descendants of Martin Serrano ultimately became known as "Martines," though by the nineteenth century descendants had changed the *s* to a *z* and thus became known as "Martinez."

Oñate and his colonists brought the first sheep and goats to this region. The livestock thrived and became a source of food and clothing for settlers. Some three hundred years later, they also became a significant, though short-lived, source of wealth for Naunny's father, José Julio Martinez.

According to historians, over one-half of Oñate's men were from Spain and considered themselves to be of "purer" Spanish descent, and they retained the class system that had been in place since the Spaniards set foot in the New World in the late 1400s. Over time, however, there was much intermingling with Indian and mestizo women, many of whom were slaves and servants of the colonists. Nonetheless, in his book *The Hispano Homeland*, Robert Nostrand concludes that this Spanish connection left Hispanos with "an Iberian legacy" that made them culturally unique.

Whether or not Naunny's ancestors were direct descendants of the Martin Serrano family, they definitely lived in what is now New Mexico for many generations. Life in this region remained relatively unchanged for many years, because the colony of Nuevo Mexico was 1,500 miles from Mexico City and several hundred miles from the closest Spanish settlements, so the primary communication with Mexico came through royal decrees rather than regular contact with other colonists.

Due to this detachment from Mexico, the Spanish colonists in New Mexico were more independent and isolated than any other group of colonists in the Spanish New World. In fact, life in New Mexico during the eighteenth century was very similar to life during the seventeenth century, as native Hispanos worked in an agricultural-based society and practiced various Catholic rituals.

Naunny's Martinez ancestors lived in northern New Mexico for many generations until the 1870s, when her grandparents and their children—including Naunny's father as a very young boy—homesteaded to the village of San Miguel near the town of Trinidad in what is now southern Colorado. By the time they settled there, however, the region had undergone major changes. While the eighteenth century might have been similar to the seventeenth century for the Hispanos of New Mexico, the nineteenth century was radically different from the eighteenth century. Mexico had gained its independence from Spain, so New Mexico and southern Colorado had become part of the newly established Mexican nation and its citizens were officially "Mexicans." The opening of the Santa Fe Trail increased trade between Mexico and the United States and led to the era of Anglo fur trappers and "Mountain Men" like Kit Carson and Jim Bridger as well as Trinidad legend "Uncle Dick" Wooten. Less than thirty years later, New Mexico and southern Colorado (as well as Arizona and California) became part of the United States following Mexico's loss in the Mexican-American War in 1848, and the Hispanos of New Mexico, whose families had lived there for generations, became Mexican Americans.

By the late 1800s, American Anglos and immigrants from Italy, Poland, Greece, Ireland, Mexico, and other lands arrived to work for railroads, lumber mills, coal mines, and commercial agriculture and herding ventures. These changes dramatically disrupted—and in many cases ended—life in the Hispano villages.

These and other historical changes also led to adjustments in the ethnic identity of the native Hispanos, adjustments that are still prevalent in New Mexico and southern Colorado to this day. These adjustments influenced my grandmother's ethnic identity for most of her life, and she passed on this sense of ethnic identity to her children and grandchildren, some of whom still maintain it to this day.

AT DIFFERENT TIMES in my life I have filled out forms for job applications, financial aid, surveys, and other paperwork. Whenever the form asked me to indicate my ethnicity, I was always confused. I am a mixture of ethnic groups, because my mother is Polish and my father is, as Naunny always used to tell us, Spanish. Most of these forms made me pick a single ethnic group, and I usually selected my Spanish ancestry, because my last name is Hispanic.

Even though I identified more with the Spanish side of my family, I was never sure what ethnic label to use on forms, because "Spanish" was never listed as an option. The labels used for Spanish ancestry also changed every few years: sometimes it was "Latino," sometimes it was "Chicano," sometimes it was "Mexican" or "Mexican American," and sometimes it was "Hispanic."

No matter what I checked off, I always felt a little uneasy about the choice I had made and about not knowing exactly what my real ethnic identity was.

Chapter 5

NAUNNY'S ETHNIC IDENTITY

Racismo occurs in a curious form in New Mexico. A large group of
people, who claim they are descended from the early Spanish
settlers of the area, call themselves Hispanos. They insist that their
Spanish ancestry distinguishes them from Mexican-Americans,
whom they consider racial and cultural inferiors.
      —EARL SHORRIS, *Latinos*

I remember one time somebody in the family said that we were
Mexican. And Grandma said, "Why are you saying we're Mexican?
No one in our family is from Mexico. We have never been from
Mexico. We're Spanish." She said that we were descendants of the
Conquistadores. I thought, "OK, that sounds fine. We're Spanish,
then."
      —GRANDDAUGHTER

Ethnic identity is an important part of one's overall identity and
sense of belonging.

Sociologist Herbert Gans has argued that for many Americans, especially for third and fourth generations of Americans in
the United States, ethnic identity is largely *symbolic*, with expressive rather than instrumental meaning. He writes that these
symbolic ethnic identities establish the uniqueness of a group of
people without requiring individuals actually to participate in
those groups because the allegiance is to the symbol and not to
the ethnic group.

A key component of an individual's symbolic ethnic identity
is the *label* used to signify membership in an ethnic group. Labels provide a name for an ethnic identity and a way to manage
that identity with others, and attitudes about particular ethnic
groups are partly a function of the label associated with that
group. As such, it is not surprising that the labels used to identify various racial and ethnic groups change over time. For example, the labels "Mexican," "Chicano," "Latino," and "Hispanic" have been used at different points in U.S. history, as have
"Negro," "Black," "Afro-American," "African American," and
others.

It appears that Naunny's ancestors, like other Hispanos of
New Mexico, did change the labels they used to identify their

ethnicity when confronted with the changing ethnic landscape of the late 1800s and the various prejudices that accompanied those changes. Hispanos started to refer to themselves as "Spanish" and "Spanish American," and they tried to integrate into the new American nation by taking on a "white" way of life. As someone who was born and raised in this area soon after these changes in ethnic identity were made, Naunny's family adopted both of these strategies and passed them on to their children and grandchildren.

Elsie walked into the coffee shop where she had applied for a second job to make some extra money to pay for her boys' musical instruments and lessons.

The owner, a burly man with a bad cough, looked over her application as they sat at a table in the back of the coffee shop.

"Everything looks fine," he said. "Trujillo? Is that Mexican?"

"It's Spanish," Elsie said.

"Spanish?" the man said and laughed. "You from Spain?"

"No," Elsie said, "but I'm not from Mexico, either. I'm from Colorado."

"I know somebody else from Colorado, and he calls himself Spanish, too. How come you people don't just call yourselves Mexicans? That's what you are."

"Because we're Spanish."

"You think you're better than Mexicans?"

"We're just different."

"You eat beans, right?" he said.

"Yes," Elsie replied politely, though her patience was wearing thin.

"And tortillas," he said, now smiling. "Ain't that what Mexicans eat?"

"Like I said, I'm Spanish."

He paused and looked at her application one last time. "OK, Spaniard," he said, coughing another laugh. "You got the job."

Elsie thanked the man and then exited the coffee shop, never to return. She found a job at another restaurant where the owner was not as interested in her ethnic background.

I played baseball when I attended college at USC. One day before the season started, the head coach asked me about my last name.

"Are you Italian?" he asked.

"No, I'm Spanish," I said nervously, wondering why the head coach, a rather arrogant man of French ancestry who had spoken very little to me during the winter months of practice, was asking about my ethnicity.

"Spanish?" he said with a sarcastic tone of voice. "Is that Mexican?"

"Yeah, I guess so," I said, tentatively.

"I guess I'll call you 'Tortilla,' then," he said and laughed. "Now go hit some fungoes to the outfielders, Tortilla."

From that point on, the head coach called me "Tortilla," and I am certain that he did not use the label affectionately. Every time he yelled out, "Tortilla," most of my teammates laughed, except for a couple of Mexican players. Some players started to call me Tortilla as well. I felt uncomfortable every time someone yelled out that nickname, but I couldn't criticize anyone for doing so because the head coach had coined it. I remember wishing that I had told him I was Italian, but then he probably would have called me "Tortellini."

"Spanish," Not "Mexican"

Chubby Grandma always used to say she was Spanish? I mean, around here [in Los Angeles], everybody's Mexican. But Chubby Grandma heard me say that I was Mexican one time, and she said, "No, you're not Mexican. You're Spanish!"

—GREAT-GRANDSON

Nancie González writes that many native New Mexicans call themselves "Spanish" rather than "Mexican" because they believe that they are direct descendants of the original Spanish colonists with "purer" lineages than native Mexicans. González calls this widespread belief the "New Mexico legend."

In actuality, the use of the label "Spanish" is related less to the original Spanish colonization of New Mexico in the 1500s and more to the Anglo-American occupation of the area in the late 1800s. Robert Nostrand writes that during the period of Mexican occupation of New Mexico following independence from Spain (1821–1843), Hispanos actually called themselves "Mexicans" and did not believe that they were that different from Mexicans in Mexico. But after American occupation and the development of American industries in the late 1800s, the terms *Spanish* and *Spanish American* came into favor as tens of thousands of Mexican immigrants came to the area for work.

Most of the Anglo-Americans in this changing region considered Mexican immigrants to be of a much lower class than other ethnic groups, and those Mexicans suffered from prejudice and discrimination in the Anglo-run industries. For example, in 1908—one year after Naunny was born—an official from the U.S. Labor Bureau wrote that Mexicans were "lacking in thrift, ambition, and strength, and filled only with listlessness, unsteadiness, and indolence" and that they were the "scavengers of the mining industry, picking up the positions left by other classes of workers."

Given how badly Mexican immigrants were treated by the Anglo-Americans, it is not surprising that Hispanos, who were born and raised in New Mexico not Mexico, made a distinction between themselves and these immigrants, using the labels "Spanish" or "Spanish American" to disassociate themselves from Mexicans.

As native Hispanos of New Mexico, Naunny's relatives adopted these labels, along with the "New Mexico legend" of their Spanish heritage. As one of Naunny's nephews who grew up in southern Colorado told me, "The people on my mother's side called themselves 'Spanish.' They were actually from the original settlers who came from Spain." A niece, whose mother (Naunny's sister) also grew up in the region, echoed the same view, though she expressed ambivalence about the label yet revealed its lasting influence:

> My mother said we were Spanish. But I never knew what the difference was. I always heard that people who were Spanish with Indian blood were Mexican. And we're Spanish with Indian blood? So I don't know why everyone said we were Spanish? But I still say I'm Spanish, because that's the way I was raised.

Unfortunately, in the process of using the label "Spanish" to distance themselves from Mexican immigrants, some of Naunny's relatives—and no doubt many native Hispanos—may have developed some of the same prejudicial views of Mexicans held by Anglos. As Naunny's son recalled:

> I remember when I went to Colorado [as a young boy] and one of my cousins said, "The Spanish Americans live over here, and on the other side of the tracks is where all the Spics live." I said, "What's a Spic?" She said, "They're the Mexicans." I guess that's what her parents had told her.

Ironically, or perhaps fittingly, while these "Spanish Americans" of New Mexico thought that they were different from the "Mexican" immigrants, many of the Anglo-Americans in the region did not recognize this difference. Although the Hispanos did enjoy a few benefits that Mexicans did not enjoy—like getting haircuts in Anglo barbershops—a majority of Anglos did not make a distinction between the two groups, and whatever distinction had been made diminished during the 1910s as the push for Americanism strengthened.

Consequently, the Spanish Americans of New Mexico suffered from much of the same prejudice and discrimination that the Mexican immigrants experienced. In the process, Naunny's father, who once had been a wealthy man with a sizable flock of sheep and other businesses, lost everything and became dependent on his sons and other family men who worked, side by side, with "Mexicans" and other immigrants in the coal mines.

When Naunny and her new husband Charley left southern Colorado in 1924 and moved to Los Angeles, they took the "Spanish" label with them and continued to use it to characterize their ethnic identity. If this label was dubious in New Mexico and Colorado, it was even more problematic in Los Angeles. Although Spanish colonists had also settled California, the labels Spanish and Spanish American never really caught on in California, even with those who could legitimately claim to be descendants of the original Spanish colonists. In California, all people of Hispanic descent, whether born in California or Mexico, were called "Mexicans." Neither Anglos nor California Mexicans were aware of any special identity or distinction for Hispanics that were born in New Mexico and Colorado, and California Mexicans thought the term *Spanish* was an insult, used by Hispanics who thought they were better than Mexicans were.

Naunny's two sons learned this lesson firsthand when they went to school with a variety of ethnic groups in Lincoln Heights, including Mexicans. My father told me that even though he is Spanish, he told his friends that he was Mexican, because he didn't want them to think that he thought he was better than they were. Her other son admitted the unfortunate consequences of being raised with this sense of ethnic identity:

> To tell you the truth, I was kind of ashamed to say that I was Mexican. Mexicans were considered lower class. Most of my friends in Lincoln Heights were Italian, and they bragged about being Italian. They didn't even call themselves "American"; they said they were "Italian." I always wondered how come I wasn't proud to be Mexican.

One of Naunny's nieces, who was born in Colorado, also admitted she was ashamed to say that she was Mexican when she moved to California, adding "that prejudice was embedded in us in Colorado."

Sadly, this prejudice is one of the enduring legacies of the "Spanish" label that Naunny accepted and passed on to her children, grandchildren, and even great-grandchildren. In their stories, relatives reconstructed a grandmother who maintained this prejudice for much of her life. I do not believe that my grandmother ever held overtly prejudiced attitudes about Mexicans or any other group of people. She was a loving woman who accepted every person as an individual, and no one in the family ever heard her make any prejudicial comments about Mexicans—unless they were fat, and then she made jokes about their weight but not their ethnicity. Moreover, she did not decide on her own to use the label "Spanish" to differentiate herself from Mexicans but was socialized as a child to believe that she was Spanish and, thus, different from Mexicans.

However, as Naunny passed on this label and its pernicious connotations to her descendants, we, too, were socialized into believing that we were different—and, in some unstated way, better—than Mexicans. Most of us disassociated ourselves from

Mexicans and distanced ourselves from our Mexican heritage rather than embracing it with pride. My uncle Chuck admitted that for the race/ethnicity category on the most recent 2000 census, he checked "other" and wrote in "Spanish American." As one of Naunny's granddaughters said, "Since it was ingrained into my head since the time I can remember, I still consider myself Spanish. I hate to say it, but because of the distinction that was made from my earliest recollection, I almost feel embarrassed about being Mexican. I also have told my daughter that she is Spanish."

And so the label and the legend—but hopefully not the prejudice—continue.

Elsie's two young boys, Charlie and William Lee, were shooting marbles on the ragged lawn in the backyard of their rental house in Lincoln Heights with the two little blonde girls who lived in the house behind them. They had only been playing for a few minutes when the girls' mother looked through the kitchen window and saw them all together.

"Girls!" she yelled through the window. "Come back inside. I don't want you playing with those dirty Mexicans."

"Sorry," one of the little girls said to Charlie and William Lee, then went home with her sister.

"Dirty Mexicans?" Charlie said to his little brother. "Let's go inside and tell Mom."

The two boys went inside and found their mother chopping an onion in the kitchen while their grandmother was rolling dough for tortillas.

"Mom," Charlie said, hesitantly. "The lady next door called us dirty Mexicans and told us not to play with her kids."

Elsie glanced over at her mother, but Grandma Catalina turned away and looked down at the floor. Elsie took a controlled breath and looked back at Charlie and William Lee.

"Come with me," she said and headed for the back door, still with the chopping knife in her hand.

Elsie led her two boys out the back door and toward the neighbor's back door that faced them. She knocked on the door briskly. No one answered, but Elsie saw the kitchen drapes move and knew that the lady was home.

"I know you're in there!" Elsie shouted and knocked again.

Finally, the lady answered the door, cracking it just enough to see out. Her eyes widened when she saw the knife in Elsie's hand.

"Did you call my boys dirty Mexicans and tell your daughters not to play with them?" Elsie asked. She didn't wait for an answer. "We are not Mexicans; we're Spanish. And I want you to know that my boys are as good as anybody, and they can play with anybody. I don't ever want to hear you call my boys dirty Mexicans again!"

Elsie did not wait for a response. She turned abruptly and escorted her two boys back to their house.

"Don't worry about that lady," she said. "You boys are as good as anybody, and don't let anybody tell you that you're not."

One day at USC, my girlfriend, a buxom blonde of Polish descent, and I were walking across campus, talking about our families. I had mentioned earlier when we started dating that I was Spanish, but on this walk I said that my dad was Mexican.

"Mexican?" she said in a surprised and strangely offensive tone. "I thought you were *Spanish*."

"Spanish, Mexican, what's the difference?" I replied.

"It's no big deal," she said. "I just didn't know that you were Mexican."

The topic never came up again, but we broke up about a month later.

Spanish Americans as "White" Americans

I remember one time when I was about twelve or thirteen and a bunch of classmates and I went to Big Bear Lake. We stayed at some Presbyterian Center by the lake. This one really cute girl had a crush on me. Her parents were German, but she had olive skin. One guy in the cabin was interested in her and asked if she was my sister. One of my Anglo buddies told him, "She's not his sister; he's Mexican." I never forgot that. He could have just said she wasn't my sister, but he had to point out that I was Mexican and she wasn't. I didn't even consider myself to be Mexican. I considered myself to be white.

—SON

Many native Hispanos of New Mexico also took on an "Anglo" way of life to counteract the discrimination they felt. When Naunny and her husband moved to Los Angeles in the 1920s, they definitely took on such an Anglo way of life. Although they continued to call themselves Spanish when describing their ancestry, they thought of themselves as white, the label they used on their marriage certificate in 1924 to describe their race. They spoke *English*, not Spanish, and they listened to swing and other big band music, not Latin music, in an effort to assimilate themselves and their two young boys into mainstream American culture.

When Charley died in 1934, Naunny continued to raise her sons as white and as Americans. As Naunny's daughter-in-law told me:

> Your dad didn't know Naunny as an Hispanic woman, because they weren't raised that way. Naunny wanted them to be all-American types. The only thing really suggestive of her Hispanic background was that she made beans and tortillas. Otherwise, she cooked American food, and she didn't speak Spanish unless she was around somebody from the neighborhood who spoke Spanish.

However, many of the Anglos in Los Angeles did not consider Naunny and her two boys to be white, or even American, but Mexican. This label was reinforced by the U.S. government, when in the 1930 census, all persons of Mexican origin were classified as Mexican, even though most Hispanos from New Mexico considered themselves to be white Americans of Spanish, not Mexican, descent.

Mexicans in Los Angeles in the 1930s and 1940s, whether born in California, Mexico, or elsewhere, suffered from some of the same prejudice and discrimination that Mexican immigrants suffered in New Mexico. In a 1930 report, sociologist Emory Bogardus wrote that Americans "still treat Mexicans as laborers and not as full-fledged human beings and potential citizens." During the 1940s, prejudice against Mexicans intensified even more, culminating in the so-called zoot suit riots of 1943 when groups of Mexican youths, who called themselves "Pachucos" (or "Chucos" for short), clashed with white servicemen who found the nontraditional dress and behavior of these Mexican youths to be unpatriotic.

Even though Naunny and her two boys did not seem to suffer greatly from this prejudice and discrimination, they certainly were not immune from it. Both of Naunny's sons remembered when they were young boys and a lady in the neighborhood would not let them play with her daughters because they were "dirty Mexicans." My uncle also remembered a time several years later when he was dating a young girl of Irish-Swedish ancestry who would become his wife, and he overheard a lady in her neighborhood ask her mother whether she was upset that her daughter was going out with a Mexican. Years later when they were married and going to buy their first house, his mother-in-law said that he shouldn't tell the owners of the house that he was Mexican.

In their stories, then, relatives reconstructed a grandmother who denied her Mexican heritage and considered herself to be white yet was never completely accepted as a full member of Anglo-American culture. Although Naunny's grandchildren and great-grandchildren have become far more Americanized with each subsequent generation, most of us still have not embraced our Mexican heritage, either. As Rodolfo Acuna concludes, "It is more than a cliché that many Mexicans and Latinos want to be white, or at least consider fairer skin to be better," adding that some Mexicans are proud that they are classified as Caucasian.

Fortunately, while Naunny continued to call herself Spanish when asked directly about her ancestry, some relatives said that she did become more accepting of her Mexican heritage later in life.

WHEN I WAS in college, I remember speaking—or trying to speak—Spanish with Naunny to help me with my language requirement. I also remember enlisting her help when I did an anthropology paper on mural art in East Los Angeles. Naunny served as the navigator while I drove around the neighborhoods in my green Volkswagen Beetle, photographing examples of mural art that seemed to be on almost every corner in the area.

I took several pictures of different images of the Virgin Mary, and Naunny explained to me that they were images of the Virgin of Guadalupe who had appeared to an Indian peasant named Juan Diego in Tepeyac, Mexico. When I asked about all of the eagles on the murals, she told me that they represented the sun god, Quetzalcoatl. I was impressed that she knew so much about these and other symbols of Mexican culture.

Although these visits did not completely change my sense of our family's ancestral identity as Spanish, they did engender at least a limited identification with our Mexican heritage. I only wish that I had spent more time trying to speak Spanish with Naunny and learning more about her beliefs about our ethnic background.

WHEN NAUNNY BECAME A MEXICAN

It's funny, because my mother never listened to Latin music. She liked big band stuff. But when she married Pete, she got into the Latin thing. I remember [my wife] once asked me, "When did your mother become a Mexican?"
—SON

After her husband's death in 1934, Naunny did not marry again until the late 1950s when she married Pete Alcaraz. Perhaps it was fitting that Pete was born in Mexico and that they lived most of their life in a predominantly Mexican American section of East Los Angeles where he grew up after moving to California with his family. During those years, Naunny spoke Spanish with her neighbors and attended a little church down the street in which Mass was said in Spanish and which served the Mexican soup *menudo* after Mass. She also listened to Latin music, at least in part because her husband was a piano player on a Latin jazz band.

Several relatives recalled a running joke they shared with Naunny and other relatives around this time. The joke came in the form of a question they asked of her: "When did you become a Mexican?" As her daughter-in-law remembered:

Naunny became Hispanic when she moved to East L.A. with Pete. We used to joke, "Hey, Mom, when did you become Mexican?" That was funny. I think a lot of it had to do with the neighborhood. It was an exclusively Mexican neighborhood, except for the Chinese people who owned the grocery store. But the lady who did her hair was Mexican. And Pete was getting more into his Mexican roots, too. So they started changing. She acted totally Mexican there. It was very strange for us. We got a kick out of it.

A grandson recalled that one time he drove over to Naunny's house with some friends, and she said, "Did you come by to see your little Mexican grandmother?" Her son added that when she lived in East L.A., she used the term *Mexican* to describe herself, adding, "I don't think the distinction between Spanish and Mexican mattered as much to her anymore."

While writing this book, I have found it difficult to recognize that Naunny was brought up to hold some prejudicial attitudes about Mexicans. I am comforted that she never said a bad word about Mexicans as a group of people and, more important, that she eventually rejected those negative attitudes. It may have taken her fifty years to become a Mexican, but it was an identity that she ultimately embraced with pride. And when she died at age eighty-six and my cousin Tim hired a Mariachi band to play at her funeral, everyone in attendance could feel the spirit of our little Mexican grandma dancing to the music.

Naunny walked up the hill on 6th Street in East L.A. where they lived. She was on her way to the nearby Star Market to get some chorizo and fresh tortillas because some of the grandkids were going to come by for breakfast the next morning.

The moment Naunny entered the store, she greeted the cashier at the counter.

"Hi, sweetie," Naunny said and touched the middle-aged Mexican woman on the shoulder.

"Elsie!" she said with a smile. "Que pasa?"

"Muy bien," Naunny said. "Mis jitos are coming for breakfast tomorrow so I need some fresh torts and chorizo."

Naunny grabbed a cart and headed for the chorizo. She heard Mariachi music coming from an AM radio in the back of the store, and she danced up and down the aisles.

When she finished her shopping, she visited again with the cashier as she checked out.

"Know any new jokes?" the cashier said, in Spanish.

"No, but I know some old ones," Naunny said in Spanish, laughing. Then she told the following joke, in Spanish.

"You know the old story about Mary and Joseph, right?" Naunny asked, not waiting for an answer. "When Mary got pregnant, she told Joseph, 'We've got to think of a name because this is going to be a special baby.' So Joseph says, 'How about Michael after the Archangel?' She says, 'No, there's already a Michael. We've got to come up with a unique name.' So, after a while she says, 'I finally came up with a name.' He says, 'What's that?' She says, 'Jesus.' He says, 'Jesus? Do you want everybody to think he's a Mexican?'"

"That's a good one, Elsie," the cashier said and laughed. "Have a good visit with your jitos.*"*

A few years ago my department hired an assistant professor who was born in Mexico. Before he arrived, I mentioned to another colleague that it would be good to have another Mexican on our staff.

"Yeah," my colleague said, "but he's a *real* Mexican."

I did not say anything in response, in part because I did not know what to say and in part because I think my colleague was right. For my entire life I did not call myself Mexican, I grew up in a white middle-class neighborhood, and I do not speak Spanish. Although this research has given me some insights into my Mexican heritage that I did not have before, a single study cannot change an ethnic identity that has been constructed over a lifetime.

As a culture, we call ourselves Spanish when referring to ourselves as a linguistic group and when copping out. . . . We call ourselves Hispanic or Spanish-American or Latin American or Latin when linking ourselves to other Spanish-speaking peoples of the Western hemisphere and when copping out. We call ourselves Mexican-American to signify that we are neither Mexican nor American. But more the noun "American" than the adjective "Mexican" (and when copping out).
—GLORIA ANZALDÚA, *Borderlands La Frontera*

We're obviously Mexican.
—GRANDSON

Grandparents are important links to our ethnic heritage, and when they die and/or when subsequent generations move away from their grandparents, we lose this vital link. Arthur Kornhaber writes that grandparents have important roles in teaching family members about their ethnicity but concludes that those roles are dissolving because of social mobility.

Of course, in the process of learning about the roles our grandparents play in shaping our ethnic identity, we may discover some unsettling information. I have come to the disturbing realization that the term *Spanish*, the label my grandmother used for most of her life to describe our ethnic heritage, is based less on ancestral lineage and more on prejudice and politics. Even more disturbing is the fact that Naunny passed this label on to her children, grandchildren, and great-grandchildren, most of whom still continue to use it.

Unfortunately, the use of this label and the prejudice against Mexicans continue today, in New Mexico as well as California. In New Mexico, middle- and upper-class Hispanics still refer to lower-class Hispanics as Mexican, and in southern California, Mexicans and Mexican Americans alike are sometimes called "illegal aliens."

Although Naunny may have bought into the "New Mexico legend" for most of her life, I am very sad that she is no longer here to talk about our family's ethnic background. I would love to be able to discuss my research with her and to tell her that I will never again use the term *Spanish* to describe my own ethnic identity. Although it still sounds a little strange, I am proud to say that *I am a Mexican American*. I am also proud to say that I am Polish American, though I feel far less affinity to that ethnic identity because my name is Trujillo, not my mother's family name of Zwolinski, and because I did not spend much time in the Polish American neighborhoods of Chicago where my mother was born and raised. That is another story to be told at another time.

A Frail, Old Woman

Disruption of the social bond occurs as the body fails, self-identity becomes harder to hold together and the normal expectations of human relations cannot be fulfilled.
> —CLIVE SEALE, *Constructing Death*

She didn't take to old people. She called them "old fogies." After she went to retirement housing, I said she should get involved with the activities like cards and gardening. Her reply was, "Why would I want to hang around all those old fogies?" She despised getting old. She started to refer to herself as a "shriveled up bag of bones."
> —GRANDSON

Naunny and Pete were watching a rerun of The Rockford Files, *one of their favorite television programs of all times. She was feeling a little rundown, but not bad for a seventy-three-year-old woman, she thought. She had been sniffling a bit as well, and she wondered whether she was getting a summer cold.*

She went to get Pete another beer from the kitchen. She felt a sneeze coming on but simply willed it away.

"You are not going to get sick this summer," she scolded herself.

As she reached into the refrigerator, she got a chill and felt another sneeze coming. She placed her finger under her nose to stop the sneeze as she pulled the beer out of the fridge with her other hand. This time, however, she could not stop it. Her body contorted awkwardly as she sneezed, and she heard a strange cracking sound. She did not think anything of it until she closed the door of the refrigerator and realized that she had a sharp pain in her chest.

She delivered the beer to Pete and told him about the pain in her chest. Pete made her call her son, and Chuck came over to take her to the doctor.

The doctor examined her then sent her out to get X-rays. When the X-rays came back, he told her that she had cracked a rib.

"From a sneeze?" Naunny asked incredulously.

"Your body is very fragile, Elsie," the doctor said softly but sternly. "You only weigh one hundred pounds. Maybe if you gained a little weight, your bones wouldn't be so brittle."

"But then I wouldn't have this girlish figure," she said and smiled.

The doctor smiled politely but then added, "I'm serious, Elsie."

"I know," she said and looked away.

The doctor asked a nurse's aide to wrap Naunny's ribs, and then Chuck took her home.

Leah and I went to my parents' house in Las Vegas for Christmas of 1992. It would be a special holiday because both grandmothers would be there. "Naunny Los Angeles" spent every Christmas with us, but "Naunny Chicago" rarely came to Las Vegas for Christmas. The only time we went to Chicago for Christmas was in 1968, and Naunny L.A. came with us. It was brutally cold in Chicago that year, and Naunny L.A. came down with pneumonia and spent Christmas in the hospital.

Having both Naunnies in Vegas would be very special in any year, but in 1992 it was even more meaningful because everyone knew that it might be the last time that both Naunnies came to our house for Christmas. Naunny L.A. was eighty-five years old, Naunny Chicago was seventy-seven years old, and neither one of them was in good health.

I was very excited when I knocked on the door of the house after the ten-hour drive from Sacramento. My mom greeted us at the door, and then I rushed in to see my grandmothers. I was stunned. Both of them looked *ancient*. I had not seen Naunny Chicago since 1985, but she looked like she had aged twenty years in the seven years since I last saw her.

Naunny L.A. was seven and a half years older than Naunny Chicago was, but she looked about twenty years older. She was frail, stooped over, and frighteningly skinny. When I hugged her I could feel her bones. Her hair was withered, and her skin seemed slightly yellow. She obviously had not been taking care of herself.

Throughout her visit, Naunny L.A. also kept repeating herself. She would tell a story and then repeat it several minutes later. She looked at pictures of her own grandchildren and great-grandchildren and asked, "Who's that?" My mom and I shared our beliefs that she was suffering from some form of dementia.

My dad did not seem to recognize Naunny's condition. Every time she repeated herself, he would say, "What's wrong with you? You already told that story."

I pulled him aside and said that Naunny probably had dementia and that he should be more sensitive.

"Don't be a drag, man," he said, invoking the jazz musician expression that he has used throughout his life. He continued to ask his mother what was wrong with her every time she repeated a story.

Despite the frail minds and bodies of both Naunnies, we all had a wonderful visit that Christmas. When I hugged and kissed my grandmothers good-bye, however, I wondered whether I would ever see either one of them again.

THE GRANDMOTHER AS FRAIL, OLD BODY

What definition of bodily experience do we wish to have to live up to when we no longer enjoy the bodies we now inhabit?
—ARTHUR FRANK, "Bringing Bodies Back In"

The last few years of her life, she looked really old.
—GREAT-GRANDDAUGHTER

As time passed, my grandmother did what every grandparent who lives a long life does: She got old, and her body and her mind deteriorated. For family members, then, part of my grandmother's meaning is as an old, frail woman.

Not surprisingly, my grandmother's relatives interpreted the meaning of her frailty and declining health in different ways. For younger relatives such as her great- and great-great-grandchildren, Naunny *always* was a frail, elderly woman.

"To be honest, I always saw her as an old lady," a great-granddaughter admitted. "She was never young to me. She was always skinny and having problems with her health, so I don't really remember seeing much of a change in her as she got older."

Older relatives, however, did notice a significant change in her as she aged, though they varied on when they noticed this change and what it meant. Some family members became aware of Naunny's deterioration in health when she was in her seventies, especially when her husband Pete was suffering from a host of ailments in the late 1970s and early 1980s. As one granddaughter remembered:

> Grandma liked us to spend the night at her house when Uncle Pete was in the hospital. One night she said, "Do you want to wear a bandanna?" I agreed. She said, "I wear a bandanna around my head, and I wrap it real tight because that makes my head feel better." I put a bandanna on her head and felt her skull. She had this huge soft spot on the top of her head. I guess she was losing so much calcium that it was like her skull was receding. I remember combing her hair and thinking, "Oh, my gosh." She really was in bad shape.

Naunny's daughter-in-law recalled that Naunny was starting to show signs of dementia around this time. She remembered when Naunny took the bus downtown to get her hair done but then got lost coming back and had to take a cab home.

"That's about the time she stopped taking care of herself, too," Uncle Chuck added. "I'd go over there to take her to a party or somewhere, and she was in something that she dragged out of the closet from twenty years ago that was missing a button and was stained. I'd say, 'That really doesn't match, Mom—why don't you put on these over here,' you know, in a diplomatic way."

"One of the tip-offs of problems with the elderly is when they stop taking care of themselves," Aunt Penny said, finishing the point. "Your grandma had always been immaculate, dressed to the nines. She'd have bunions on her feet but would still be in high heels. But she stopped taking care of herself and just stayed in her pajamas most of the time. That's when we knew she was starting to really deteriorate."

Other relatives believed that Naunny changed after the death of her husband in the mid-1980s. Researchers have written that the effects of widowhood can be devastating, especially for the elderly. In her book on death in contemporary America, Kathy Charmaz notes that *loneliness* is the major problem for many widows, because they are "structurally isolated" and feel "psychological abandonment."

Several relatives talked about Naunny's decline after becoming a widow. Many of them said that she went into seclusion after Pete's death, not only because Pete died but also because many of her friends and relatives had also died or had Alzheimer's disease.

Whether or not my grandmother's health started to deteriorate before or after the death of her husband, her health really suffered the last few years of her life as she battled dementia. Naunny was never formally diagnosed with Alzheimer's, and it is unclear whether she "merely" had senile dementia or Alzheimer's disease. Naunny repeated herself constantly, and although she could recall stories from her childhood, she could not remember what had happened just minutes before. She spent most of her days just sitting on the couch in her living room watching television. She also had stopped eating regularly, consuming mere crumbs of food but sneaking cigarettes, wine, and cough syrup whenever she could do so. She was still living by herself in her one-bedroom apartment with daily help from Ophelia, the woman my uncle had hired to fix her meals and check up on her. But everyone in the family knew it would not be long before she was completely unable to take care of herself.

Naunny had gone to bed a little earlier than usual that night. Chuck had confiscated all of the wine that Naunny had asked Ophelia to buy for her, so Naunny drank some cough syrup that evening and was feeling woozy. She had one last cigarette in the living room during the ten o'clock news and then staggered off to bed.

She woke up at one o'clock in the morning, jolted by the backfire of a passing car. Once she recognized that everything was fine, she tried to fall back asleep. After a few moments, though, she realized that she had to go to the bathroom, but she did not really want to expend the energy to do so. She closed her eyes and tried to fall asleep, but she was afraid that if she did not go to the bathroom she might pee in bed later that night. Reluctantly, and very slowly, she pulled herself out of bed.

The room was pitch black, as usual. Naunny loved to keep her entire house dark at all times, especially at night. Even the slightest light shining through the bedroom window bothered her, so she kept her blinds pulled together tightly.

She gently placed her right foot on the floor and tried to feel for her soft pink slippers that she always kept on the floor near the right side of the bed. She was still a bit disoriented from the cough syrup, so she misjudged where her slippers were located. She placed her other foot on the floor but still could not feel them. She moved her body forward, still sitting on the bed, and reached out again with her right foot. Finally, she felt the side of one slipper. She tried to place her foot in the slipper at the same time that she stood up, but that required too much coordination for an eighty-four-year-old frail woman who had drunk too much cough syrup. Naunny slipped, twisting awkwardly, and fell onto the floor of the bedroom.

The fall startled her, and she lay on the carpet in silence. After a few moments, she regained her composure and tried to get up. She felt a sharp pain throughout her body but could not determine its source. She tried to get up from another angle, but the pain intensified. She lay back down on the floor and thought about what to do.

She decided that she would crawl out of the bedroom. She tried to roll over to get a better angle for crawling, but the pain was still too sharp. She thought about yelling out for help, but she did not want to wake up her neighbors. She decided to lie there until Ophelia arrived in the morning.

She tried to fall back to sleep, but she was in too much pain on the hard floor. She said an Our Father and a few Hail Marys but then stopped praying, remembering that neither God nor Mary had saved her husband Pete from dying a few years earlier, so it was doubtful that either of Them would help her now. She craved a cigarette but realized that she would not be able to crawl to the living room to get one. The more she tried to put the craving out of her mind, the more she wanted that cigarette. She tried to crawl again, but the pain was just too severe. She lay back down on the floor and closed her eyes.

To pass the time, she tried to remember the birthdays of her children and grandchildren. She remembered the birthdays of her two sons but could not remember the birthdays of any grandchild. She then tried to figure out the leftover words from the previous day's crossword puzzle but could not remember them, either. She was getting more and more frustrated, and the cravings for that damn cigarette would not go away. She tried to cry herself to sleep, but she couldn't even do that.

Several hours later, Naunny heard someone open the door of her apartment.

"Elsie?" Ophelia said quietly. "Elsie? ELSIE!"

"I'm in here," Naunny said, feeling the sharp pain echo throughout her body.

Ophelia came into the bedroom. "O mis Dios," she said frantically and rushed over to Naunny. "Ay, Jesus."

"Jesus isn't the one who fell down," Naunny said.

"Don't move," Ophelia said and called 911. She shouted into the phone for an ambulance and then held Naunny's hand while they waited.

About fifteen minutes later, the paramedics, two cute males in their late twenties, came into the room and knelt down by Naunny.

"How you doing, ma'am?" one of them asked.

"Terrible," Naunny said. "Can you get me a cigarette? I've been stuck on the floor here all night, and I couldn't even reach my smokes."

The paramedics smiled and then lifted Naunny—and what turned out to be her broken hip—onto a gurney. They placed her in the ambulance and took her to the hospital, but, to her dismay, they never gave her that cigarette.

Uncle Chuck finally realized that Naunny could no longer take care of herself in her own apartment. "One night she called me and said, 'I can't pee,'" he told me. "I said, 'I'll take you to the hospital in the morning.' She said, 'No, I really can't pee, I'm going to burst.' I said, 'Mom, it's two o'clock in the morning.' She said, 'OK, come over in the morning when you have a chance, and if you find a body in a puddle of pee you'll know what happened.'" He smiled, recalling how my grandmother could combine humor and guilt so strategically. "So I came over and took her to the hospital. After about a half-hour in the waiting room, she said, 'Why are we waiting here?' I said, 'Because you had a bladder problem.' She said, 'I did? Well, I don't have any problem now. Let's go home.' I said, 'Well, as long as we're here, why don't you let them check you out.' So they put a catheter in her and got about one ounce of urine out of her. She might have had a bladder infection or even cancer, but at her age they didn't want to run any tests or anything, and she was in too weakened a condition to undergo chemotherapy or any treatment like that anyway. So they just sent her home."

Uncle Chuck was the person who visited her the most during this period, and he realized that she finally had become a danger to herself. "She was physically limited," he said. "She started to forget what she had plugged in or turned on. I'd go over to the house and it would be really hot. She'd have all the burners on because it was cold that morning, but in the afternoon it was hot. She'd say, 'It's really hot today.' I'd say, 'Yeah, it's hot because you've got all the burners on.' She didn't even remember that she had put them on."

The final straw came when Naunny fell out of her bed in the middle of the night and broke her hip. She was admitted to the hospital for the injury, but once the injury was treated, she could no longer stay in the hospital. At that point, Uncle Chuck finally decided to put her in a nursing home because she could not be on medical insurance since she was not sick anymore, but she could not support herself.

"She needed somebody to bathe her, take her to the bathroom—all that stuff," Uncle Chuck said. "She refused to come live with Penny and me, so I had to put her in the convalescent home."

When I first heard that Naunny was being moved into a nursing home, I thought it would be on a temporary basis until she recovered from her hip injury. I figured, naively, that she would take a few months to recover and then move back to her apartment.

When I found out that the move to the nursing home was permanent, I was very disheartened. I knew that Naunny would want to go back to her place—her "pad," as she called it—as soon as possible. However, I also knew that she could not take care of herself and that she would not want to live with Uncle Chuck and Aunt Penny or with my parents.

Even so, a permanent move to a nursing home sounded so final. Old people die in nursing homes, I thought. I wondered whether she would be able to go to Las Vegas for Christmas that year and whether that would be the last Christmas she would live to enjoy.

Naunny was already bored with her daily routine after just two weeks in the nursing home, and it looked like this day would fit the pattern. She woke up around 6:30 A.M., and, even though she was ready to get out of bed, she had to wait for the nurse to arrive at 7:00 to open the protective gates on the sides of her bed and take her, by wheelchair, to the bathroom. Then it was breakfast in the dining area where she ate the usual tasteless serving of bland oatmeal, runny eggs, and dry toast. Even though she had not been eating much before she was put into this place, she had a craving for some beans and tortillas.

After breakfast, the nurse carted her back to her room, where she wrote in her journal and watched television. As usual, she listed the programs that she watched in her journal: Regis and Kathy Lee, *8:00 A.M.;* Family Feud, *9:00 A.M.;* The Price Is Right, *9:30 A.M.;* Magnum P.I., *10:00 A.M.;* The Young and the Restless, *11:00 A.M.;* Joan Rivers, *12:00 noon.*

At 12:30 P.M., the nurse came back and wheeled Naunny to the bathroom again where she managed to pee but could not force out a bowel movement. Then it was back to the dining area to have lunch. This time it was boiled meat, boiled carrots, and boiled potatoes that tasted like the oatmeal and eggs she had eaten that morning. As usual, Naunny ate just a few bites before asking the nurse to take her back to her room.

Then it was more TV: Highway Patrol, *1:00 P.M.;* 21 Jump Street, *2:00 P.M.;* Sally Rafael, *3:00 P.M. She was watching* Hunter *at 4:00 P.M. when the physical therapist came and took Naunny to a room with other residents where they all had to hit balloons to each other. Naunny thought it was a stupid game and demanded to be taken back to her room.*

She was watching the five o'clock news when the nurse interrupted her and told her it was time for dinner. Naunny told the nurse that she wasn't hungry, but the nurse carted her down to the dining area anyway, where she ate a few bites of bland chicken and even blander rice. After dinner, the nurse took her to the bathroom, but nothing would come out.

Then it was back to the room, where she watched Full House *at 6:00,* Family Matters *at 6:30,* Jeopardy *at 7:00, and* Wheel of Fortune *at 7:30. She was about to watch* Matlock *at 8:00 when Chuck and Penny arrived for their nightly visit. They had a wonderful visit, but the hour went by too fast for Naunny. Chuck and Penny said good-bye, told Naunny that they would see her tomorrow, and left.*

The nurse came by and took Naunny to the bathroom one last time. She could not force out a pee or a bowel movement. The nurse wheeled Naunny back to her room and helped her get into bed.

Naunny wanted to watch more television, but the nurse told her it was bedtime, turned out the lights, left the room, and closed the door.

Naunny tried to cry herself to sleep, but she could not even force out a tear.

COPING WITH "LIFE" IN A NURSING HOME

To know, literally, that you could not go home again raised the curtain on the final act of life.
—JOEL SAVISHINSKY, *The Ends of Time*

I hated to see her get that dementia. I felt sorry because she was realizing it, too—that she couldn't remember things and that she couldn't take care of herself anymore.
—SON

Naunny left the hospital in early November 1993 and was admitted to a nursing home in South Pasadena, close to where Uncle Chuck and Aunt Penny lived. They had checked out the place before admitting Naunny and were confident that it was a quality facility. It was clean, the staff seemed to take good care of the residents, they had monthly meetings for families, and they sponsored many activities for residents such as bingo games and music. Naunny was placed in a room with two other women, but neither woman could engage in any meaningful conversation because they both had Alzheimer's disease. So every day, Naunny watched television, wrote in her diary, and waited for the staff to feed her and take her to the bathroom. And she cherished every visit from Uncle Chuck, Aunt Penny, and other family members.

Naunny initially believed that she would be there only until she was well enough to go back to her apartment. In the meantime, however, Uncle Chuck and Aunt Penny had to let her apartment go because it was in a government-subsidized complex, and there was a long waiting list to get in. However, Uncle Chuck instructed family members not to tell Naunny that her apartment was gone in the hope that she would keep her spirits up and stay motivated to get better if she thought she would be going home.

Everyone who visited Naunny tried to maintain the lie, but as the weeks passed, she began to doubt whether she still had her apartment. As the husband of her former daughter-in-law admitted:

> When we went to visit her, she looked at me with those big eyes and asked, "Is my pad still there?" We told her that if she ate her food and got better, she could go back to her pad. But I think she probably knew that her pad wasn't there. It may have been the best thing for her to go home, but there was no one there to take care of her.

In late December, Naunny came down with the flu, and word spread among a few of the relatives that she was sick. Several family members made special trips to L.A. to see her, some feeling that it might be the last time they saw her. Two of her granddaughters, Terese and Cathy, visited her around this time.

"My sister and I had a picnic with Grandma," Terese recalled. "We stopped at Trader Joe's and got all these goodies and a bottle of red wine. We wheeled her around the place and then went back to her room. We put goodies all over the bed, little chocolates, nuts, red wine. We were just talking and chit-chatting."

"We had a wonderful time," Cathy said, continuing the story. "She was really happy, kind of like her old self. She was laughing and joking and eating, because she was forgetting her situation. But everybody was getting sick in there, and I thought, 'This isn't good.'"

"The hardest part was when we said good-bye," Terese said, blinking back tears. "For some reason, I just knew I was saying good-bye to Grandma. I looked back and didn't want to leave. I had a feeling that I wasn't going to see her alive again. So I went back to the bed, and she said, 'I've been so lucky. Look at these beautiful granddaughters. I'm so lucky.' Rather than dwelling on the fact that she was there, dying in a nursing home, and she'd lost her pad, she talked about how lucky she was."

I knew that Naunny had come down with a cold, but I did not find out how serious her sickness was until it was too late. Like other relatives, though, I knew that she did not want to be in a nursing home. But I don't think any of us truly understood the depth of Naunny's despair while she existed in that place. I only discovered how badly she felt after her death, when Uncle

Chuck gave me the diary he asked her to keep so she would remember what happened each day. This diary contains a log of the TV shows she watched each day, her commentary on how the staff was treating her, and glowing reports of visits from various family members. But it is also filled with sorrowful accounts of her feelings, and it is very clear that her despair intensified as the weeks passed.

EXCERPTS FROM NAUNNY'S NURSING HOME DIARY

Sunday, Nov. 7

Lucy is my nurse. Chuck and Penny arrived at 11:30 and brought a TV.

The nurse's aid came to change me. I've seen sacks of potatoes handled more gently.

Hunter 2 PM

Saved by the Bell   3:00 PM

My Timmy came over at 5 PM and left at 5:30.

Chuck and Penny came over this evening. Such a beautiful family! . . .

Tuesday, Nov. 9, 1993

The nurse just took me to the potty. Not much happened, just a small turd, the size of a cork top. Well, I haven't eaten much, so I can't have too much kacky in me!

A therapist came and had me toss a balloon back and forth. I wonder what that's for?

Hunter 2 PM

I have to go potty, but I can't reach the bell!

In the Heat of the Night 3 PM

Chuck and Penny arrived at 6:45 PM. God bless them. They never forget the old lady. They left at 7:30 PM. . . .

Another miserable day.

Short walk with the help of the doctors at 10 AM

Joan Rivers at Noon. I can't stand her, but she does have interesting guests.

Highway Patrol 1 PM

They had me walk, holding onto a wall board at 1:30 PM. Took a shower and I was shaking. It was so cold!

I want to go home!

Had supper at 5:30 PM. Everything tastes the same, like wet cardboard. . . .

Pee pee time   8 AM.

Hope the nurse brings the pan. I don't want to start wetting the bed, at my age.

Nurse took me pottie. I made a big totie and pee pee!

I wonder how much longer I'll have to stay here? Or if I'll still have a pad to go to? I don't want to ever have to move in with my kids, God Bless them, as great as they all are.

Jeopardy 7 pm

Wheel of Fortune 7:30 pm. . . .

                            Wednesday, Dec 1st, I think.

Another day. Dear Lord, how much longer will I have to stay here. I want to go home, wherever that is.

Robin Williams

Phil Donohue

The lady in the next bed to mine sits and chews on her tongue. Good thing she doesn't have any teeth, she wouldn't have a tongue left.

Sally Rafael at 3 pm

My Charley just got in, 3:30 pm.

Had a bite to eat at 6 pm. Not too hungry.

Jeopardy 7 pm

Wheel of Fortune 7:30 pm. . . .

8:25 am

My kingdom for a cig! What kingdom?

Same old scrambled eggs, cream of wheat, milk, prune juice, and coffee.

I want out. I feel like I'm in prison! How long have I been here? Oh Lord, get me out of here! I'm wondering if I still have a pad to go to?

"My Fair Lady" at 2:30 pm

They just gave me 3 more pills. What are all the pills for when I don't feel sick?

Numero uno Chuck just stopped in at 4 pm and took me out for a bit.

A Frail Old Woman

Chuck left at 5 pm. God Bless him and Bill and all the rest of my beautiful family! . . .

Another day. I don't even know what day it is. . . .

I just sneezed (twice). God Bless me. Wonder if I'm catching cold? Oh well. So what else is new?

Just ate, now potty time. But I have to wait until someone can pull down the sides of the bed. This is worse than being in jail (I guess). I've never been in jail.

I asked the guy that visits his wife if he could turn my light on for me, and he said he doesn't work here! He'll get his reward in hell. . . .

Another day in this hell hole! I want to go back to my pad, if I still have one to go to. It seems as if I've been here forever, and that I have no one that cares what happens to this old bag. I just told my nurse's helper, "I want to go home." She said, "This is home for now, so make the best of it." I'd better quit making a pest of myself, and try to make the best of a bad bargain. What bargain? I just took 5 pills, all at one swallow. I don't know what they're for, but if they will help me get out of here. I'll take ka ka if they tell me to!

The young nurse's assistant just took me to the shower. Now if I could just have a cig, I'd be happy! . . .

Another boring day ahead, unless my Charley takes me to my apartment, where I can have a boring day there. I've got to pee pee, but I don't have a buzzer. I guess I bothered them too much, but if they have to clean up my mess, they'll return it!

Why can't I go back to my pad? Or do I have a pad? I wish I knew for sure. It's the uncertainty that's driving me nuts!! And will I have to spend Christmas here? Oh, Lord, get me out of here! . . .

Another day. Woke up with a slight headache! Maybe it will go away after I eat. And I sneezed again. Had prune juice and milk. I can't eat anything this early.

8:30 am. Have to go ka ka.

Went ka ka. Wonder why it's so black?

Joan Rivers, noon.

Chapter 6

At the risk of sounding like a broken record, I'll repeat. I want to go back to my pad, and I pray I still have one to go back to. My helper came in at 1 pm to check up on me. She said she's going to tell Chuck that I'm starving myself. Maybe he'll believe her and get me out of this hell hole! I've never been a cry baby, but lately the tears seem to be right on the surface.

A group came by and sang Christmas songs. They made me cry. All my lights are on, but they put up the sides on my bed and I can't get out. I want to go back to my pad. And will I have to spend Christmas here?

My bed has both sides up. I don't know how I'm going to go potty.

Chuck and Penny got here 7:20 pm

I have to go pee pee. Hope the helper hurries. I don't want to pee in bed!

I should have peed in bed. The helper came in grumpy, because I'd disturbed her dinner. . . .

Woke up at 7:30 am. I don't want to turn on the TV because I don't want to wake up the old ladies on each side of me. I'll just lie here and wait for breakfast. How exciting. . . .

Have to go potty, but all the girls are busy serving breakfast, so I'll have to wait until someone can open my prison gate!

Went potty at 8:30 am.

Magnum P.I. 10 am

The loneliest Christmas I've ever had. The tears just keep coming! (I only pray that my Chuck and Bill and the rest of the family are having a fun day).

Watching Oprah. Maybe by next Christmas I won't be here? I can't even hear my TV. The lady in the bed to my left has her radio or TV on. . . .

Happy New Year.

Chuck came by at 3:30 and told me about the movie he saw last night, then we watched the Rose Bowl (boring!). He left at 4:30 pm.

God Bless him and all the rest of my beautiful family.

My helper arrived at 5:30 pm. Had a bite to eat. Not too hungry.

Woke at 7 pm. Don't know what happened after that. My memory isn't what it used to be. . . .

According to those who have studied life in nursing homes, the words that my grandmother expressed in this diary are not unusual but represent the experiences of many elderly people who live in these facilities. Most important, these elderly residents have left their homes, never to return. As Daniel Krause puts it, "A true appreciation for the negativism about old age institutions requires an understanding of one obvious fact, that the institution is not home; for most residents, it will never be looked as such."

Naunny's journal presents an elderly woman clearly concerned about the loss of her home. She wrote frequently about her desperate wish to go back to her "pad." As her daughter-in-law told me, "We kept telling her that she had her pad, but I'm not sure if she believed us. I don't think she had the hope that she would get better and go back to her pad anyway." I believe that this loss of home—and loss of hope—contributed to Naunny's continued deterioration and ultimately to her death.

Residents in these places are not simply away from their homes; they exist in *institutions* where they have little or no control over their lives. Researchers describe the nursing home as a "total institution," especially for residents like my grandmother who are physically and/or mentally restricted and are totally dependent on nursing assistants. Residents do not have control over their schedules, their meals, or even their own bodies. In this regard, the nursing home can feel like a prison to residents, regardless of the quality of the home itself or the kindness of the attendants. Naunny's journal reveals that she did view her facility as a prison or, as she also put it, "as worse than a jail." She expressed despair over the constraints and the powerlessness that she felt in that facility; she even had to rely on assistants to let her out of the "prison gates" surrounding her bed so she could go to the bathroom. As one of her granddaughters said, "Grandma didn't like being there at all. She liked being independent. Whenever I was there, she kept saying, 'Get me out of this joint.'"

Due to the redundancy of the daily routines, residents in nursing homes also lose track of time and ultimately experience a tedious and indeterminate existence. Jaber Gubrium writes that patients consider every day to be the same, experienced by periods of eating, sitting around, and sleeping. Naunny's journal reflects this tedium and timelessness, and she often began each new entry in her diary with the phrase "Another boring day." At one point she also wrote, "I don't even know what day it is." This timelessness, coupled with the loss of her pad and the loss of control, must have made each day excruciatingly monotonous for her.

Finally, some residents in nursing homes experience detachment from others as well as isolation. Residents want interaction with others, and for those who do not make the effort to meet other residents, life can be very lonely in the nursing home. Naunny had always been a very sociable person, but apart from occasional family visits and very brief and formal interactions with staff members, she mostly lay in her bed and watched television. As Uncle Chuck said, "On either side of her were women who were suffering from Alzheimer's, so she didn't even have anybody to talk to on a regular basis. That's what she really missed."

In some ways, however, Naunny probably contributed to her own misery and isolation in that place. Researchers have found that some residents actually improve their health in a nursing home, but only when they make an effort to eat and participate in activities with other residents. Unfortunately, Naunny would not eat much and refused to join in any activities. As her granddaughter recalled:

I remember going to the convalescent home to visit her. It was not too long before she passed away. She was really depressed. I wheeled her over to a place where they were celebrating birthdays. We were sitting at this table, and across from us was another older woman. And Grandma looks at me and asks, "Do I look as old as her?" I said, "Uh, no, she looks older." We left after that because she didn't want to stay there with all those "old fogies."

Of course, Naunny managed to put on a happy face for fam-

ily members whenever they visited her. Perhaps she was just doing what she always did—saying that she was "peachy keen"
when she was really suffering. Perhaps she was trying to give
family members peace of mind or relieve our guilt for having
put her there in the first place. Or perhaps she was just trying to
hide her suffering, enacting what sociologists call the "mask of
aging" whereby some elderly people conceal their feelings in an
effort to hide their aging from others (and from themselves) and
retain whatever dignity and autonomy they can salvage. Whatever the case, perhaps if Naunny had confided her true feelings
to the relatives who visited her, they might have been able to
bring about some changes that might have helped her to feel at
least a little better.

Even though Naunny probably contributed to her own misery in that nursing home, her diary is still a haunting reminder
of the extent to which she suffered there. It is also a lasting reminder of the incredible naiveté I displayed by assuming that
she could actually feel "peachy keen" in such a place.

When I first read Naunny's nursing home diary shortly after
her death, I had several negative reactions. I was sad that she
had suffered so much during the last few months of her life. I
was angry with the staff at the nursing home for not having
helped her feel more comfortable and more empowered, and I
wondered whether that facility was one of the more than five
thousand nursing homes cited by the U.S. General Accounting
Office for harming their residents. I also felt guilty about not
calling her more often and for not making the trip to L.A. to
visit her one last time before she died. I was not comforted by
the fact that what Naunny experienced is common for many
residents in these institutions.

As I have had time to reflect on Naunny's diary and to read
some of the literature on nursing homes, however, my feelings
have changed considerably. I still feel a little sad, angry, and
guilty, but I also have developed more understanding and com-
passion about her situation. I feel far more empathy and com-
passion for the staff at the nursing home. I recognize that it was
very easy for me to feel anger toward them initially, especially
since I never made the trip to the nursing home to visit
Naunny, and they remained nameless, faceless individuals about
whom Naunny complained in her diary. As I read more about

nursing homes, though, I gained a new appreciation for the valuable and thankless services that these people perform. If I thought Naunny's life in the nursing home was tedious, imagine the lives of employees who clean urine and feces from beds and bodies several times every day. As Joel Savishinsky reminds us, "The people who provided for the physical and social needs of residents needed considerable amounts of emotional support themselves."

The flu spread quickly throughout the nursing home that Christmas. It was a particularly nasty strain, and in her weakened condition Naunny was an easy target. She caught the flu, and by the next week her flu had turned into pneumonia. The doctor prescribed antibiotics and gave her an oxygen mask to help her breathe. She struggled for each breath, and the wheezing and crackling in her lungs told her and her relatives that she was very sick.

She slept most of the time, getting up only to go to the bathroom. The aides brought her meals of soup to her room, but she would sip just a few spoonfuls and then fall back asleep. She could not even stay awake for Joan Rivers, whom she found incredibly annoying.

The doctor told Chuck to call any relatives who should be there to see her alive. He called his brother Bill, and he flew from Las Vegas to Los Angeles to be with his mother.

Bill, Chuck and Penny, and Tim and Jimmie took turns being with Naunny at her bedside. She was in and out of consciousness for the next couple of days.

The "old-old," the majority of whom are women and who are at the greatest risk of frailty and institutionalization, are the fastest growing segment of the elderly population.
—BRYAN TAYLOR, "Frailty, Language, and Elderly Identity"

I was afraid that she wasn't going to last very long when she went into that nursing home.
—GRANDDAUGHTER

In their stories, Naunny's relatives reconstructed an elderly grandmother who hated getting old, especially after she was placed into a nursing home. In her diary, Naunny revealed her feelings as an elderly person who felt trapped and had given up hope.

Many grandmothers and grandfathers have experienced and will continue to experience those feelings. As the average life expectancy in the United States continues to increase, so does the number of elderly people who require institutionalization in nursing homes and hospitals. According to some researchers, approximately 25 percent of the elderly in the United States are functionally disabled, requiring daily assistance with routine tasks such as shopping, eating, and bathing. Although the vast majority of these elderly people still live at home, the number of them that are being placed in nursing homes has tripled in the last two decades. Over 1.5 million elderly and disabled Americans receive care in over 1,600 nursing homes in the country, and researchers estimate that over 40 percent of all older Americans will require institutionalization at some point in their lives.

Researchers who have studied nursing homes have made numerous recommendations. Some have called for more community involvement with nursing homes through the establishment of boards and councils that include staff members, residents and their relatives, and community leaders. Others have recommended increased salaries for staff members and the development of programs to give more power and autonomy to residents. Others have advised nursing homes to provide more education to family members of patients.

My own relatives also made suggestions based on their experiences with Naunny and other family members who have been institutionalized in nursing homes. When I asked these relatives what they might have done differently had they known how much Naunny was suffering in the nursing home, most of them said that they would have visited her more often. Uncle Chuck and Aunt Penny, who visited her almost every day, said they would have paid the extra money to get her a private room so she would have had more autonomy. However, as Uncle Chuck admitted, "I feel that my mother didn't want to live anymore. She seemed to have lost hope, even before we put her in the convalescent home. So I really don't know if being in a room by herself would have made any difference."

One of Naunny's nieces from Colorado did not visit Naunny

in the nursing home but recalled her own mother's stay in a similar facility. She offered these recommendations based on her experience:

Do whatever you can for your parents while you still have them. Sometimes you may have to put them in a nursing home, especially if you don't have certain facilities that they need like wheelchairs, medical people on staff, and others. No matter what, though, if you have to put them in a home, see them as often as you can. That will make them feel better, and the people who care for them are more apt to check on them and care for them if they know you're coming around often. Don't be afraid to call attention to things that need to be done for them or things the staff haven't done. They may be ignored if you're not calling their attention to it.

I also have thought about what I might have done differently. Although I do not punish myself with guilt, I still do—and always will—wish that I had called Naunny more often and, most important, that I had gone to Los Angeles to see her one last time before she died.

I have also thought about what will happen to my parents if they are afflicted with disabilities and/or dementia. Both of my parents are in their seventies, and they both are in relatively good health. However, that may not be the case if they live into their eighties or nineties when they may have to be institutionalized. Leah and I expect to pay the bulk of any future nursing home expenses not paid by their insurance, because, unlike my two sisters and their husbands, we do not have the cost of raising children. We hopefully won't have to make these decisions in the near future, but we likely will have to make them at some point.

I have also thought about what will happen if Leah and I are lucky enough to grow old. At the time of this writing, I am forty-eight years old and Leah is fifty-four, old enough to be planning for our retirement but not for institutionalization as demented elderly. We do not have any children, so we do not have any dependents who might feel the responsibility to help us if we get dementia or cancer or become disabled in an automobile accident. Thus, we have recently purchased insurance for long-term care. As two full professors with no children, we can afford such a "luxury."

What is far more difficult, though, is imagining life as an elderly demented person in a nursing home. You cannot buy an insurance policy for that. Hopefully I will have a few more decades to prepare for that possibility.

One Last Gasp

When a person dies, his or her family has a story to tell about the events surrounding the death. Such stories are meaning laden, but few researchers have talked about the presence or significance of these meanings.

— JANICE NADEAU, *Families Making Sense of Death*

I sure hope that when my time comes, I'll go quickly, like Aunt Alice. She was 86, and active to the last! She and two girl friends went out to dinner, and as they were going to sit at the table, Alice collapsed. She was taken to the hospital, and she died three days later.

—from Naunny's journal

Naunny sat on the couch in her government-subsidized apartment, staring at the morning news show on television. She sipped some Chablis and started to cry.

It had been over two months since Pete died, and she still missed him badly.

She thought about taking a shower but decided not to do so. "What's the point?" she mumbled to herself. She thought about finishing the crossword puzzle that she had started the day before but rejected that idea as well. She just stared at the television.

After a commercial break, Regis and Kathy Lee appeared on the screen, meaning that it was now nine o'clock. Pete usually woke up at nine, and Naunny would always fix him a couple scrambled egg burritos and some coffee.

Naunny grabbed a Kleenex and blew her nose. She thought about making a scrambled egg burrito for herself since she still had not eaten anything.

"What's the point," she mumbled again to herself. She took an-

other sip of Chablis and continued to stare at the fake smiles of Kathy Lee.

THE DEATH OF A GRANDMOTHER

Over time, everything about the very ill person deflates; the skin, the bones, even the personality begins to fade. But at the same time, another pulse seems to grow ever larger and stronger, a something, a someone, who knows it is time and who wants to let loose.

—ROBERT L. MARRONE, *Death, Mourning, and Caring*

For the last couple of years, Grandma wasn't really there. I think she was just waiting to die.

—GRANDSON

Naunny's Social and Symbolic Death

Naunny suffered a "symbolic" or "social" death well before she stopped breathing. Kathy Charmaz defines such a death as a condition in which the self is invalidated, noting that it is a "death of meaning." According to researchers, three groups of people in particular experience symbolic deaths, including people in the latter stages of a terminal illness, the frail elderly, and people suffering from dementia or Alzheimer's disease. Although Naunny was not suffering from a terminal illness per se, she was a frail, elderly woman afflicted with senile dementia and was a prime candidate.

Naunny likely experienced a form of symbolic death even before she was placed in the nursing home. After Pete died, she was a lonely widow who was showing signs of senile dementia. She mostly sat on the couch in her apartment, watching television and waiting for occasional visits and phone calls from relatives.

One of Naunny's nieces from Colorado came to visit Naunny around this time. She told me how she felt when she saw how badly her Aunt Elsie had deteriorated:

The last time I saw her was when she was living in her apartment. All the blinds were drawn, and it was very dark. I asked her, "What do you do?" She said, "Oh, I just sit here and watch television." She was frail and stooped, and it seemed like her spirit was broken. I suppose that comes with old age, but it was so sad to see because she had so much energy and vitality. I felt so heartbroken. She was just existing, but not really participating in life.

If Naunny had not experienced a complete social death before entering the nursing home, she definitely suffered one after she was placed in that institution. Naunny simply lay in her bed every day at the nursing home, watching television, writing in her journal, and waiting for the staff to feed her and take her to the bathroom.

Naunny clearly was "just existing" in that nursing home, waiting for her biological death. As one of Naunny's grandsons said, "She'd tell me in the nursing home, 'The only way I'm getting out of here is feet first. I don't want to end up like that one next to me, with her tongue hanging out.'" Soon enough she would get her wish.

Chuck was sitting on the edge of his mother's bed in her room at the nursing home, holding her hand. Naunny was struggling to breathe through the oxygen mask that the doctor had ordered several days earlier when he diagnosed her illness as pneumonia.

The doctor had also told Chuck to call any family members who might want to see Naunny one last time, as her condition was deteriorating rapidly. Chuck had called a few of his children who lived in the area as well as his brother Bill, who was at that very moment on a flight from Las Vegas.

"Mom," Chuck whispered and stroked his mother's hand. "Mom," he repeated when she did not respond.

Naunny slowly opened her eyes and looked over at her eldest son. Her eyes were dark and heavy, and Chuck could see that she might not hang on for much longer.

"I've got to go now," he said, enunciating his words so that she could understand him. "I've got to pick up Bill at the airport."

Naunny reached up and pulled off her oxygen mask. Chuck leaned in to hear his mother's words.

"Ooh, that sounds ominous," she said, smiling.

Chuck laughed softly, amazed that his mother could keep her unique sense of humor, even as she lay on her deathbed.

Naunny's Biological Death

You hate to see somebody you love die in a convalescent hospital. People should go out with more dignity. It's nicer to die in your own home than in a hospital, but there was no other choice.
—SON

Like many residents in the nursing home, Naunny caught a cold in December 1993.

"I just sneezed twice," she wrote in her journal on December 23 and then asked, "I wonder if I'm catching cold? Oh well, so what else is new?" The next day she wrote, "I'm still sneezing. I hope I'm not getting a cold on top of everything else!"

On New Year's Eve, one of her granddaughters visited and wrote in her journal, "Grandma has a cough so we stopped smoking and went in."

Within a few days, her cold had turned into serious influenza. Naunny already had been weakened by a lifetime of smoking and a bad diet, and her frail condition provided the perfect home for a life-threatening virus. Within a few days after her granddaughter's visit, her flu had turned into pneumonia.

Pneumonia is a serious disease for all humans, young and old, but it is especially dangerous for the elderly. William Osler, a pioneering author of one of the first comprehensive textbooks of medicine in the late 1800s, describes pneumonia as "the special enemy of old age." Dr. Sherwin Nuland explains why this disease is so devastating for the elderly:

> More than any other organ system excepting skin, the lungs of elderly people are subjected to every insult out polluted environment is capable of inflicting. . . . [T]he passage of time results in a decreased ability to inflate or deflate completely. . . . The microbes of pneumonia lie in wait for the appearance of any added

insult that might inhibit further the already-damaged defenses of the aged. . . . Pneumonia triumphs.

As the pneumonia conquered her lungs, Naunny became weaker and weaker. She had trouble breathing, so the doctor prescribed an oxygen mask. According to Uncle Chuck, she was also starting to get scared. "She was very frightened near the end," he said. "You could tell it in her eyes. She didn't want to be there. She would ask me, 'Am I dying?' I'd tell her, 'No, you're not dying. You just have a broken hip.' 'Well, then when am I going back to my pad?' It was pretty tough."

As her condition deteriorated further, her doctor asked Uncle Chuck whether he wanted to put her on life support. He told him not to do so, because Naunny did not want to be on life support. The doctor then told him to call anyone who should be there and tell them to come as soon as possible. As my father remembered, "Chuck called me and told me that Naunny didn't have long. I don't even remember how I got down there. I just grabbed a couple of things and took off."

The Moment of Naunny's Death

I was there with her the day she died. I had a picture of the Virgin Mary, and I kept saying the rosary over and over and holding this picture over her. She was still alive in a coma, but I knew that my mother was gone. It was so sad. Then Tim walked in and saw me doing this, so I left and went back to Uncle Chuck's house and he went back to the nursing home. I was only there for fifteen or twenty minutes when Uncle Chuck and Tim came in and said that Mom had passed away.
—SON

My uncle Chuck and cousin Tim were the only family members in the room at the moment of Naunny's death. She had been in a coma all morning long, and my dad was there until Uncle Chuck came to relieve him. Tim had not planned to go there that morning but for some reason decided to do so.

I asked Uncle Chuck how he felt at the moment of her death. "When she actually died, I guess I felt a combination of things," he said. "I was sorry to see her go, because I'd never get a chance to talk to her again. But I didn't want to see her suffer, either, so there was kind of a feeling of relief. . . . Not that it all happened at exactly the same time."

Tim also shared his feelings about that moment:

I honestly think there was a higher power maneuvering the situation there. I mean the coincidences were so bizarre. I had a sense that she was planning her own departure. I wasn't even planning to go there that morning, but I woke up and just thought I'd stop in to see how she was doing. Uncle Bill's there, but she probably knew that he couldn't handle it, so he went back to my dad's place. Then my dad comes in. I really think that the people who were supposed to be there were there.

Among other qualities, Tim is known for his dramatic stories, and his story about a "higher power" present at the moment of Naunny's death may seem to be overly exaggerated. But researchers who study people who were near death report similar experience. Here is how Raymond Moody describes the moment of near death:

A man is dying and, as he reaches the point of greatest physical distress, he hears himself pronounced dead by his doctor. He begins to hear an uncomfortable noise, a loud ringing or buzzing, and at the same time feels himself moving very rapidly through a long dark tunnel. After this he suddenly finds himself outside of his own physical body. . . . He glimpses the spirits of relatives and friends who have already died, and a loving, warm spirit, . . . a being of light, appears before him. . . . [H]e finds himself approaching some sort of barrier or border, apparently representing the limit between earthly life and the next life.

Some people who have near-death experiences also say that deceased family members or friends serve as escorts and that they felt a lifetime of memories. Robert Marrone writes that these people also experience intense positive emotions as they relive moments in their lives and then feel a great sense of calm as the life passes from them.

Obviously, no one knows what my grandmother experienced at the moment of her death. However, after reading accounts of near-death experiences, I am oddly comforted that she might have had a rich and meaningful experience even as she took her last breath.

My cousin Cathy arrived at the nursing home just minutes after Naunny died. As she recalled:

> I went to my dad's house first, but your dad was there, and he said they were at the convalescent home. I drove over there but just missed my dad and Tim. They had just left. I walked in the room, and I looked at her bed and this sheet was over her, but her bed was flat. She was still in the bed. She had just died. I was kind of standing there, and this doctor or somebody came in and said, "Your grandmother just passed away. If you want to look at her, that's fine." I lifted the sheet, and it was like her body had just collapsed. There was hardly anything left of her anyway, but it was like her spirit was gone. She was still warm, and I said good-bye to her.

When my cousin Tim said that he thought the people who were "supposed to be" at Naunny's deathbed were there, I could not shake the feeling that I should have been there as well. It may be a bit arrogant to say, but I was the "numero uno" of her second son, and several relatives have told me that they thought Tim and I were Naunny's favorite grandchildren. Her two other "numero unos"—her first kid and her first grandkid—were there, so shouldn't her other numero uno have been there, too?

I wasn't there, however, because my father didn't call me until after Naunny died. He certainly knew how much I loved Naunny. The one time I asked him about it, he told me that it happened too fast for him to think of anything but getting to Los Angeles to see her.

At first I actually believed that he did not call me to get back at me for the strained relationship that we have had over the years. But knowing my dad, he probably was so overwhelmed by Naunny's impending death that he couldn't think of anyone else.

In the several years since her death, I have reflected on Tim's comment about who was "supposed to be there." When he said that during my first interview with him, I was a little offended that he didn't think I should have been there, too. But I have come to believe that Tim was right. I tend to remember the last time I saw someone, and I know that I would not cherish the memory of Naunny taking her last breath. Perhaps, as Tim suggested, a higher power—or Naunny herself—knew that.

I also think that if I were there and saw my dad placing a picture of Our Lady of Guadalupe on Naunny's forehead, I would have told him to stop it and let her die in peace, and then we might have reenacted another fight. Perhaps Naunny or some higher power did not want my dad and I to have an unpleasant scene at her deathbed.

I also recognize that Naunny's true numero unos were in fact there. Uncle Chuck is her first child, and Tim is her first grandchild. Although I like to think of myself as one of her cherished "numero unos," the first born of the second born is not exactly a true numero uno.

It took me a few years to admit it, but I believe that Tim was absolutely correct: He and his father should have been the only people present at Naunny's side when she died. I am very thankful that they were there.

Elsie was in and out of consciousness, but she could still sense that something profound was happening to her. She somehow knew that she was taking her last breaths, though she could not feel any pain. In fact, she could not feel anything. It was more of a presence within her that was acutely aware of what was happening, but she could not hear or smell or see anything. The presence within her was ephemeral, beyond her earthly senses.

Elsie experienced the sensation of looking down on herself in the nursing home bed. She knew her numero unos were in the room with her. Some part of her wanted to reach out and touch them, to hold them one last time and to reassure them, but she knew that they would be fine.

She also experienced a sensation of intense light. She felt as though she was passing through a tunnel of light, but she could not tell whether she was moving or whether the tunnel was moving. The light seemed to be in front of her while, at the same time, it surrounded her.

As she passed through this tunnel of light, she experienced simultaneously many moments of her life, past, present, and future. She sat on her father's lap as a young girl while a photograph was taken—she could actually feel his power and wealth and his love for her. She saw her mother as a beautiful young woman, even before Elsie herself was born, helping her mother, Elsie's grandmother, in the kitchen; at the same moment, she saw her mother as a stooped old woman, smoking her hand-rolled cigarettes and making tortillas in the kitchen of Elsie's house in Los Angeles. She danced with Charley, her first husband, where they first met in Berwind, Colorado, and, at the same time, she felt his moment of terror as his jugular vein was severed when he was thrown through the windshield of the car in an auto accident in Los Angeles. She experienced the tragic birth of her stillborn daughter and the triumphant birth of her two boys. She was surrounded by the beautiful sounds of the song "Amapola" from the piano that her second husband Pete loved to play for her, while, at the same time, she felt the life go out of his old feeble body at the Veteran's Hospital in Long Beach. She experienced the birth of every single grandchild, great-grandchild, and great-great-grandchild in a single beat of her failing heart. And she reveled in the sensation of dancing on her own gravestone as a Mariachi band played at her funeral. These images, even the violent ones, were strangely serene and calming.

After Elsie had experienced these and other images of her life, she sensed that she was coming to the end—or was it the beginning—of the light. Another presence seemed to be emerging from—or in—the light. It had no particular shape or form, but it was so familiar to Elsie. Although she could not see the image, she recognized it as her mother.

It's time, Eloysa, the image somehow communicated to Elsie without words.

Elsie felt an overwhelming sense of joy, as the last vestiges of life exited her body.

The next task for Uncle Chuck and other family members was to inform relatives that she had died. Although everyone was sad to hear the news, relatives responded in various ways. One of her grandsons remembered the call from his father in this way:

My dad called and said, "Your grandma died today." It was sad. But then he started talking about how she had the oxygen mask on the day before, and he told her that he was going to pick Bill up at the airport, and she takes the mask off and says, "That sounds kind of ominous." So it felt good to know that she had kept her sense of humor to the end.

One of her granddaughters reported a different experience:

Mom called me. I was at work. I remember I was at my desk when she called. As much as I knew she was getting old and wouldn't be with us much longer, when I got the word that she had died, I cried right there at my desk. I was very sad. My boss came in, and I told him that my grandmother had just died, and I was very grief-stricken, and he said to just go home. So I left and went home for the day. I was very sad. I don't remember what I did when I got home. I just remember thinking about the loss, because Naunny was such a beautiful, special person in my life.

I, too, remember that fateful call. I heard about Naunny's death in a message from my father on my answering machine. I fell to my knees and started crying and praying for her. I could not believe that she was actually gone.

When I got up off my knees, I called Uncle Chuck. I called him because I did not want to confront my dad about why he did not call me earlier and because I knew that Uncle Chuck would be making the arrangements for her rosary and funeral. He told me that he would have called me before she died but that he thought my dad was going to call me, which, of course, didn't make me feel any better. He also told me the details about her services. Then he asked me whether I would do the eulogy at her funeral.

Without hesitation, I said yes. But when I hung up the phone, a wave of panic washed over me. What could I possibly say to capture the essence of this beloved woman? I knew that words would fail me, but all I had to work with were words.

For most of the night I thought about the words that I might use during the eulogy. Then I remembered that I still had some of *Naunny's* own words. I found her family history journal, but I could not find the tape recording I had made of her talking about that history. I stayed up most of the night reading her

journal and wishing that I could hear the words in her wonderful voice. Yet as I read page after page of her story, I wondered
what I should include in her eulogy.

The mortician stared for a moment at Elsie's pale corpse on the stain-
less steel table in the chilled basement of the funeral home. She was
less than eighty pounds when she died, and now that all of the fluids
had been drained from her body, she weighed about seventy pounds,
and she seemed to be about an inch thick. He knew that it would be a
challenge to restore her fullness and color.

"At least it's not a total reconstruction," he mumbled to himself,
thinking about the traffic accident victim whom he had worked on
the night before in which a third of the victim's head had been sliced
away.

He started to pump formalin, a solution of formaldehyde and wa-
ter, into Elsie's body. As the embalming fluids went in, her body
started to rise as if he were pumping up a deflated inner tube. He had
a picture of Elsie that he was using as a rough guide, but he had done
this so many times that he had an innate sense of how to present the
body to family members.

When he was satisfied with the fullness of the body, he added a
bit of rouge on her cheeks to add color to her pale exterior.

He held up the picture and took one last look at the body. Then he
turned out the lights and left the mortuary.

He stopped off for a burger and fries before going home to watch a
rerun of Seinfeld.

Naunny's Rosary and Funeral

They had a closed casket at the rosary, but your mother and I
wanted to look at her face and tell her good-bye. Your
grandmother was from a time when that was a tradition. She
wasn't like modern people where death is so damn untidy. She
dealt with death head-on. So your mother and I both knew that
your grandmother would have wanted it to be open, and we sort
of goaded each other.
—FORMER DAUGHTER-IN-LAW

The next time any of us saw Naunny was at her rosary and funeral, though none of us were actually supposed to see her there. As Uncle Chuck explained:

> When she died, she looked really skinny and didn't look good at all. I told the mortician that it would be a closed casket, that we'd put a picture of her when she was younger, and people could remember her that way. But then at the rosary, your mother asked if she could see her. I asked the mortician, and he said sure. And she looked great! Your mother and aunt went up there and came back and said she looked great. So I went up there and thought, Wow! Maybe this happens a lot? I wondered why they had her fixed up so nice if this was going to be a closed coffin? Just in case, I guess.

My mother recalled the story this way:

> Uncle Chuck was firm about a closed casket. That bothered me. I think everybody in that room wanted to see her. So Aunt Robyn and I talked and we asked the funeral director, "There are some of us who would like to see her, and would you open it up just briefly?" And so he did, and it was a barrage of people immediately. They clamored to see her, hold her hand, kiss her. I was so glad. Uncle Chuck came over to me afterward and thanked me for doing that. He said that was the right thing to do.

It is not surprising that my mother and aunt insisted that Naunny's casket be opened up for a viewing. The open casket funeral is a very common one among some nationalities in the United States and in other countries. Researchers suggest that such viewings dramatize the seriousness of the funeral, allow relatives and friends to say farewell to the deceased, and provide an opportunity for those in attendance to demonstrate their relationships with the deceased and with others at the funeral. My mother explained why she wanted to see Naunny's body one last time:

> It's closure. When you can't say good-bye, it leaves things open. It's unfinished business. . . . It's part of my history to do this, and I think it's appropriate. . . . I just kissed her and said that I loved her and will always love her. And it was sure terrific knowing

you. I kind of talked to her like she was still alive. She looked a little different. The essence of the person isn't there. But you respect the house that they lived in. She looked like herself. She didn't look emaciated, because the morticians have a way of making people look their best.

Other relatives shared similar views. As one of Naunny's granddaughters told me:

I do remember that I touched Naunny. It's always weird to touch a dead person, because they're so cold and hard and stiff. That's just the way it is. . . . I guess I touched her just for a sense of closure. A way of expressing love, just to touch. I sure loved her a lot. Even though I believe her spiritual body was not in the casket, just physically touching her as a way of saying I loved you and good-bye. I touched her hands and her head.

I am glad that several relatives were able to find closure by looking at, and even touching, my grandmother's body in the casket. I do, however, find it rather ironic that several relatives said that Naunny looked "skinny" and "not very good" at the end of her life but "nice" and "cute" in death, suggesting that the "mask of dying" may be even more powerful than the "mask of aging."

I was the only family member who did not look at Naunny's body at her rosary or her funeral. I am not afraid or grossed out by dead bodies in caskets. I saw many dead bodies in my youth, especially when I was an altar boy serving at Catholic funerals. I also can appreciate the sense of closure that many relatives felt after they looked at and touched her body.

The reason I did not look at Naunny's body one last time is that I tend to remember the very last time I saw someone. I simply would rather not have the memory of a lifeless corpse in a casket to be the last time that I saw a friend or family member. So, when they opened up Naunny's casket at the funeral home after the rosary, I did not go back into the room to see her. And when they opened up her casket at the end of her funeral service in the church, I gracefully left my pew and exited the church.

I have never regretted my decision not to look at Naunny's body one last time, though I have questioned this decision after reading some of the literature about death and dying. Several authors, including Elisabeth Kubler-Ross, have suggested that America is a "death-denying" culture. We use euphemisms such as "passed away" and "laid to rest" to describe death, and we mostly have removed death from our homes and placed it into hospitals and funeral parlors where death professionals rather than family members prepare the body for burial or cremation.

I do not believe that my reluctance to look at Naunny's dead body was a form of death denial, but it ultimately does not matter. I do know that the last time I saw Pete and my grandfather on my mother's side, they were stiff, lifeless bodies in a casket. To this day, I still do not like those memories, regardless of whether they might have provided me with some ambiguous sense of closure.

On the other hand, I will always cherish the memory of the last time I saw Naunny. She was in the front seat of Uncle Chuck's car, waving good-bye to me as they drove away, following a wonderful visit to our house in Sacramento.

Naunny's Funeral

I thought her funeral was just tremendous. Everybody loved that funeral.
—FATHER OF FORMER DAUGHTER-IN-LAW

Naunny's funeral occurred the day after her rosary at a Catholic church near her former apartment in East Los Angeles. My dad started the service by playing a medley of songs on his saxophone, including "Somewhere over the Rainbow," as a tribute to his mother. "If she hadn't bought me that tenor and encouraged me to play and got me those lessons, I don't know how I would have wound up," he said.

My cousin Tim also hired a Mariachi band that played some of Naunny's favorite Mexican songs as well. A Catholic funeral mass followed, during which I gave the eulogy, reading extensively from her family journal. After the mass, we all drove in a procession to Calvary Cemetery, where Naunny was buried.

Relatives who attended the funeral agreed that it was a wonderful service. "I have never seen a funeral like that before," a nephew said. "It was just right for her. I enjoyed it very much. . . . It wasn't so much of a mourning as it was just a saying good-bye." His wife added, "It was like a celebration, and she would have been very happy."

A granddaughter described the scene at the cemetery on that January day:

> All the graves were decorated for Christmas; the breeze was blowing; the Mariachi band was playing; the kids were dancing. It was like a Fellini movie—it was so surreal. It was really sad, but it was also so beautiful. And when they played that song, "Amapola," "My Little Poppy," that Grandma loved so much . . . well, you know how music is when you're feeling emotional. My eyes were all blurry, and all the kids were dancing on the gravestones. What a legacy to leave behind. People don't usually say that they love funerals, but I loved Grandma's funeral. It was a beautiful funeral. I felt like Grandma was there, dancing in the breeze and sweeping over us.

I, too, believed that Naunny was there, and I, too, felt her presence there. The very last image I had of my grandmother was of her spirit dancing at the cemetery the day she was buried.

THE GRANDMOTHER AS SPIRIT

Grandma Flo landed in our house. Although we couldn't see her, the scent was unmistakable. . . . One morning, the "Grandma Smell," as it came to be known, permeated the garage. . . . Dad was elated. Confirmation at last! The mother he feared he'd lost forever was showering us with her celestial essence. . . . "She's letting us know she's all right," Dad winked. "She's looking out for us."

—JAN HENRIKSON, "The Empress of Scents and Non-Scents"

She checks in on us every now and then.
—GRANDDAUGHTER-IN-LAW

The final, yet most enduring, identity that relatives reconstructed in their stories about Naunny is the grandmother as spirit. For the most part, their views about Naunny's spirit were dependent on their religious beliefs or lack thereof.

Several of Naunny's relatives were raised Catholic, and

Catholicism strongly influenced the beliefs of those that still practice this religion. For example, one of her granddaughters said this when I asked, "Where do you think Naunny is now?"

> In heaven. I knew that she believed in the Lord Jesus as her Savior, so that gave me great peace to know that she is in heaven. . . . I believe heaven is a place of joy and peace and fulfillment. I believe that Naunny is experiencing that. And I know that someday I'll see her there.

Other relatives who were raised Catholic but no longer practice Catholicism were more ambivalent about Naunny's afterlife. As one grandson put it:

> Well, if there's a heaven, she's there, no doubt about it. She was a religious lady, so that's the way she lived most of her life. I'm hoping there's an afterlife. We were raised Catholic, so we believed certain things. Then you grow up and become an adult and become cynical.

On the other hand, relatives who are agnostics or atheists had very different views on the possibility of Naunny's afterlife. Uncle Chuck said this:

> I don't believe in an afterlife. It's like a bug: When you get squashed, that's it. You do the best you can during your life. I suppose there could be a spirit. There are electrical things going on in the body. . . . But one of my favorite stories is about a preacher who addresses a congregation: "How many of you believe in heaven?" And everybody raises their hands. "And how many of you want to go to heaven right now?" And nobody raises their hands.

As one of Naunny's nieces put it, "It's just like my father used to say: 'When you die, you're like a fart. You smell for a while, and then you're gone.'"

Regardless of where Naunny may or may not be, she is still with us on earth, in our memories. Many relatives told me that they continue to think about Naunny. As my father said on a tape recording:

I think about my mother all the time, like Christmas. She loved Edie Gormet. She used to do her little dance step. It was so cute. She'd wake up in the morning when she stayed with Mom and me and she'd have a song. I'd say, "Hey, Mom, what's the song of the day?" She'd sing some song. She couldn't remember what happened ten minutes ago, but she could remember songs from 1930, Tin Pan Alley songs.

A granddaughter expressed a similar view:

I still talk to her sometimes. Like last Christmas, I was making tamales and I couldn't remember the recipe. So I started asking her, "Come on, Grandma, how'd you used to make them?" I think she helped me out. They came out fine. So I visit with her every now and then.

Some relatives even believe that Naunny's spirit visits them from time to time. Tim and his wife Jimmie share such a belief.

"After she died, it was weird," Jimmie said. "Tim went to bed and closed the door, and we could smell her."

"No doubt about it," Tim said. "I smelled it, but I thought I maybe was imagining it, and I didn't want to scare Jimmie, and then Jimmie goes, 'I smell your grandma.'"

"I wasn't even afraid," Jimmie said. "I just said, 'Hi, Grandma.'"

"Then a couple years later it happened again," Tim said. "It was just this pleasant smell that reminded us of her."

"Yeah," Jimmie concluded. "She checks in on us every now and then."

Naunny's spirit will always be with us. If there is a heaven, Naunny must be there because of the way she lived her life. I certainly hope there is a heaven, and I hope that I will join her there one day . . . but not anytime soon.

A few weeks before writing this chapter, I was talking to Leah about the literature I had been reading about near-death experiences. When I told her that some people who have had these experiences reported being guided by the spirit of deceased friends or relatives, she asked, "So who would you want to guide you when you die?"

"Naunny," I answered without hesitation.

"Naunny?" Leah said in surprise. "What if I die first? Wouldn't you want me?"

"Nope," I said, perhaps too bluntly.

"Why not?"

"Because Naunny loved me unconditionally."

Leah laughed. "I guess that makes sense," she said, knowing that however great her love for me is, it comes with at least some conditions.

Obviously, I don't know what is going to happen to me when I die. I have rejected most of the Catholic beliefs that were pounded into my head in my youth, though I retain a belief that there is some form of afterlife. And if there is such an afterlife, I hope to God that Naunny is the one who will guide me and that her cool hands on my face is the last sensation that I experience as I take my last breath. With her guidance, I know that I will not fear the Shadow of the Valley of Death. . . .

We expect death to be shattering (often it is) and final, but for many granddaughters, death was also a window through which lessons and living (and even humor) continue to illuminate.
—VALERIE KACK-BRICE, "A Stitch in Time"

In an earlier time, you had a lot of generations in a household, and you had more caregivers, so an older person could die in the home. But you don't have that anymore. So you have convalescent homes, and they aren't the same.
—DAUGHTER-IN-LAW

Death, of course, is a universal experience for all of us earthly beings. And members of various families across the country and around the world deal with the loss of their grandparents every day. In the United States, over one million people age sixty-five or older die every year. Like Naunny, more and more of our grandparents are dying in nursing homes and hospitals, since fewer and fewer of our elderly relatives die at home.

I am not suggesting that we should return to the days when elderly people spent their final days, weeks, and/or months at home, being cared for by family members. Most families are not equipped to care for the elderly, especially those who are frail or require serious medical attention. We all need to recognize, however, that a nursing "home" is not experienced as a *home* and that we should do everything we can to make those places more meaningful for our elderly loved ones.

I believe that we also should honor our grandparents with funerals and other death rituals that celebrate their lives and convey to family and friends in attendance how meaningful their lives were to us. This can only occur when family members take an *active* part in these rituals. Naunny's funeral was more of a celebration, but only because family members had active roles in opening the casket, selecting the music, doing the eulogy, and other activities. Kathy Charmaz cautions that if family members do not take an active role, they might end up with "the commercialized funeral of today" in which there are "alienated human beings who passively and unquestioningly perform their expected tasks."

Regardless of how our grandparents die and how we organize their funerals, whenever these important family members do die, we should take time to truly grieve the loss and to truly reflect on the meaning of their lives. Thomas Attig advises that if we do this, we can "bring new meanings into existence as we grieve."

In the final analysis, I suppose that my search for the meaning of Naunny's life and death was an extended part of my grieving process. I still miss Naunny very much, yet as I talked to my relatives about her, they helped me bring new meanings of her into existence. For that, I will be forever grateful.

The Search Continues

We can learn more about those who died through researching
their lives, exploring diaries, letters, and other records they left
behind, and the like. And we can extend and modify our individual
memories through exchanging, discussing, and exploring
memories with others. . . . Sometimes we find in their memories
understandings and meanings that complement our own.
Sometimes we come to new perspectives on their lives and make
new sense of what we find in them.
    —THOMAS ATTIG, "Relearning the World"

She was the glue that held everybody together.
    —NIECE

December 30th, 1982

Dearest Jitos Lindos—

We had the best time ever in Vegas! Christmas Eve with the
lumpy potatoes and gifts, Christmas Day with Mass and a super
turkey dinner at home Sunday. Monday, your parents took us
to a matinee of "Tootsy" with Dustin Hoffman. (You must see
it! Best movie we've ever seen). Then they took us to a Chinese
restaurant for dinner. Then on Tuesday, just before going to the
bus, I hit a hundred dollar jackpot at the Golden Gate, then I
put in another dollar to play it off and hit for another 10.

    I received a beautiful black suit from Bill & Claudia, a black
flowered blouse from Lisa, a pair of black socks from Mishe,
then Christmas Day I got this stationery from Santa, plus some
knives and forks and spatulas!

    Before we left L.A., I called my friend Faith. She said she
was spending Christmas alone, so I invited her to go with us.
She declined, but said "Let me know when Bill plays for
Liberace and I'll go." (She likes him even if he is a fag!) I told
Bill what she said, and he said "It just so happens that I'll be

playing for him from the 10th of January for 2 weeks." So when we got back, I told her, and she was thrilled. So I'll be going back there with Faith from the 12th to the 15th of January. I have to be back, as Pete is being admitted to the VA Hospital on the 17th for major surgery.

Laura hasn't had her baby yet, so no news in that direction. Lupe came over last night, and brought us a big box of Knott's Berry Farm products (cheese, jams, salami, and thin crackers), a box of See's chocolates, and a bottle of Lambrusco red wine! We received 65 cards and much goodies.

Pete read the TV Bloopers book that you gave him on the bus, and tittered and laughed all through it. Once in a while he'd laugh out loud, and the passengers were looking at him.

Thanks mucho for the stationery. You know that as long as I'm able to write, you'll get letters, even if you don't always have time to answer.

> God Bless.
> Love ya a ton,
> Naunny
> *Xxxooo*

My search for the meaning of my grandmother's life and death took me to many places. I made a trek to her birthplace, where I walked around the ruins of the ghost town that used to be her childhood home. I traveled to libraries in three states, where I conducted genealogical research on her ancestry and historical research on the eras during which she lived. I tracked down over fifty relatives in four states, where I heard wonderful stories about her and ate beans and tortillas like the ones that she had always made for me whenever I visited her. I searched boxes in my closet where I found old photographs and letters. And I walked around the cemetery in which she is buried, where, with the help of a son, another grandson, and a great-great-grandson, I finally found her grave.

My search revealed that Naunny had many meanings to her relatives, and I have discussed some of her most important meanings in this book. She was a family historian who passed down stories about our ancestors, providing a link to our past and lessons about what it means to be a family. She was a blue-collar worker of low socioeconomic means who somehow managed to provide virtually everything for her two boys and for relatives who visited her. She was a sexy, sensual woman who was loved by several men and who suffered from anorexia as she tried to maintain her sexual appeal. She was a server and a giver who sacrificed her own needs to fulfill the needs of other family members. She was a Latina who denied her Mexican heritage until very late in life. She was an old, frail woman with dementia who spent the last few months of her life feeling trapped in a nursing home. At the very end, she was a dead body in a casket and, most important, an enduring spirit who will live forever in the hearts and minds of her many friends and relatives.

These were just some of Naunny's meanings. She also was a storyteller who entertained us whenever we visited her. She was a baby-sitter who looked after her very young grandchildren, great-grandchildren, and great-great-grandchildren. She was a playmate who played cards and games with us. She was a safe haven, especially for her grandkids after their mother and father got divorced and for me when I had conflicts with my father. She was a spiritual leader who read her Bible every day, told us stories about Jesus and Mary, and took us to her little church down the big hill from her house. She was the family gatekeeper who kept relatives informed about other relatives. She was all of these things and so much more.

Like many of our grandmothers, Naunny was also a woman who experienced oppression and alienation during her lifetime. As a working-class minority woman, Naunny may have suffered from what some researchers have called "triple oppression," having been denied privileges because of her gender, class, and ethnicity. As she aged, she experienced a fourth oppression as well, because the elderly in this country suffer in a society that clearly emphasizes youth. Toward the end of her life, Naunny lost partial control of her mind to dementia and then lost complete control of everything else when she was placed against her will in a nursing home and needed help even to go to the bathroom.

Although she may have suffered as a poor, elderly, Mexican woman, she never complained to family members, and she always managed to find joy and humor in her life. As one granddaughter concluded:

Whenever she talked about anything, even the hard times, she always found the humor in it. Some people can be bitter about it and be unhappy, but she always told everything in a humorous way. I imagine at times things were pretty terrible for her, but she'd always try to make you laugh by the stories that she would tell.

Other researchers have argued that oppression is not an additive phenomenon, because gender, class, race/ethnicity, and age blend together in unique ways that make each individual life experience *qualitatively* different. Clearly, Naunny had such a unique life experience. Yet many of the experiences that she had throughout her life were and still are shared by many grandmothers across the country. Like Naunny, many of our grandmothers have experienced various combinations of poverty, menial employment, sexual objectification, anorexia, abortion, marriage, service to family, widowhood, racism, old age, dementia, and, ultimately, death. In this way, then, Naunny's life experiences were unique to her and, at the same time, representative of the experiences of many grandmothers.

Of course, this book is not about my grandmother's life experiences per se but about how her many relatives have reconstructed her life experiences and her meanings in the stories they tell about her. Above all else, Naunny's relatives described a grandmother who dearly loved them, and their stories revealed their own love and admiration for this wonderful woman.

Some relatives did present an overly romanticized view of the grandmother in their stories. Author Lois Banner has cautioned against such a view, because it oversimplifies our grandmothers as well as grandmother–grandchild relationships.

Other relatives, however, reconstructed a more complex image of the grandmother, one filled with tensions and contradictions. Naunny was a thin woman who struggled to maintain her "girlish figure" through anorexia, even when she was older and of ill health. She was a working-class widow of little means who spent whatever money she had and maxed out her credit cards so that she could buy presents for relatives and show the world that she had "made" it, even though she was very poor. She spent much of her time satisfying the needs and desires of others while denying her own needs and desires. She was a descendant of New Mexican Hispanos who denied her Mexican heritage for most of her life. In the end, she was a frail, elderly woman who refused to be around "old fogies" and who desperately wanted to leave her convalescent facility and go back to a home that no longer existed. As Janet Yerby, one of the reviewers of this book, wrote, Naunny "is both spirited and poignant, living in poverty most of her life but refusing to be defined by it, determined to provide for her sons without submerging her sexuality, maintaining her sense of independence even as she succumbed to anorexia and the frailty of her body."

In their stories, relatives not only reconstructed my grandmother's meanings but also reinforced, no doubt unintentionally, certain ideologies of the grandmother in society. For example, relatives who reconstructed a simple portrait of Naunny as not much more than a nice old lady who served them, gave them presents, and spoiled them reinforced a very limited view of the grandmother. Mike Featherstone and Mike Hepworth argue that we often place elderly people in roles "which do not do justice to the richness of their individual experiences and multifacets of their personalities." As Elisa Facio notes about Hispanic grandmothers, the word *abuela* (grandmother) represents a romanticized image of older Hispanic women that "serves to disempower women within their families and among the community."

I have to admit that I had seen my grandmother in this stereotypical way for most of my life, and, in so doing, I had been marginalizing the meaning of the very grandmother that I loved so much. It took years of research for this book to see Naunny—and every grandmother—in a way that recognizes the richness of her life.

Even those relatives who reconstructed a more complex portrait of the grandmother in their stories also reinforced other ideologies related to gender, class, ethnicity, and age. In their stories about Naunny's ancestors, relatives reinforced a patriarchal division of labor in which men's work is more important than women's work. In their stories of Naunny's service, relatives reinforced the subordinate status of the grandmother as someone whose primary concern is—and should be—serving others in the family. In their stories of Naunny's sexual identity and anorexia, they reinforced cultural stereotypes about "beauty" and may have naturalized eating disorders among women. In their stories of Naunny's working-class jobs and her spending habits, they reinforced the "myth of affluence" that equates the acquisition of consumer goods with a higher social class. In their stories about Naunny's ethnic identity, they reinforced the myth of "Spanish" superiority over "Mexicans."

As relatives reinforce these and other ideologies in their family stories, they may also *reproduce* these ideologies in their own families. Critical theorists have argued that stories not only are told in the context of power structures but also reinforce those power structures. In her book on mothers, Nancy Chodorow states that when children are raised in families with strict divisions of labor based on gender, they are more likely to reproduce those gendered divisions of labor in their families when they are parents.

Ideologies are especially likely to be reproduced when family stories are told to subsequent generations of family members. For example, when passed down to family members, stories about the gendered division of labor among Naunny's ancestors may reinforce the continued belief that women's work "always" has been restricted to household duties. Stories about Naunny's "Spanish" background may reproduce the belief that we still are different from—and better than—Mexicans. Stories about Naunny's "girlish figure" and her attempt to maintain it through anorexia may reproduce the belief that women should strive to be thin, even if they must endure eating disorders. Stories about Naunny's poor socioeconomic status and her spending habits may reproduce the belief that family members should spend as much as they can on other relatives, even if it means going into more debt. Stories about Naunny's service and sacrifice may reproduce the belief that grandmothers and other women in the family need to serve others and subordinate themselves, at least if they wish to be seen in the same loving terms by their relatives. These and other ideologies may be reinforced whenever we tell family stories to each other.

I do not wish to be overly critical of my relatives for reinforcing these and other ideologies in their stories about Naunny. After all, Naunny herself reinforced many of these beliefs in the stories that she told relatives, and some of these relatives have simply retold these stories to other relatives. I realize that this point may be ironic, because one of my primary goals in writing this book was to honor my grandmother's importance (and power) as the matriarch in my extended family, yet she herself may have undermined that goal (and her own power) in her family stories and journal entries. As one of the reviewers of an article based on chapter 1 pointed out, "Naunny is both privileged as matriarch and dethroned through the depictions of her."

Even though Naunny herself may have reinforced certain ideologies in the stories she told to her relatives, her relatives can retell her stories in different ways. We can retell stories about our ancestors' work, emphasizing how the family was dependent on the labors of *men, women, and children* for survival. We can retell stories about Naunny's courtship and marriage to Charley, emphasizing that she was the one who accepted his advances, brought him home to meet her parents, and chose to start a new life with him in California. We can retell stories that honor Naunny's service in her roles as "housewife" without reifying that service as women's "natural" role and by emphasizing that she also was a primary "breadwinner" of the family for most of her life. In this book, I have tried to open up these and other alternative possibilities for retelling and reframing our family stories, and I encourage my relatives to think of other possibilities.

THROUGHOUT MY SEARCH for the meaning of the grandmother, I have asked myself why Naunny was so important to me. I think part of the reason was that Naunny lived in Los Angeles, so a visit to her house meant taking a trip to California. Even though she lived in a tiny house in a relatively poor area, it was exotic to a kid growing up in a middle-class neighborhood in Las Vegas. I also think part of it was that she was so incredibly fun to be around. She sang to us and told stories and gave us beer shampoos. And we had epic 500 Rummy games that lasted for hours.

If I dig deeper, however, I think the main reason Naunny was so important to me is that my relationship with her was so very different from my relationship with my father. With Naunny I could be myself and she could be herself, and we truly enjoyed each other's company. Her home was always a peaceful sanctuary from the drama and defensiveness of my father. And Naunny herself was the most loving and peaceful—and the least dramatic and defensive—person that I have ever known. She never ordered you around or told you what to do or how to think. She didn't ask you how much you weighed or criticize you. And you never had to worry about what you said or how you said it. Her love seemed truly unconditional.

I wish I could report that after writing this book about Naunny, my father and I repaired our strained relationship, but that is not the case. I'm sure Naunny would be very happy if we had done so, though I'm just as certain that she would be happy to see that we have avoided the major conflicts we experienced many years ago. Above all else, Naunny hated conflict. She rarely raised her voice, and whenever anyone argued in the house, she would leave the room. When her two kids fought with each other, she would pack a suitcase and threaten to go back to Colorado. In a sense, then, the fact that my dad and I have not had a big fight for many years may be a tribute to my grandmother and our mutual love for her.

I know that it is much easier to develop positive relationships with one's grandparents than with one's parents. Researchers have found that the conflicts characterizing the parent–child relationship are usually absent from the grandparent–grandchild relationship, except in cases where the grandparent functions as the parent in the primary caregiving role. Grandchildren usually do not see their grandparents as much as they see their parents, so they are less likely to experience the daily tensions of living together. And grandparents do not have the authority of parents, so issues of control are less likely to color the grandparent–grandchild relationship. Whatever the case, I loved going to my grandmother's house, and I still dread going to my father's house.

I also recognize that some people do not develop close relationships with their grandparents. Some grandparents die before their grandchildren can get to know them, while others live too far away and do not see their grandchildren very often, as was the case with Naunny and Grandpa Chicago. Still other grandparents remain cold, aloof figures throughout a grandchild's life. I can only express my sorrow to people who never got the chance to know their grandparents or people who have chosen not to develop close relationships with them. Of course, I also express envy at people who had or have a close relationship with their fathers.

In closing, I still miss my grandmother very much. I am glad that I did the research for this book, because I learned a great deal about her that I never knew. I only wish that I had started my search while she was still alive so that I could talk to her about her life.

I no longer have any living grandparents, so I no longer have an identity as a grandchild. I miss that identity. In addition, since I do not have any children, it is virtually guaranteed that I will never be a grandfather. I will never know what I will miss by not experiencing this role.

My guess is that many readers of this book do have at least some living grandparents, especially since people are living longer and are more likely to become and remain grandparents. In addition, many readers are likely to become grandparents in the future. Unfortunately, as author Laurie Arliss reminds us, the trend in our culture has been to attach less importance to the grandparent–grandchild relationships.

I encourage you to break this trend by contacting your grandparents if they are still alive or, if you are a grandparent, by contacting your grandchildren. Perhaps you can even interview your grandparents for posterity, adapting some of the questions that I asked my relatives. If your grandparents are no longer alive, you still can celebrate their lives and learn more about them by asking relatives to share stories about their lives with other family members. If you do, I am confident that you will find your "search" to be personally rewarding. I also encourage you, even if you are in your teens or twenties, to think about what kind of grandparent you wish to be. My search indicates that there are many options.

Chapter 8

**When Grandmother died in 1966, a part of me was lost; although
now when I go to her grave in the exact spot where she told me it
would be, I have my own cascade of memories of her.**
—ROBERT ARCHIBALD, "A Personal History of Memory"

I wish I was more like my mother.
—SON

I have finished my search for the meaning of my grandmother,
though I know that the search for her meaning will always continue. I end with a poem that expresses some of the feelings
evoked by this study.

500 Rummy

I'm sorry, Naunny, that I didn't behave well
the one time you did not let me win at 500 Rummy,
when I was a young boy.

I'm sorry that I didn't answer most of the letters
you continued to send to me,
when I was away at school.

I'm sorry that I didn't call you more often
to say hi and small talk,
even though you never really had much to say.

I'm sorry that I didn't visit you
during your brief stay in the nursing home,
before you died so unexpectedly.

I only wish that you were still alive,
so that years from now I could feel even more guilt
about not doing these things.

Studying Naunny

Does the recollection that is ethnography ease the pain of the loss evoked by the recollection? No, certainly not; ethnography is only another form of mourning.
> —RICHARD QUINNEY, "Once My Father Traveled
> West to California"

What are you going to do with all those interviews?
> —DAUGHTER-IN-LAW

September 29, 1986

Dearest Nick and Leah—

Last week was not the best! Emma had back surgery. My sister-in-law Cruz had a 6-hour open-heart surgery and your Dad was in the hospital with an infected bladder condition. They did a ream job on him and he hemorrhaged! Michelle had her wallet stolen, with all her credit cards, bus pass and 50 bucks. Good thing she hadn't cashed her 200 and some paycheck. And Jimmie had her car stolen! And I've got a doozy of a chest cold. Other than that, everything else is Peachy Keen!

I hope you're both OK.

Love & Blessings Always,
Naun

THE EVOLUTION OF "THE NAUNNY PROJECT"

[T]he traveler metaphor sees the interviewer as on a journey from which he or she will return with stories to tell, having engaged in conversations with those encountered along the way. . . . The route may be planned ahead of time, but will lead to unexpected

twists and turns as interviewer-travelers follow their particular
interests and adjust their paths according to what those met along
the way choose to share.
    —BARBARA HEYL, "Ethnographic Interviewing"

What a great idea, tracking down all our relatives.
    —SON

My search for the meaning of Naunny's life and death took me
several years to complete and culminated in this book. But I certainly did not start out with this in mind.

After Naunny's funeral back in January 1994, I felt empty,
not only because of the loss of my grandmother but also because the eulogy I delivered did not seem to me to be enough of
a tribute to her. However, I returned home to Sacramento and
soon fell back into business as usual. There were books and articles to write, classes to teach, bills to pay, and so on. Every now
and then I would think of Naunny, rattle off a quick "Hail
Mary" in her honor, and get back to what I was doing.

Before I knew it, the one-year anniversary of her death had
arrived. I paused to reflect on her life and to say a few prayers,
and then I got back to work.

A few months later, however, something happened. It was
not exactly an epiphany, but it definitely changed my perspective. Leah and I were grading papers one night while the Acad-
emy Awards were on in the background. When Elton John won
an Oscar for his song "Can You Feel the Love Tonight," from the
movie *The Lion King*, he dedicated the award to his grandmother, who had died recently.

I stopped grading and stared at the TV screen.

"I've got to do something," I mumbled.

"What?" Leah asked, still reading a paper.

"I've got to do something," I said, and paused. "For *Naunny*."

Leah put down her favorite purple grading pen and looked
up at me.

"What do you want to do?"

"I don't know. *Something*."

That night, I tossed and turned in bed, thinking about what I
could do to honor Naunny. If I were a painter, I would have
done her portrait. If I were a musician, I would have composed
a song in her honor. But I am a researcher.

So I decided to do a study about her.

The next day I composed a letter to Naunny's relatives and friends. I asked them to write down their memories of Naunny and send them to me. I mailed the letter to about seventy-five relatives and friends and hoped that maybe fifteen of them would write back.

I was amazed by the response. Most of the relatives responded with written tributes. Some of them also sent pictures. A couple of them even sent cassette tapes with their recorded memories. It was a beautiful reminder that Naunny had touched many lives.

Several others, many from southern California, called me and said that they wanted to write down their memories, but they had too much to say. So a few months later I drove there to conduct interviews with almost twenty of these relatives. I asked a variety of questions: What is your first memory of Naunny? What do you remember most about her? Can you describe some times when you were with her? (What did you do with her? What did you say to each other?) When was the last time you saw her? (What did you do? Say?) How would you describe her defining qualities? What was her significance to the family? What will you miss most about her?

I tape-recorded all of these interviews and returned home to Sacramento, eager to transcribe the tapes. But then I had to start teaching a summer class and meet deadlines for other projects. Before I knew it, the regular semester had started and the Naunny tapes remained untranscribed. And "The Naunny Project," as I called it, was on the back burner.

The Naunny tapes remained in a box in my closet for many months. I did not even look at these materials again until nearly two years later, in the fall of 1997, when I directed a collaborative study on consumer behavior with several graduate students. For the final project, we wrote a paper together, titled "Shopping for Family," in which each of us wrote a personal vignette about how shopping and family were intertwined in our lives. One student wrote about shopping for a birthday card for her suicidal grandfather; another wrote about visiting with her father at a shopping mall, the last time she saw him alive before he died of cancer; others wrote about how shopping had defined their family lives in various ways.

For my vignette, I wrote about buying Emeraude perfume for Naunny every Christmas and about how her identity was defined, in some ways, through her gift giving. To complete my vignette, I retrieved the box of Naunny materials and began rereading the letters and listening to the tapes. I finished my brief section of the paper, titled "Emeraude," and, after several rounds of revisions, we submitted the paper for publication. It was published two years laters.

Listening to the tapes and rereading the relatives' letters for this article rekindled my resolve to get back to The Naunny Project, and I decided to write a full-length article about how family members reconstructed Naunny's meaning after her death. I transcribed all of the tapes, and I called up several relatives and conducted brief telephone interviews to fill in some of the gaps from those interviews.

In that article, titled "In Search of Naunny's Grave," I discussed some of the meanings of my grandmother and critiqued the ways in which relatives—including me—subordinate her meaning in the stories that we tell, especially when we define her importance in terms of how she served us.

I was a bit apprehensive about how the article would be received, especially by family members whom I had interviewed and to whom I sent copies. I was again overwhelmed by the response. All of my relatives—even my father—loved the article. Many of them called or wrote to say that as they read the article they laughed, they cried, and they learned. They were not upset that I had revealed my grandmother's anorexia or that I had critiqued how we all have subordinated her meaning.

I also was surprised when colleagues from around the country corresponded with me after the article was published. They said that it helped them to remember their own "Grammies," "Gagas," "Nanas," and "Nonnas."

With the publication of that article, I thought The Naunny Project had come to fruition. But I was moved that the article had resonated with so many friends and relatives, and I decided to continue my research and write this book.

The Naunny Project thus evolved in unexpected ways. What started out as a eulogy progressed into an excerpt in an article, an entire article, and, finally, this book. The process is a reminder that researchers should be open to pursuing research projects that are personally as well as professionally meaningful and to pursuing them in ways that are unplanned.

Collecting and Analyzing Family Stories about Naunny

Whereas natural science tends to taxonomize natural phenomena and causally or probabilistically explain the behavior of things, human science aims at explicating the meaning of human phenomena and at understanding the lived structures of meaning.
—JOHN VAN MAANEN, *Tales of the Field*

The methods used in any study always depend on the research questions that the investigator seeks to answer. I was interested in answering two broad questions: What are the meanings of my grandmother, as represented in stories about her? How do these stories privilege certain meanings of my grandmother over others and reinforce certain ideologies of the grandmother in the family?

I could have answered these questions based solely on my own memories of stories that Naunny told to me, and I could have written a purely autobiographical account. But I knew that Naunny had also told stories to other relatives and that those stories likely would represent other interpretations that I had never made. Thus, I used interview methods to generate stories about Naunny from her relatives from which I could develop a more complex image of my grandmother.

Using Naunny's address book and referrals from other family members, I tracked down as many relatives as I could find. There is no magic number of interviewees needed to conduct such a study, and I ended up with a little over fifty interviewees. Most of the interviews were face-to-face; some—especially follow-up interviews—were on the telephone; and a few were conducted through letters, e-mail, and even tape recordings. For example, I did not feel comfortable interviewing my father, so I sent him a letter with a list of questions and a cassette tape. I interviewed most of the relatives one time, but some key people—such as Uncle Chuck and Aunt Penny, Aunt Robyn and her husband Ed, and my cousin Tim and his wife Jimmie—were interviewed several times.

I expanded my initial list of general questions, adding ones about Naunny's ancestors, childhood, jobs, boyfriends, ethnicity, religious beliefs, and other topics, and about my relatives' feelings about her. Some relatives, especially elderly ones and very young children, could not remember many specifics about Naunny, whereas others elaborated extensively on every question. Some relatives were uncomfortable talking to me about certain things, such as the inside jokes Naunny used to tell about her boyfriends' and husbands' body parts, whereas others told me *everything* they could remember.

There are some limitations to the information gathered in such interviews. As scholars who study memory point out, what we remember is not objective, but subjective and dependent on a variety of personal and political factors. However, I was less concerned with the accuracy of the details that Naunny's relatives remembered and more with how relatives reconstructed her meaning to them—in a sense, how they reconstructed their own memories of her.

I transcribed all of the tape-recorded interviews myself—a very tedious process. I believe that transcribing familiarizes the researcher with the language of the interviewees and helps the identification of patterns and themes in the analysis.

I also searched the literature for information about grandparents. Literature searches also can be tedious, but they almost always turn up information helpful to a research project. I found that early research on grandparents was informed by a clinical perspective and that scholars often concluded that grandparental influence on children was negative because it occurred outside the boundaries of the nuclear family unit. I learned that subsequent research has been interdisciplinary in nature and has examined many positive and negative dimensions of grandparenting, including children's views of grandparents, grandparent perceptions of grandparenting, grandparenting styles, gender and ethnicity differences in grandparenting, grandparent diversity, grandparent communication, and others.

I found the body of research on grandparent *roles* to be the most relevant for this book, because that research emphasizes the types of activities grandparents perform and the meanings assigned to those activities by grandparents and grandchildren. Grandparenthood itself is a general role because grandparents have a particular identity *as* "grandparents," and they perform this identity in the specific activities they perform with their grandchildren. Researchers have found that grandparents play roles as diverse as fun seekers, surrogate parents, educators, care-givers, rescuers, mediators, mentors, nurturers, playmates, role models, wardens of culture, and others.

However, I was not interested in the actual roles that Naunny had performed during her lifetime but in how her grandchil-dren and other relatives have reconstructed her roles as they as-signed meaning to her life and death. In this regard, I treat roles not as properties of individual persons but as cultural expecta-tions about individuals who hold particular positions. Although the roles my relatives assigned to Naunny are reflective of my grandmother's actual behaviors, I believe they are more repre-sentative of their cultural expectations about grandmothers and other women in the family. That is why I believe this book is not just a study of a particular grandmother but also a study of what the concept "grandmother" means to family members.

I analyzed the interview data in two ways. First, I conducted a *cultural* analysis to identify how relatives assigned meaning to my grandmother. Researchers that adopt cultural (or "interpre-tive") perspectives assume that reality is socially constructed and examine how people assign meaning to—how they *interpret*—their social reality. Thus, I coded the interview data into categories that represented how relatives socially con-structed—or reconstructed—my grandmother's meaning. This type of analysis is an iterative process that involves induction and deduction, as researchers are influenced by the data as well as by their own viewpoints and by the literature they read.

I generated a large list of categories that represented the many meanings that Naunny had for relatives, including story-teller, family historian, server, giver, nurturer, teacher, playmate, baby-sitter, joke teller, cook, counselor, religious leader, family gatekeeper, television watcher, driver, worker, housewife, sex ob-ject, purveyor of ethnic identity, victim of poverty, alcoholic, anorectic, old and frail woman, dead body, spirit, and others. During subsequent analysis of the data, I reduced this list to the categories that I believed represented recurrent patterns from the interviews and key concepts from the literature.

I also conducted a *critical* analysis. Researchers that adopt critical perspectives assume that reality is a *site of ideological struggle* in which certain meanings are privileged over others.

Thus, I critiqued how relatives emphasized certain meanings of Naunny over others and how relatives reinforced certain ideologies of the grandmother in the family. This type of analysis focuses on meanings that are marginalized in—and even absent from—the text, especially those involving gender, class, ethnicity, and age. For example, relatives told many stories about how Naunny cooked for them, washed their laundry, and did other tasks for them. From a cultural perspective, these stories suggested that relatives interpreted one of Naunny's roles to be that of a server. However, from a critical perspective, these stories can be seen as reinforcing the subordinate status of the grandmother as someone who is—and should be—focused on serving the family. Throughout this book, I have tried to deconstruct these and other sets of stories to reveal how relatives reinforce and reproduce various ideological positions.

WRITING THE NAUNNY PROJECT

[W]riting is not just a mopping-up activity at the end of a research project. Writing is also a way of "knowing"—a method of discovery and analysis. By writing in different ways, we discover new aspects of our topic and our relationship to it.
—LAUREL RICHARDSON, "Writing"

In the last few decades, many scholars have questioned traditional forms of social science writing. Informed by feminism, postmodernism, and other contemporary approaches, these scholars argue that researchers should use forms of writing that can convey the complexities of the phenomena we study.

In this book, I used multiple forms of writing to try to present a complex image of the grandmother. I used traditional social science writing and critical forms of argument to present the "results" of my analysis and critique. Although social scientific and critical approaches differ greatly in terms of research goals and methods, they are similar in terms of writing. The author is usually absent from the text and serves as the omnipotent observer who analyzes the subjects' points of view or critiques how their views marginalize others and reinforce certain ideologies.

I also included autoethnographic writing through my own confessional stories and emotional reflections. Autoethnography combines autobiography and ethnography in a way that reveals the connection between the personal and the cultural. In addition, I revealed my feelings about the research process itself, including how I struggled over my decision to include certain stories about my grandmother (and other family members).

I included impressionistic and literary writing as well. Sociologist Laurel Richardson and others have argued that contemporary researchers should use fiction-writing techniques, such as character development, flashbacks, and dialogue. I used many of these techniques when I wrote narrative fragments of various moments in Naunny's life based on the stories that relatives told me and/or on my own imagination of what Naunny might have experienced. I included these passages because Naunny now exists for family members in the stories of her life that we tell each other. Upon her death, Naunny's life on Earth became but a series of fragmented stories that her descendants remember and imagine.

I combined all of these forms of writing to create what Carol Ronai calls a "layered" account, one that produces for the reader "a continuous dialectic of experience, emerging from the multitude of reflexive voices." I hope that this layered account is evocative and that it has personalized my grandmother and encouraged you to think about your own grandmothers.

ETHICAL CONCERNS

[I]t is axiomatic that the rights, interests, and sensitivities of those studied must be safeguarded.
> —American Anthropological Association's "Principles of Professional Responsibility"

You're not going to use that in the book, are you?
> —NIECE

Protecting Naunny and Other Relatives

Whenever researchers study an individual or a group of people, they will usually uncover information that is embarrassing or harmful to that individual or group. In the case of research about one's own family, you are bound to uncover so-called family skeletons. During the course of my research, I uncovered some of those skeletons. Several family members knew some of this information, whereas very few relatives knew other information—at least very few relatives admitted that they knew this information. One ethical dilemma that I confronted was whether to reveal this information.

Researchers agree that one should always try to protect individuals who provide information for a study. I wondered about the extent to which I even needed to protect Naunny. She was, after all, deceased, so by definition I could not harm her. But by disclosing certain information about her, I could harm her memory, which, in turn, could hurt some of the living family members who knew and loved her.

My biggest dilemma was whether to reveal that Naunny might have had an abortion during the Depression. Only one relative told me this information relatively early in the project, but then almost one year later, another relative confirmed that she also had been told about Naunny's abortion.

I avoided making a decision on whether to include a reference to Naunny's abortion for many months. To help me make this decision, I asked many colleagues around the country for their advice. Not surprisingly, I received conflicting suggestions. Some people told me that I should not reveal it because Naunny herself kept it a secret. As one colleague pointed out, the secret "was hers to keep."

Others insisted that I should write about it as part of what was uncovered during fieldwork. One colleague said that it might "open up personal connections for readers who have faced similar dilemmas in their lives."

Perhaps the most interesting suggestion started with the provocative question "What does your grandmother say?" This colleague explained that she was serious and that I should ask Naunny what to do.

One night, I sat on the back patio and looked into the heavens without any distractions. I said a few "Hail Marys" and then meditated in silence for several minutes. Then I asked, "Naunny, what should I do?"

"Whatever you want, *jito lindo*," I heard in my head, something Naunny would always say to me whenever I asked her for something. But I couldn't tell whether I was hearing her or just hearing words that I reconstructed for her.

After agonizing over this decision, I ultimately chose to include a reference to Naunny's alleged abortion, because my grandmother was one of many thousands of poor women during the Depression who had to make gut-wrenching decisions that went against their beliefs in order to survive. I also suspect that most of the women who had abortions when it was illegal kept their decisions a secret from their children and grandchildren, as my grandmother seems to have done. Even though abortion has been legal for many years, it still is a very personal decision that few are willing to discuss openly, even with family members.

I hope that the disclosure of my grandmother's abortion makes readers think about the difficult choices their own grandmothers and/or great-grandmothers had to make during their lifetimes and that my own relatives understand my reasons for writing about Naunny's family secret.

Objectifying Naunny

I also thought about the ways in which I objectified my grandmother and the many relatives that shared stories about her. In some ways, Naunny ultimately became an object of study rather than the beloved grandmother that I wanted to honor. There were times when I heard something unexpected about her and treated it as "good data." And *I* was the one who had the final say on what should and should not be included in this book, even against the will of some of Naunny's relatives as in the case of her abortion. As Bud Goodall writes, "[T]o observe [or interview] others is to *colonize* them. To write their experiences in your book or article is to *use* them. It is to place yourself, as author, in a *superior relationship* to the persons you are observing, hearing, and analyzing."

Although I obtained feedback from relatives throughout the process and used Naunny's own voice throughout the book, I was the one with all the power—the power to find, select, interpret, and critique my relatives' stories and the overall meaning of my grandmother.

It may also be ironic to some readers that I am a male, telling the story of a woman and drawing on feminist literature to do so. A reviewer of an article based on the gender issues raised in chapter 1 posed these questions in her initial review: "[W]hat does it mean when a man tells a woman's story? . . . Does it reconfigure her life/narrative in ways a woman's telling does not?

. . . Most importantly, does it provide yet another example of how insidious and normalized the patriarchal lens has become?" In a subsequent review, the same reviewer added, "Frankly, it concerns me that male researchers wearing the mantle of feminism feel that their ideological position grants them license to tell women's stories unselfconsciously."

This reviewer made me think more consciously about how I have told the story of Naunny's life and the story of this very research project. On reflection, I admit that I may have used a masculine frame to tell this story. Some readers might say that I have written a story about a grand*son* (a family hero?) on a search (a quest?) to discover (rescue?) the meaning of his grandmother (a damsel in distress?). In the end, I recouped (reclaimed?) her meaning (her honor?) from relatives (villains?) who marginalized and subordinated (imprisoned?) her in the stories they told about her.

Would this story have been written differently if I were a woman? Undoubtedly, but it is impossible for me to know how differently because my name is Nick, not Nikki. All I can say is that I did not consciously write this book as a male; I wrote it as a cultural-critical scholar who analyzed how family stories about a grandmother reconstructed her meaning and reproduced particular ideologies. In fact, part of me wrote this book as a *feminist*, because I interpret "feminism" as a way of thinking that is not determined by one's biology. I did not consciously write this book as a grand*son*, either, but as a family member who wanted to keep the memory of our grandmother alive and to encourage relatives to reflect on the kinds of family stories that we tell each other. In the final analysis, these are the meanings that I wish to privilege in my story of my relatives' stories about my grandmother.

Writing about My Father

Finally, I have very mixed feelings about my decision to write about the strained relationship that I have with my father. I was not pleased when the reviewer, one of the series editors, and the publisher read the first draft of the book and all agreed that I needed to discuss this relationship in more depth. I was reluctant to do so, because I did not want to take the focus away from Naunny and because I did not want to cause another fight with my dad. One of my goals in middle age has been to avoid another big blowout with him that might destroy the veil of civility we have managed to maintain for the last several years, and I fear that writing about our relationship might destroy that veil.

Carolyn Ellis, one of the series editors, suggested that writing about our relationship might provide an opportunity to improve that relationship, and she expressed disappointment when that did not happen. As she put it in an e-mail after reading the second-to-last draft, "[C]an't you give us any hope that reconciliation is possible?"

It would be easy enough and truthful to write that I do hope that my dad and I will communicate with less tension in the future. It is harder and more truthful to write that I have doubts about that possibility. We have had a strained relationship for over thirty years, and I do not believe that either one of us is willing to put in the time and energy with a therapist that it would take to dramatically improve our relationship. We see each other once or twice a year and mostly avoid conflict, and that seems to be the best we can hope for, at least for the foreseeable future.

In my response to Carolyn's e-mail, I said that I could not offer a Hollywood ending in which my dad and I reconcile our differences and communicate happily ever after. I believe that relationships among family members, especially between fathers and sons, are far more complicated than that. Family relationships often are paradoxical, enacted with love, comfort, and support as well as sibling rivalry, parental control, teenage defiance, marital codependency, and, in some cases, physical or sexual abuse. Although my dad and I both loved Naunny very much, even our mutual love for her isn't powerful enough to resolve years of conflict.

I don't know what will happen when my dad reads this book. Perhaps it will lead to a fruitful discussion, but I doubt it. Perhaps it will lead to a final blowout fight, though I hope not. My guess is that we will just continue to avoid conflict. And I will continue to postpone that search for a later time.

Notes

INTRODUCTION

1   Arthur Kornhaber, 101.

4   Terry Hargrave and Suzanne Midori Hanna, 52. According to researchers, life expectancy in the United States is more than seventy years for men and almost eighty years for women. There are over forty million Americans who are age sixty-five or older, and researchers estimate that they will represent at least 14 percent of the U.S. population by 2010 and 25 percent by 2020. Researchers also have estimated that 80 percent of older people in this country are parents and that 94 percent of these parents are grandparents (see William Anderson).

5   For a review of the research on grandparenting, see Maximiliane Szinovacz.

8   Hope Edelman, 24.

17 Gunhild Hagestad and Linda Burton, 471.

18 For a discussion of family stories, see Karen Baldwin; Elizabeth Stone.

19 Arthur Bochner and Carolyn Ellis, 22.

CHAPTER 1

20 Laurie Arliss, 161.

24 Kristin Langellier, 268. For a discussion of social memory, see Jacob Climo and Maria Cattell. For a critical analysis of family stories, see Kristen Langellier and Eric Peterson.

26 Although my grandmother suggests that the demise of the sheep industry happened in one year under President Taft when he allowed the importing of wool from Australia, the situation was far more complicated than that. For example, in his historical discussion of sheep in the western United States, Edward Wentworth argues that a series of tariffs and other legislation from 1866 to 1930 impacted the price of wool, though he points out that in the late 1800s and early 1900s, Australia did come to dominate the wool market, which put severe constraints on the domestic wool industry.

28 Sarah Deutsch, 21.

32 Duane Smith calls the mining accidents of the era an American "holocaust" (94). For a discussion of the history of mining in Colorado, see also Carl Abbott; Michael Jenkinson.

33 For a discussion of the Mother Jones riot and the Ludlow Massacre, see Howard Gitelman; George McGovern and Leonard Guttridge; and Leon Stein and Philip Taft. The George West report is quoted by Stein and Taft.

36 For a discussion of how stories can be used to trivialize women, see Robin Clair.

41 Elizabeth Stone, 17.

CHAPTER 2
44 Mary Ann Lamanna and Agnes Riedmann, 357.

45 Maureen Honey, 20.

48 Leslie Reagan, 133. For a discussion of abortion, see Angela Bonavoglia; Ellen Messer and Kathryn May.

53 "Fleeing Motorist Killed."

54 The "Mexican Expert" is quoted in Douglas Monroy, 29–30.

55 For a discussion of working women during World War II, see Karen Anderson; Sheila Rowbotham. The statistics on the drop in women working are cited by Sherna Gluck.

62 J. Ross Eshleman, 212. For a discussion and critique of the "feminization of poverty," see Paula Dressel; Meredith Minkler and Kathleen Roe; Renee Feinberg and Kathleen Knox.

68 Elisa Facio, 61.

CHAPTER 3
70 Chris Barker, 236.

71 Tara Masih, 36

72 The AARP studies were reported by Karen Uhlenhuth. For a discussion of sexual objectification, see John Berger; Sarah Gamble.

84 Susan Bordo, 147. For a discussion of anorexia and other eating disorders, see Kim Chernin; Nancy Etcoff.

85 Chernin, 61.

87 Bordo, 120.

91 Chernin, 2.

CHAPTER 4
94 Sibylle Bergemann, 41.

96 Jean Miller, 61; Facio, 92.

98 Bordo, 122.

101 Stephanie Golden, 13; see also Mary Bateson.
101 Wood, 26.
105 Wood, 25.
108 Miller, 50.
110 Coontz, 63.
111 See Evelyn Keller for a discussion of alternative models of women's service.

CHAPTER 5

113 Edelman, 93. For a review of research on Hispanic grandparents, see Facio; Norma Williams and Diane Torrez.
114 Nancie González, xi.
116 Robert Nostrand, 31. For a discussion of Spanish colonization of New Mexico and Colorado, see Marc Simmons.
117 For a discussion of the history of Trinidad, Colorado, see Barron Beshoar.
118 Earl Shorris, 167. For a discussion of ethnic labels, see Rodolfo Acuna.
120 González, x.
121 The U.S. Labor Bureau official is quoted in Deutsch, 36; see also José de Onis.
126 The Bogardus study is quoted in Ricardo Romo, 75.
127 Acuna, 8–9.
130 Gloria Anzaldúa, 84.
131 Kornhaber, 42.

CHAPTER 6

132 Clive Seale, 149.
134 Arthur Frank, 143.
135 Kathy Charmaz, 309.
141 Joel Savishinsky, 175.
147 Daniel Krause, 68. For a discussion of nursing homes, see Tim Diamond; Jaber Gubrium; Maria Vesperi.
149 Mike Featherstone and Mike Hepworth discuss the "mask of aging." Deb Riechmann describes the U.S. General Accounting Office report on nursing homes.
150 Savishinsky, 245, emphasis deleted. Bryan Taylor, 186.
151 For a discussion of the number of elderly people who will require institutionalization, see Peter Kemper and Christopher Murtaugh.

CHAPTER 7

154   Janice Nadeau, 2.
155   Robert Marrone, 88. Charmaz, 80.
157   William Osler is quoted in Sherwin Nuland, 60.
158   Nuland, 69.
159   Raymond Moody, 16–18.
168   Jan Henrikson, 181.
171   Valerie Kack-Brice, 151.
172   Charmaz, 204; Thomas Attig, 34.

CHAPTER 8

173   Attig, 47.
175   For a discussion of "triple oppression," see Denise Segura.
177   Featherstone and Hepworth, 382; Facio, 100.
178   For a discussion of the "myth of affluence," see Lillian Rubin.
181   Arliss, 160.
182   Robert Archibald, 67.

APPENDIX

183   Richard Quinney, 381; Barbara Heyl, 371.
186   See Communication Studies 298.
187   John Van Maanen, 4. For a discussion of interview methods, see Jaber Gubrium and James Holstein.
188   For a discussion of memory, see Climo and Cattell. For a discussion of early research on grandparenting, see Ernest Rappaport; for recent research on grandparenting, see Vern Bengtson and Joan Robertson; Andrew Cherlin and Frank Furstenberg Jr.; Kornhaber; and Angie Williams and Jon Nussbaum.
189   For research on grandparent roles, see Bernice Neugarten and Karol Weinstein; Meredith Minkler and Kathleen Roe; Eva Kahana and Boaz Kahana; Helen Kivnick. For a discussion of cultural or interpretive approaches, see Norman Denzin and Yvonna Lincoln; Paul Atkinson, Amanda Coffey, Sara Delamont, John Lofland, and Lyn Lofland.
190   For a discussion of critical approaches, see Chris Barker; and Paul Marris and Sue Thornham. Laurel Richardson, 923. For a discussion of writing in the social sciences, see James Clifford and George Marcus; Clifford Geertz. For a discussion of autoethnography, see Carolyn Ellis; Deborah Reed-Danahay.
191   Carol Ronai, 396. The American Anthropological Association is quoted in James Spradley, 35.
193   H. Lloyd Goodall Jr., 110.

Bibliography

Abbott, Carl. *Colorado: A History of the Centennial State*. Boulder: Colorado Associated University Press, 1976.

Acuna, Rodolfo F. *Occupied America: A History of Chicanos*. 4th ed. Reading, Mass.: Addison-Wesley, 1999.

Alvarez, Rudolfo. "The Psycho-Historical and Socioeconomic Development of the Chicano Community in the United States." In *Beyond 1848: Interpretations of the Modern Chicano Historical Experience*, ed. Michael R. Ornelas. Dubuque, Iowa: Kendall/Hunt, 1999, 3–26.

Anderson, Karen. *Wartime Women: Sex Roles, Family Relations, and the Status of Women during World War II*. Westport, Conn.: Greenwood, 1981.

Anderson, William T. "Dying and Death in Aging Intergenerational Families." In *The Aging Family: New Visions in Theory, Practice, and Reality*, ed. Terry D. Hargrave and Suzanne Midori Hanna. New York: Brunner/Mazel, 1997, 270–94.

Anthony, Carolyn, ed. *Family Portraits: Remembrances by Twenty Distinguished Writers*. New York: Doubleday, 1989.

Anzaldúa, Gloria. *Borderlands La Frontera: The New Mestiza*. 2d ed. San Francisco: Aunt Lute, 1999.

Archibald, Robert R. "A Personal History of Memory." In *Social Memory and History: Anthropological Perspectives*, ed. Jacob J. Climo and Maria G. Cattell. Walnut Creek, Calif.: AltaMira, 2002, 65–80.

Arliss, Laurie P. *Contemporary Family Communication: Messages and Meaning*. New York: St. Martin's, 1993.

Atkinson, Paul, Amanda Coffey, Sara Delamont, John Lofland, and Lyn Lofland, eds. *Handbook of Ethnography*. London: Sage, 2001.

Attig, Thomas. "Relearning the World: Making and Finding Meanings." In *Meaning Reconstruction and the Experience of Loss*, ed. Robert A. Neimeyer. Washington, D.C.: American Psychological Association, 2001, 33–53.

Baines, Carol, Sheila Neysmith, and Patricia Evans, eds. *Women's Caring: Feminist Perspectives on Social Welfare*. Toronto: McClelland & Stewart, 1991.

Baldwin, Karen. "'Woof!' A Word on Women's Roles in Family Storytelling." In *Women's Folklore, Women's Culture*, ed. Rosan A. Jordan and Susan J. Kalcik. Philadelphia: University of Pennsylvania Press, 1985, 149–62.

Banner, Lois. *In Full Flower*. New York: Vintage, 1993.

Barker, Chris. *Cultural Studies: Theory and Practice*. London: Sage, 2000.

Bateson, Mary C. *Composing a Life*. New York: Penguin Plume, 1990.

Beck, Warren A. *New Mexico: A History of Four Centuries*. Norman: University of Oklahoma Press, 1962.

Bengtson, Vern L., and Joan F. Robertson, eds. *Grandparenthood*. Beverly Hills, Calif.: Sage, 1985.

Bergemann, Sibylle. "Luise Maria Liss." In *Our Grandmothers: Loving Portraits by 74 Granddaughters*, ed. Linda Sunshine. New York: Welcome, 1998, 41.

Berger, John. *Ways of Seeing*. New York: BBC and Penguin, 1972.

Bernardes, Jon. *Family Studies: An Introduction*. London: Routledge, 1997.

Beshoar, Barron B. *Hippocrates in a Red Vest: The Biography of a Frontier Doctor*. Palo Alto, Calif.: American West, 1973.

Bochner, Arthur P., and Carolyn Ellis. "Talking over Ethnography." In *Composing Ethnography: Alternative Forms of Qualitative Writing*, ed. Carolyn Ellis and Arthur P. Bochner. Walnut Creek, Calif.: AltaMira, 1996, 13–45.

Bogardus, Emory S. "The Mexican Immigrant and Segregation." *American Journal of Sociology* 36 (1930): 74–80.

Bonavoglia, Angela, ed. *The Choices We Made: Twenty-Five Women and Men Speak Out about Abortion*. New York: Random House, 1991.

Bordo, Susan. *Unbearable Weight: Feminism, Western Culture, and the Body*. Berkeley: University of California Press, 1993.

Bourdieu, Pierre. *Distinction: A Social Critique of Judgement of Taste*. London: Routledge & Kegan Paul, 1984.

Charmaz, Kathy. *The Social Reality of Death: Death in Contemporary America*. Reading, Mass.: Addison-Wesley, 1980.

Chavez, Angelico. *The Origins of New Mexico Families in the Spanish Colonial Period: In Two Parts, the Seventeenth (1598–1693) and the Eighteenth (1693–1821) Centuries*. New York: Gannon, 1982.

Cherlin, Andrew J., and Frank Furstenberg Jr., eds. *The New American Grandparent: A Place in the Family, a Life Apart*. New York: Basic, 1986.

Chernin, Kim. *The Obsession: Reflections on the Tyranny of Slenderness*. New York: Harper & Row, 1981.

Chodorow, Nancy J. *The Reproduction of Mothering: Psychoanalysis and the Sociology of Gender*. Berkeley: University of California Press, 1978.

Clair, Robin Patric. "The Use of Framing Devices to Sequester Organizational Narratives: Hegemony and Harassment." *Communication Monographs* 60 (1993): 113–36.

Clifford, James, and George E. Marcus, eds. *Writing Culture: The Poetics and Politics of Ethnography*. Berkeley: University of California Press, 1986.

Climo, Jacob J., and Maria G. Cattell, eds. *Social Memory and History: Anthropological Perspectives*. Walnut Creek, Calif.: AltaMira, 2002.

Communication Studies 298. "Shopping for Family." *Qualitative Inquiry* 5 (1999): 147–80.

Coontz, Stephanie. *The Way We Never Were: American Families and the Nostalgia Trap*. New York: Basic, 1992.

Coward, Rosalind. *Female Desires: How They Are Sought, Bought, and Packaged*. New York: Grove Weidenfeld, 1985.

Cunningham-Burley, Sarah. "Constructing Grandparenthood: Anticipating Appropriate Action." *Sociology* 19 (1985): 421–36.

de Onis, Jose, ed. *The Hispanic Contribution to the State of Colorado*. Boulder, Colo.: Westview, 1976.

Denzin, Norman K., and Yvonna S. Lincoln, eds. *Handbook of Qualitative Research*. Thousand Oaks, Calif.: Sage, 1994.

Deutsch, Sarah. *No Separate Refuge: Culture, Class, and Gender on an Anglo-Hispanic Frontier in the American Southwest, 1880–1940*. New York: Oxford University Press, 1987.

Diamond, Tim. *Making Gray Gold: Narratives of Nursing Home Care*. Chicago: University of Chicago Press, 1992.

Dressel, Paula L. "Gender, Race, and Class: Beyond the Feminization of Poverty in Later Life." In *Critical Perspectives on Aging: The Political and Moral Economy of Growing Old*, ed. Meredith Minkler and Carroll L. Estes. Amityville, N.Y.: Baywood, 1991, 245–52.

Edelman, Hope. *Mother of My Mother: The Intricate Bond between Generations*. New York: Dell, 1999.

Ellis, Carolyn. "Evocative Autoethnography: Writing Emotionally about Our Lives." In *Representation and the Text*, ed. William G. Tierney and Yvonna S. Lincoln. Albany: State University of New York Press, 1997, 115–39.

Eshleman, J. Ross. *The Family: An Introduction*. 7th ed. Boston: Allyn & Bacon, 1994.

Espinosa, Aurelio M. *The Folklore of Spain in the American Southwest: Traditional Spanish Folk Literature in Northern New Mexico and Southern Colorado*. Norman: University of Oklahoma Press, 1985.

Etcoff, Nancy. *Survival of the Prettiest: The Science of Beauty*. New York: Anchor, 1999.

Facio, Elisa. *Understanding Older Chicanas: Sociological and Policy Perspectives*. Thousand Oaks, Calif.: Sage, 1996.

Featherstone, Mike, and Mike Hepworth. "The Mask of Ageing and the Postmodern Life Course." *The Body: Social Process and Cultural Theory*, ed. Mike Featherstone, Mike Hepworth, and Bryan S. Turner. London: Sage, 1991, 371–89.

Feinberg, Renee, and Kathleen E. Knox. *The Feminization of Poverty in the United States: A Selected, Annotated Bibliography of the Issues, 1978–1989*. New York: Garland, 1990.

"Fleeing Motorist Killed." *Los Angeles Times*, September 10, 1934, Pt. II, p. 1.

Foucault, Michel. *Discipline and Punish: The Birth of the Prison*. New York: Vintage, 1979.

Frank, Arthur W. "Bringing Bodies Back In: A Decade Review." *Theory, Culture, & Society* 7 (1990): 131–62.

Gamble, Sarah, ed. *The Routledge Critical Dictionary of Feminism and Postfeminism*. New York: Routledge, 1999.

Gans, Herbert. "Symbolic Ethnicity: The Future of Ethnic Groups and Cultures in America." *Ethnic and Racial Studies* 2 (1979): 1–20.

Garcia, Alma M. "Studying Chicanas: Bringing Women into the Frame of Chicano Studies." In *Chicana Voices: Intersections of Class, Race, and Gender*, ed. National Association for Chicano Studies. Albuquerque: University of New Mexico Press, 1990, 19–29.

Geertz, Clifford. *Works and Lives: The Anthropologist as Author*. Stanford, Calif.: Stanford University Press, 1988.

Gitelman, Howard M. *Legacy of the Ludlow Massacre: A Chapter in American Industrial Relations*. Philadelphia: University of Pennsylvania Press, 1988.

Gluck, Sherna Berger. *Rosie the Riveter Revisited: Women, the War, and Social Change*. New York: Meridian, 1987.

Golden, Stephanie. *Slaying the Mermaid: Women and the Culture of Sacrifice*. New York: Three Rivers, 1998.

González, Nancie L. *The Spanish-Americans of New Mexico: A Heritage of Pride*. Albuquerque: University of New Mexico Press, 1967.

Goodall, H. Lloyd, Jr. *Writing the New Ethnography*. Walnut Creek, Calif.: AltaMira, 2000.

Gubrium, Jaber F. *Living and Dying at Murray Manor*. New York: St. Martin's, 1975.

Gubrium, Jaber F., and James A. Holstein, eds. *Handbook of Interview Research: Context and Method*. Thousand Oaks, Calif.: Sage, 2001.

Hagestad, Gunhild O. "Problems and Promises in the Social Psychology of Intergenerational Relations." In *Aging: Stability and Change in the Family*, ed. Robert W. Fogel. New York: Academic Press, 1981, 11–46.

Hagestad, Gunhild O., and Linda M. Burton. "Grandparenthood, Life Context, and Family Development." *American Behavioral Scientist* 29 (1986): 471–84.

Hargrave, Terry D., and Suzanne Midori Hanna, eds. *The Aging Family: New Visions in Theory, Practice, and Reality.* New York: Brunner/ Mazel, 1997.

Harris, Katherine. *Long Vistas: Women and Families on Colorado Homesteads.* Niwot: University Press of Colorado, 1993.

Henderson, J. Neil, and Maria D. Vesperi, eds. *The Culture of Long Term Care: Nursing Home Ethnography.* Westport, Conn.: Bergin & Garvey, 1995.

Henrikson, Jan. "The Empress of Scents and Non-Scents." In *For She Is the Tree of Life: Grandmothers through the Eyes of Women Writers,* ed. Valerie Kack-Brice. Berkeley: Conari, 1994, 180–83.

Hesse-Biber, Sharlene, and Gregg Lee Carter. *Working Women in America: Split Dreams.* New York: Oxford University Press, 2000.

Heyl, Barbara Sherman. "Ethnographic Interviewing." In *Handbook of Ethnography,* ed. Paul Atkinson, Amanda Coffey, Sara Delamont, John Lofland, and Lyn Lofland. Thousand Oaks, Calif.: Sage, 2001, 369–83.

Honey, Maureen. *Creating Rosie the Riveter: Class, Gender, and Propaganda during World War II.* Amherst: University of Massachusetts Press, 1984.

hooks, bell. *Yearning.* Boston: South End, 1990.

Hutter, Mark. *The Changing Family.* 3d ed. Boston: Allyn & Bacon, 1998.

Janeway, Elizabeth. *Man's World, Woman's Place: A Study in Social Mythology.* New York: Delta, 1971.

Jenkinson, Michael. *Ghost Towns of New Mexico: Playthings of the Wind.* Albuquerque: University of New Mexico Press, 1967.

Kack-Brice, Valerie. "A Stitch in Time." In *For She Is the Tree of Life: Grandmothers through the Eyes of Women Writers,* ed. Valerie Kack-Brice. Berkeley, Calif.: Conari, 1994, 151.

Kahana, Eva, and Boaz Kahana. "Theoretical and Research Perspectives on Grandparenting." *Aging and Human Development* 2 (1971): 261–67.

Keller, Evelyn Fox. *Reflections on Gender and Science.* New Haven, Conn.: Yale University Press, 1985.

Kellner, Douglas. *Media Culture: Cultural Studies, Identity and Politics between the Modern and the Postmodern.* London: Routledge, 1995.

Kemper, Peter, and Christopher Murtaugh. "Lifetime Use of Nursing Home Care." *New England Journal of Medicine* 324 (1991): 595–600.

Kivnick, Helen Q. *The Meaning of Grandparenthood.* Ann Arbor: University of Michigan Press, 1980.

Kornhaber, Arthur. *Contemporary Grandparenting*. Thousand Oaks, Calif.: Sage, 1996.

Krause, Daniel R. *Home Bittersweet Home: Old Age Institutions in America*. Springfield, Ill.: Thomas, 1982.

Kubler-Ross, Elisabeth. *On Death and Dying*. New York: Scribner's, 1997.

Lamanna, Mary Ann, and Agnes Riedmann. *Marriages and Families: Making Choices in a Diverse Society*. 6th ed. Belmont, Calif.: Wadsworth, 1997.

Langellier, Kristin M. "Personal Narratives: Perspectives on Theory and Research." *Text and Performance Quarterly* 4 (1989): 243–76.

Langellier, Kristin M., and Eric E. Peterson. "Family Storytelling as a Strategy of Social Control." In *Narrative and Social Control: Critical Perspectives*, ed. Dennis K. Mumby. Newbury Park, Calif.: Sage, 1993, 49–77.

Lerner, Gerda. *The Creation of Patriarchy*. New York: Oxford University Press, 1986.

Macdonald, Myra. *Representing Women: Myths of Femininity in the Popular Media*. London: Arnold, 1995.

Marris, Paul, and Sue Thornham, ed. *Media Studies: A Reader*. 2d ed. New York: New York University Press, 1996.

Marrone, Robert L. *Death, Mourning, and Caring*. Pacific Grove, Calif.: Brooks/Cole, 1997.

Masih, Tara L. "Scrim-Shaw." In *For She Is the Tree of Life: Grandmothers through the Eyes of Women Writers*, ed. Valerie Kack-Brice. Berkeley, Calif.: Conari, 1994, 35–38.

McGovern, George S., and Leonard F. Guttridge. *The Great Coalfield War*. Boston: Houghton Mifflin, 1972.

Mead, Margaret. "Grandparents as Educators." In *The Family as Educator*, ed. Hope J. Leichter. New York: Teachers College Press, 1974, 66–75.

Messer, Ellen, and Kathryn E. May. *Back Rooms: Voices from the Illegal Abortion Era*. New York: St. Martin's, 1988.

Miller, Jean Baker. *Toward a New Psychology of Women*. 2d ed. Boston: Beacon, 1986.

Minkler, Meredith, and Kathleen M. Roe. *Grandmothers as Care Givers: Raising Children of the Crack Cocaine Epidemic*. Newbury Park, Calif.: Sage, 1993.

Monroy, Douglas Guy. "Mexicanos in Los Angeles, 1930–1941: An Ethnic Group in Relation to Class Forces." Ph.D. diss. University of California, Los Angeles, 1978.

Moody, Raymond. *Life after Life: The Investigation of a Phenomenon—Survival of Bodily Death*. 2d ed. San Francisco: Harper, 2001.

Myerhoff, Barbara. *Number Our Days*. New York: Simon & Schuster, 1978.

Nadeau, Janice Winchester. *Families Making Sense of Death*. Thousand Oaks, Calif.: Sage. 1998.

Neugarten, Bernice L., and Karol K. Weinstein. "The Changing American Grandparent." *Journal of Marriage and the Family* 26 (1964): 199–204.

Noller, Patricia, and Mary Anne Fitzpatrick. *Communication in Family Relationships*. Englewood Cliffs, N.J.: Prentice Hall, 1993.

Nostrand, Robert L. *The Hispano Homeland*. Norman: University of Oklahoma Press, 1992.

Nuland, Sherwin B. *How We Die: Reflections on Life's Final Chapter*. New York: Vintage, 1993.

O'Neill, Cherry Boone. *Starving for Attention*. New York: Dell, 1982.

Ornelas, Michael R., ed. *Beyond 1848: Interpretations of the Modern Chicano Historical Experience*. 2d ed. Dubuque, Iowa: Kendall/Hunt. 1999.

Pearce, T. M. *New Mexico Place Names: A Genealogical Dictionary*. Albuquerque: University of New Mexico Press, 1965.

Quesada, Carmen. "Wanderlust." In *Our Grandmothers: Loving Portraits by 74 Granddaughters*, ed. Linda Sunshine. New York: Welcome, 1998, 86.

Quinney, Richard. "Once My Father Traveled West to California." In *Composing Ethnography: Alternative Forms of Qualitative Writing*, ed. Carolyn Ellis and Arthur P. Bochner. Walnut Creek, Calif.: AltaMira, 1996, 357–82.

Rappaport, Ernest A. "The Grandparent Syndrome." *Psychoanalytic Quarterly* 27 (1957): 518–37.

Reagan, Leslie J. *When Abortion Was a Crime: Women, Medicine, and Law in the United States, 1867–1973*. Berkeley: University of California Press, 1997.

Reed-Danahay, Deborah. "Autobiography, Intimacy, and Ethnography." In *Handbook of Ethnography*, ed. Paul Atkinson, Amanda Coffey, Sara Delamont, John Lofland, and Lynn Lofland. Thousand Oaks, Calif.: Sage, 2001, 407–25.

Richardson, Laurel. "Writing: A Method of Inquiry." In *Handbook of Qualitative Research*, ed. Norman K. Denzin and Yvonna S. Lincoln. Thousand Oaks, Calif.: Sage, 1994, 516–29.

Riechmann, Deb. "Clinton Calls for U.S. Aid to Boost Nursing Home Care." *Sacramento Bee*, September 17, 2000, p. A10.

Riesmann, Catherine Kohler. *Narrative Analysis*. Newbury Park, Calif.: Sage, 1993.

Romo, Ricardo. *East Los Angeles: History of a Barrio*. Austin: University of Texas Press, 1983.

Ronai, Carol Rambo. "Multiple Reflections of Child Sex Abuse: An Argument for a Layered Account." *Journal of Contemporary Ethnography* 23 (1995): 395–426.

Rowbotham, Sheila. *A Century of Women*. New York: Penguin, 1997.

Rubin, Lillian B. *Worlds of Pain: Life in the Working-Class Family*. New York: Basic, 1969.

Savishinsky, Joel S. *The Ends of Time: Life and Work in a Nursing Home*. New York: Bergin & Garvey, 1991.

Scharf, Lois. *To Work and to Wed: Female Unemployment, Feminism, and the Great Depression*. Westport, Conn.: Greenwood, 1980.

Seale, Clive. *Constructing Death: The Sociology of Dying and Bereavement*. Cambridge: Cambridge University Press, 1998.

Segura, Denise A. "Chicanas and Triple Oppression in the Labor Force." In *Chicana Voices: Intersections of Class, Race, and Gender*, ed. National Association for Chicano Studies. Albuquerque: University of New Mexico Press, 1990, 47–65.

Shield, Renee Rose. *Uneasy Endings: Daily Life in an American Nursing Home*. Ithaca, N.Y.: Cornell University Press, 1988.

Shorris, Earl. *Latinos: A Biography of the People*. New York: Norton, 1992.

Simmons, Marc. *Coronado's Land: Essays on Daily Life in Colonial New Mexico*. Albuquerque: University of New Mexico Press, 1991.

Smith, Duane A. *Colorado Mining: A Photographic History*. Albuquerque: University of New Mexico Press, 1977.

Spitzack, Carol. *Confessing Excess: Women and the Politics of Body Reduction*. Albany: State University of New York Press, 1990.

Spradley, James P. *The Ethnographic Interview*. New York: Holt, Rinehart & Winston, 1979.

Stein, Leon, and Philip Taft, eds. *Massacre at Ludlow: Four Reports*. New York: Arno and the New York Times, 1971.

Stone, Elizabeth. *Black Sheep and Kissing Cousins: How Our Family Stories Shape Us*. New York: Time, 1988.

Szinovacz, Maximiliane E., ed. *Handbook on Grandparenthood*. Westport, Conn.: Greenwood, 1989.

Taylor, Bryan. "Frailty, Language, and Elderly Identity: Interpretive and Critical Perspectives on the Aging Subject." In *Interpersonal Communication in Older Adulthood: Interdisciplinary Theory and Research*, ed. Mary Lee Hummert, John M. Wiemann, and Jon F. Nussbaum. Thousand Oaks, Calif.: Sage, 1994, 185–208.

Trujillo, Nick. "In Search of Naunny's Grave." *Text and Performance Quarterly* 18 (1998): 344–68.

Tushar, Olibama Lopez. *The People of "El Valle": A History of the Spanish Colonials in the San Luis Valley*. Denver: Author, 1975.

Uhlenhuth, Karen. "Senior Romance: So Many Women, So Much of the Time." *Sacramento Bee*, March 4, 2001, p. E5.

Van Maanen, John. *Tales of the Field: On Writing Ethnography*. Chicago: University of Chicago Press, 1988.

Vesperi, Maria D. *City of Green Benches: Growing Old in a New Downtown*. Ithaca, N.Y.: Cornell University Press, 1985.

Wentworth, Edward Norris. *America's Sheep Trails: History and Personalities*. Ames: Iowa State College Press, 1948.

Williams, Angie, and Jon F. Nussbaum, eds. *Intergenerational Communication across the Life Span*. Mahwah, N.J.: Erlbaum, 2001.

Williams, Norma, and Diana J. Torrez. "Grandparenthood among Hispanics." In *Handbook on Grandparenthood*, ed. Maximiliane E. Szinovacz. Westport, Conn.: Greenwood, 1989, 87–96.

Wolf, Naomi. *The Beauty Myth: How Images of Beauty Are Used against Women*. New York: Anchor, 1991.

Wood, Julia T. *Who Cares: Women, Care, and Culture*. Carbondale: Southern Illinois University Press, 1983.

Yerby, Janet, Nancy Buerkel-Rothfuss, and Arthur P. Bochner. *Understanding Family Communication*. 2d ed. Scottsdale: Gorsuch Scarisbrick, 1995.

Index

abortion, 48-53, 192-93, 198n
"abuela," 177
Acuna, Rodolfo, 127
adultery, 35-36
Alzheimer's disease, 136, 155. *See also*
    dementia
anorexia, 84-88, 92-93, 178, 198n
Anzaldúa, Gloria, 130
Archibald, Robert, 182
Arliss, Laurie, 20, 181
Attig, Thomas, 172, 173
autoethnography, 190-91

Banner, Lois, 176
Barker, Chris, 70
"beauty myth," 72-75, 92
Bergemann, Sibylle, 94
Bochner, Arthur, 19
Bogardus, Emory, 126
Bordo, Susan, 84, 87, 98
Bourdieu, Pierre, 63
Burton, Linda, 17

caregiving, 96
Catholicism, 169
Charmaz, Kathy, 135, 155, 172
Chavez, Angelico, 115
Chernin, Kim, 85, 91
Chicanas. *See* Hispanic women
Chodorow, Nancy, 178
class. *See* social class
coalmining: accidents involving, 29-
    30, 32-33, 198n;

Colorado and New Mexico history of,
    28, 32-33, 42, 44, 46, 198n
communication studies, 185-86, 298
Coontz, Stephanie, 105, 110
critical analysis, 19, 24, 189-90, 200n
cultural analysis, 19, 189, 200n
cultural capital, 63

dances, 36-37, 56
Dawson, New Mexico, 29-30, 32, 46
death, 154, 157-62, 171-72;
    social/symbolic, 155-56
dementia, 134, 136, 155. *See also*
    Alzheimer's disease
Depression. *See* Great Depression.
Deutsch, Sarah, 28

Edelman, Hope, 8, 113
elderly, 69, 134-36, 150-53, 199n
Ellis, Carolyn, 19, 195
Eshleman, J. Ross, 62
ethical concerns, 191-95
ethnic identity, 113, 117-20, 199n;
    "Mexican" and "Spanish," 113-15,
    119-25, 129-31;
    "White," 125-27
ethnicity, 27, 62, 113, 175

Facio, Elisa, 68, 177
family history, 20, 24, 40-43.
    See also genealogy
family secrets, 52-53, 192-93

About the Author

Nick Trujillo is a professor of communication studies at California State University, Sacramento. He completed his doctoral degree at the University of Utah in 1983 and is the author of *Organizational Life on Television* (1987, with Leah Vande Berg) and *The Meaning of Nolan Ryan* (1994) as well as numerous articles on organizational culture, sports culture, and family culture. He is currently writing *The Golden Coast*, a travelogue about dog culture based on a five-week trip up the California coast that he took with his golden retriever, Ebbet. He enjoys tennis, biking, long beach walks with his wife Leah and their two dogs, and avoiding conflict with his father. He can be contacted at nickt@csus.edu.0

Made in the USA
San Bernardino, CA
20 August 2015